Dilemmas of Science Tea

Dilemmas of Science Teaching offers a unique exploration of sixteen contemporary issues in science education, in a distinctive format. Each chapter focuses on a real-life case study from the classroom, written by a teacher. The issues arising are then discussed by leading international academics, placing the everyday classroom dilemma within a wider theoretical context. The book is divided into four parts:

- Dilemmas about science: the nature and laws of science, the role of the laboratory in school science
- Dilemmas about difference: issues of gender, equity, culture and ethnicity, and power in the classroom
- Dilemmas about representation: the use of textbooks, the role of questioning, using analogies and student reports
- Dilemmas about teaching and learning: ethics, constructivism, curriculum change, teaching out of field, and science for all.

Dilemmas of Science Teaching is an exciting and accessible book that will be essential reading for anyone involved in science education. Student teachers will find it helpful in learning to review their own teaching, while practising teachers will welcome the expert insights into universal problems.

John Wallace is an Associate Professor at the national Key Centre for School Science and Mathematics at Curtin University of Technology in Perth, Australia. **William Louden** is a Professor of Education at Edith Cowan University, also in Perth.

Dilemmas of Science Teaching

Perspectives on problems of practice

Edited by John Wallace
and William Louden

RoutledgeFalmer
Taylor & Francis Group

LONDON AND NEW YORK

First published 2002
by RoutledgeFalmer
11 New Fetter Lane, London EC4P 4EE

Simultaneously published in the USA and Canada
by RoutledgeFalmer
29 West 35th Street, New York, NY 10001

Transferred to Digital Printing 2004

RoutledgeFalmer is an imprint of the Taylor & Francis Group

© 2002 John Wallace and William Louden for editorial matter and
selection; individual contributors their contribution

Typeset in Bembo by Taylor & Francis Books Ltd
Printed and bound in Great Britain by
TJI Digital, Padstow, Cornwall

British Library Cataloguing in Publication Data
A catalogue record for this book is available from the British
Library

Library of Congress Cataloging in Publication Data
Wallace, John (John William).
    Dilemmas of science teaching: perspectives on problems of
    practice/John Wallace and William Louden.
    Includes bibliographical references and index.
    1. Science–Study and teaching. I. Louden, William. II. Title.
    Q181 .W223 2002
    507'.1'2–dc21   2001034965

ISBN 0–415–23762–9 (hbk)
ISBN 0–415–23763–7 (pbk)

Contents

Introduction

John Wallace and William Louden

Teaching is an uncertain domain of knowledge. Teachers struggle to strike a balance among competing educational goals. For example, many teachers believe that students learn best when they have opportunities to construct their own meanings in their own language, but teachers also recognise the traditional value placed on formal statements of scientific principles and use of scientific language. Frequently, the attempt to strike a balance presents teachers with insoluble dilemmas. How, for example, to value the language students have and use *and* to value the language of scientific representation? The tensions inherent in the issue of language and science – like so many other issues in science education – must be worked through, optimised and traded off in practice. Teachers want students to understand that the knowledge of science is conditional and constructed *and* they want students to know about the canonical explanations found in school science textbooks. Teachers want students to understand that scientific work is a passionate and non-linear activity *and* they want students to be able to follow the protocols of writing up lab reports. Unlike the issues in more certain domains of knowledge than teaching, these dilemmas admit no permanent solution. Teachers are committed to an enterprise that requires multiple and apparently conflicting outcomes, an enterprise where excellence requires good-humoured resolution of apparently irreconcilable alternatives.

This book explores sixteen contemporary issues in science education, through an examination of the practical dilemmas the issues provoke for teachers. The distinctive feature of this book is that substantive arguments about these issues are contextualised and illuminated by case studies of students and teachers working together in science classrooms.

Preparation of this book began with discussions between the editors and some colleagues working in school science classrooms. We met in a group, two university researchers and about a dozen teachers we knew as school system consultants, exemplary teachers or graduate students. We – the editors of this book – proposed that our teacher colleagues would each write a short narrative account of a dilemma they had faced recently in their classroom science teaching. In return, we offered to work with them to develop the stories into polished narratives, and to provide them with commentaries from an international group of science education researchers. The choice of topics we left entirely to our colleagues. All that we asked they do was to tell a story they thought illustrated an important or enduring dilemma – an issue, tension or problem that had often worried them and could not be ignored or easily resolved.

Teachers chose to write about a variety of topics: constructivism, ethics, gender, lab teaching, assessment, content knowledge, analogies, and so on. We have worked with our teacher colleagues to clarify the narrative issues in their text. The kinds of questions we have asked are: What do you think the point of the story is? Where should it begin and end? How much of the context do you think needs to be told? Does the dilemma remain when the story is over, or have you rushed an easy resolution?

Our colleagues have written about issues that they have found pressing or interesting. Some of these are seemingly inescapable issues that come with the territory of the classroom, such as maintaining students' interest on sleepy summer afternoons. Teachers also have written about issues that have had a high profile in science education, such as constructivist approaches to teaching and learning. Other stories refer to issues that have concerned teachers more generally in recent years, such as the impact of gender and culture on patterns of students' learning.

Without comment on the substantive issues raised by each author, we have sent the stories to other colleagues around the world, asking them to provide a commentary. There has been some matching of stories to researchers: we expected Peter Fensham to be interested in a story the author said was about 'science for all', for Nel Noddings to be interested in a story about personal relationships in the classroom, and Reinders Duit to be interested in a story about conceptual change. However, we gave no directions to commentators about the approach they should take or the issues they should foreground in their responses. Contributors did not see other commentaries on the same story.

Commentators' responses have often problematised stories in ways that the authors might not have expected. A story, for example, that the author used to illustrate the difficulty of building his science teaching on students' experience drew sharp responses about the epistemology of science teaching and the value of students' encounters with the theoretical and imaginative world of science. Similarly, a story that the author identified as about the level of language to be used in questioning young children was read by the commentators as illustrating inequalities of power encoded in the kinds of questions teachers choose to ask young children.

While we have been working on this book, a colleague of ours and contributor to this volume – Peter Taylor – has taken to calling the project 'the alternative handbook'. He says this with a wry smile on his face, and we have never asked him the obvious question, 'Alternative to what?' But we have taken him to mean alternative to the encyclopedic handbooks of science education (e.g. Fraser and Tobin, 1998; Gabel, 1994). This book, *Dilemmas of Science Teaching,* is an altogether more modest work, no alternative to the comprehensive, authoritative and inclusive treatment of science education available in the 'real' handbooks. But it does provide an alternative reading of the issues that currently concern science educators and researchers. By starting with teachers' stories and adding commentaries on the stories, we have provoked a different set of issues. In addition to familiar concerns about teaching and learning, many commentators have touched on broader issues such as language, knowledge and power in science education.

Many commentators have focused on epistemological questions in the teaching and learning of school science. In Chapter 2, for example, Marie Larochelle argues the importance of revealing science as a social process in which people carry forward their epistemological commitments in the mediation of experience, and Jay Lemke contests the pragmatic privileging of experience over theory in school science. A second group of commentators have opened up questions about science and difference. In Chapter 5, for example, Angela Barton and Léonie Rennie explore issues of power, knowledge and gender in response to an account of girls' work in a physical science laboratory. A third group of commentators have explored dilemmas of representation in school science. In Chapter 11, for example, Brent Kilbourn discusses the way in which analogies are a particular kind of half-truth, and John Gilbert discusses the use of teaching models in schoolrooms and laboratories and the consensus models of science. Finally, a fourth group of contributors have explored teaching and learning dilemmas entailed in constructivism, science for all, curriculum change and teaching out of field. In Chapter 15, for example, Allan Harrison, Diane Grayson and Uri Ganiel provide contrasting responses to a biology teacher's description of his experience in teaching Grade 10 physics. Harrison concludes that the physics lesson is a small but significant step on the road towards improvement. Grayson has some sympathy for the teacher's attempts to move beyond equations and algorithms, but has some concerns about students left in confusion about physics concepts. Ganiel goes further, offering a detailed account of the physics content to support his argument that deep knowledge of subject matter should underpin teachers' work in science.

These are just a few of the voices in this book, and a few of the issues. More than fifty teachers and researchers from Australia, Canada, Germany, Israel, New Zealand, South Africa, the United Kingdom and the United States have contributed to the book. Our task has been to use the cases and commentaries as a way of opening up the dilemmas teachers face in science classrooms. We hope that you find the contributions as interesting to read as we have found it to bring them together.

References

Fraser, B. J. and Tobin, K. G. (eds) (1998). *International handbook of science*. Dordrecht, The Netherlands: Kluwer.

Gabel, D. L. (ed.) (1994). *Handbook of research on science teaching and learning*. New York: Macmillan.

Part I

Dilemmas about science

Chapter 1

The nature of science

Contributions by Vaille Dawson,
Norman G. Lederman and Kenneth Tobin

Editors' introduction

Teaching about the nature of science is a central thrust of many current science curriculum reform initiatives (e.g. National Research Council, 1996). However, while there is broad consensus among science educators about the merits of this movement, there is less agreement about the character of science and how it should be represented in schools (Matthews 1998; McComas, 1998). In the four decades since the publication of Thomas Kuhn's *The structure of scientific revolutions* in 1962, radical new questions have been raised about the nature of the scientific enterprise. Kuhn challenged the assumption of science based on individual enterprise, empirical evidence, rational argument, objectivity and value neutrality. Rather, he proposed that science proceeds through the socially embedded activities of its practitioners, with scientific knowledge (theories) developing through cyclic periods of consensus and dissensus among the members of the community. Science, in the post-Kuhnian era, is seen as a complex, value-laden enterprise, subject to the range of human social behaviours including ambition, care, jealousy, prudence, friendship and altruism.

Kuhn's work, and the work of many others who followed, raised a multitude of issues about participation in, and the achievements and foundations of, the scientific enterprise. Major critiques of science, led particularly by feminist and postcolonial scholars, point to the historical exclusion of women and minorities from mainstream scientific activities, and the androcentric and Eurocentric character of histories of science (Harding, 1998; Longino and Doell, 1983; Wertheim, 1995). Many examples of poorly executed, dishonest, unethical, sexist, racist and culturally inappropriate science have been documented in the literature (Allchin, 1998; Brickhouse, 1998). Other scholars point to examples of where scientific knowledge claims based on questionable practices entered the academy as unquestioned scientific lore (Stepan, 1996). In many cases, these claims are considered separately from the assumptions which underpinned the original work.

The difficulty with this kind of analysis is that it leads to dualist thinking about science (e.g. good/bad, objective/subjective, masculine/feminine, reason/emotion). Recently scholars have pointed out that cultural assumptions form the basis for claims in all kinds of science, both good and bad (Harding, 1991; Longino, 1990). Even the historic, scientific 'blindspots', so obvious in retrospect, are part of the process of understanding the nature of science (Allchin, 1998). Assumptions about gender and race, for example, are part of all aspects of the scientific process and should always be subject to critical scrutiny (Harding, 1991). Similarly, ethical questions are not confined to the more contentious activities, such as genetics research, but pervade the scientific enterprise. Making visible the assumptions behind the science is part of the process of achieving new, ethical and culturally appropriate forms of scientific 'objectivity' (Harding, 1991).

The problem for teachers is what to do with this information in a world where the dualist debate about the nature of science persists. In Kuhnian terms, we are in the midst of a revolutionary period for understanding the nature of science in science education (Duschl, 1994). In many respects, the struggle to understand the nature of science being played out in the literature is also reflected in science classrooms. On the one hand, teachers wish to convey the impression that science is rigorous, careful, inclusive, ethical and useful to humankind. On the other hand, they are faced with counter-evidence of science as sloppy, exclusive, unethical and harmful. Teachers (and their students) struggle to reconcile the traditional view of common 'textbook knowledge' as value-free with the values that were expressed in achieving that knowledge (Allchin, 1998). Teachers swing between representing science – in Kuhnian terms – as normal or stable (involving routine and confirming activity where core values are rarely questioned) and science as revolutionary and fluid (involving disagreement and debate where core values are subject to scrutiny). Often, science teachers and their students 'find themselves confronted by what to them appears to be a tangle of complexity comprehensive only to the intellectually nimble and the mathematically gifted' (Stinner and Williams, 1998, p. 1,028).

These dilemmas about teaching and the nature of science form the context for this chapter. In the following story, *What is science really like?*, Vaille Dawson recounts a brief discussion with three students about the nature of science. Vaille's own experience working within science and within science education forms the backdrop for her account and for her subsequent reflections. Several issues are raised here about how science should be represented to students. The story and the teacher's reflection are followed by commentaries by Norman Lederman and Kenneth Tobin.

What is science really like?

Vaille Dawson

I looked up from my marking as Jess, Sarah and Shannon entered my form room. These three Grade 12 students had just received their university selection papers. Shannon explained that while they enjoyed science, they were unsure about whether to embark on a career in science. Could they talk to me about their options? All three students had been in my form last year and Jess and Sarah were in my human biology class. They were all able students and it was likely that Shannon would be dux of the school despite combining a rigorous academic schedule with music, sport and debating. Shannon was studying physics, chemistry, mathematics, English literature and music. She is planning to study physics at university next year. Jess and Sarah are both considering a career in biomedical science. They are aware that I had studied biomedical science and worked in medical research for a number of years before becoming a science teacher.

'What's it really like, working in science?' Jess asked. 'Is it the same as what we do at school?'

I hesitate. What can I say? A few glib comments pop into my head, but not out of my mouth. What is it really like? I wonder as I gaze at Jess, Shannon and Sarah's expectant faces. They have all been at this private girls' school for at least five years. During that time they have constructed an image of science and how it is practised. 'What do you think it will be like?' I counter.

'I reckon it will be exciting and we'll make lots of discoveries. I don't mind working hard because I know that in the long run I can make the world a better place', responds Shannon.

So, Shannon after completing a physics degree wants to 'make the world a better place'. Should I tell her that 80 per cent of physicists are employed in defence installations?

'Yes', enthuses Sarah. 'I could develop new strains of crops and help starving people.' (We've just studied human ecology.) 'I like working with other people to solve problems.' Sarah adds finally, 'I don't want to work with animals though. You know that from the eye dissection.'

Yes, the eye dissection. In that lesson Sarah had paled when the aluminium foil was removed from the white tray to reveal twenty-four pristine eye balls. Even after explaining that the eyes had been removed from animals already killed for meat and that slicing an eye was no different to dicing meat for a casserole, Sarah had steadfastly refused to participate. Finally, she used an eye model to complete her practical work.

I recall a time when I was Sarah's age. As a Grade 11 student, during the summer vacation, I worked at the local abattoirs hosing the bone fragments from the carcasses on the assembly line. My girl friend and I walked down to where the cows were slaughtered. We watched the men in white gum boots and overalls place a hook through the heels of semi-stunned cattle and as they were dragged upside down, slit their throats. The cows screamed and the warm blood spattered the men's boots.

Two years later, employed during the university break as a laboratory assistant in clinical immunology, I was sent to the animal house to collect the kidneys, hearts and lungs from freshly killed mice, rats and guinea pigs. The technician grabbed the tail of each and swung them so that their heads hit the bench.

I completed my science degree and was initially employed in a research position in a haematology laboratory, producing antibodies against leukaemia in mice. It was difficult to get large quantities of blood from mice. A colleague taught me how to use a glass capillary tube to pierce the tissue behind the eye. This procedure could only be done twice and the mouse was left blind. I also injected large numbers (hundreds) of mice intra-peritoneally with leukaemic cells and an adjuvant to enhance the immune response. The mice developed an ascites tumour in the peritoneum from which large quantities of antibody rich fluid could be extracted. I held the mice so that their distended abdomens protruded and using a large bore needle removed as much fluid as possible. If I was fortunate I could repeat the process three to four times before the animal died. Often, knowing that a mouse was close to death I would squeeze their bodies as one would wring a sponge to extract the last few microlitres of fluid.

I do not recall ever questioning my actions. I was a research scientist and my science education at the secondary and tertiary level had instilled in me an unwavering belief that the pursuit of knowledge and truth, that is, the practice of science, outweighed any consideration of right or wrong. Although I acknowledged that some individuals may use scientific knowledge for unscrupulous purposes I believed that science was inherently good.

As well as working with animals, I spent many hours carrying out repetitive radioimmunoassays with radioactive isotopes. During these hours I worked alone with the Geiger counter ticking away beside me. I carried out numerous cell assays with cytotoxins, mutagens, carcinogens and teratogens (even while pregnant).

Over a period of eight years I never had a permanent job. Each November there was a great deal of stress in the department as researchers waited on news that their grants had been refunded for a further twelve months or in rare circumstances for three years. A career path after completion of a Ph.D. comprised reading, publishing and travelling on the conference circuit hoping to obtain a poorly paid post-doctoral position in a reputable institution. For females, combining this with a family was very difficult. Once established, usually with the help of a male mentor, one played the funding game applying for grants for yourself and your staff.

I paused in my reminiscing and stared at the girls.

'What's it really like, working in science?' Jess asked. 'Is it the same as what we do at school?'

Teacher commentary

Vaille Dawson

When I reread this story some time later, it seems to me that there are two issues here. The first is the issue of 'what is science really like?', a question which has kept philosophers busy for several hundred years and which a short story cannot hope to address, and secondly what is my responsibility as a science teacher? That is, as a teacher of science what image(s) of science should I portray to my students?

I love teaching science. What frustrates me though is the way that external forces make me teach science. Practical work is made to fit into 60-minute periods and even though the students like the opportunity for interaction and using equipment, it is not true experimentation as I (usually) know the outcome and student results in disagreement are rejected as errors.

I teach in a school where 80 per cent of the students go on to university. As a science teacher of final year students, I am often consulted by students about career options in science. This year, over 40 per cent of our graduating students entered university to embark on a degree in science or a related field. To achieve this goal, all students sit an external university entrance exam. I know that students will be asked to recall and use factual information. Thus, I ensure they know how to pass exams and answer the types of questions that are asked. What does this process do to students? They come to believe as I once did that science is a set of facts and what research scientists do is discover new facts.

To address this prevailing view, I have made little innovations. For example, I have introduced a scientific investigation into human biology which runs over a term. This helps students to experience what it is like to 'do' scientific research. But this is an addition to the regular curriculum and requires a lot of motivation from myself and the students. I also use the teaching of human evolution to demonstrate how our scientific understanding/knowledge changes over time.

Overall, the image of science I try to portray, notwithstanding the constraints, is that science is one way of understanding the world, that science is neither good nor bad, that science can solve many (not all) problems, and create others. I don't tell them about issues like sexism, etc., but I do try and boost their self-esteem enough so that they may withstand these issues regardless of their future career.

If I had to give any suggestions to a student opting for a career in scientific research (or maybe any job) I would say to get a good mentor (male or female), be intellectually honest and maintain your enthusiasm.

This story is meant to be provocative. There are many positives about working in the field of scientific research that allows one to cope with the lack of tenure and opportunities for advancement. There is the thrill of an experiment that finally works, getting a grant, a publication, a good review, the intellectual conversations with peers, the meeting of truly brilliant individuals. In my area of bone marrow transplantation, it was seeing a child who had been successfully treated with a bone marrow transplant walk out of the hospital with their family. And finally, the feeling that you might be able to make a difference.

★   ★   ★

Science is as science does? The pedagogical necessity of white lies

Norman G. Lederman, Illinois Institute of Technology

The teacher's reminiscing in response to the question posed by Jess, Sarah and Shannon strikes an all-too-familiar chord with me. I remember planning to become a veterinarian throughout my years as a high school student. I liked science, but my feelings were derived more from my attitudes about the teacher than about the subject matter. I majored in biology as an undergraduate in college, but had decided by my sophomore year not to pursue a career as a veterinarian. Up to that point in my studies biology, as well as the other sciences, were fairly routine. We were asked to do a lot of memorising and I happened to have a good memory. I took philosophy and religion courses whenever I had free electives because it was in those courses that I could satisfy my urge to debate and argue about substantive issues. We were never afforded such opportunities in science courses. It was during my junior year that I first developed a sincere love of biology and science. My animal physiology professor had designed his course so that the major activities involved collection of data, drawing conclusions and defending conclusions based on the evidence. In short, we did little along the lines of memorisation and we learned the basic principles of physiology through laboratory-oriented activities and subsequent data-based inferences. In many ways this was like the mental activities I enjoyed so much in my philosophy and religion courses.

I graduated with a B.Sc. in biology and was able to find a position as a medical technician at Bronx Veterans Hospital. I was assigned to the microbiology laboratory. I was very excited because I anticipated finally being given the chance to do 'real science'. I was going to be involved, I thought, in all kinds of interesting discoveries every day. Well after six months of doing routine blood and urine analyses each day, I realised that things weren't as I thought they would be. The work was as boring as filing index cards and the most exciting part of the day was deciding who would 'do blood' and who would 'do urine' each day as my co-workers and I gulped down the last of our morning coffee. I decided the problem was that I did not know enough to be involved in really exciting laboratory work and so I pursued a M.Sc. degree in biology.

Within months of completing my M.Sc., I resigned my position as a medical laboratory technician and took a position as a 'scientist' with a research project at Columbia University focusing on pollution on New York City beaches and respiratory ailments. This two-year position involved little more than taking pollution counts up and down the coast of New York City and Long Island. One of my responsibilities was to train individuals with little science background to take accurate pollution and chemical counts. I found pollution counts to be no different than blood counts and urine analyses. It was at this time that I turned to high school teaching, although I honestly do not remember what led me to this decision.

I thoroughly enjoyed my ten-year career as a high school teacher. 'Turning the kids on' to science and biology was more fun than anything I had done before. I enjoyed watching students learn and I felt satisfaction in affording them the opportunity to appreciate biology as I had first experienced in my animal physiology course. Interestingly, what I chose to do with my high school students was very different from my personal experiences with real science. The teacher of the three excited, but hesitant, Grade 12 students probably afforded her students similar opportunities. Both of us, however, realise that what predominated in the experiences of our high school students was far removed from our reflections on our own experiences with real science.

The final chapter (I think) of my own story is that I have been a university-level science educator for the past eighteen years. I strongly advocate science instruction that is active and motivational to students. I also advocate an instructional approach that models or is consistent with the 'nature of science'. After all, we want students to get an accurate conception of what science is really like. I work in a building that also houses departments of biochemistry, physics and assorted research laboratories. And, as I walk the halls between my classroom and office, I can look in any laboratory and typically see the real science that I experienced in Bronx Veterans Hospital and along New York City beaches. I see the same science that Jess, Sarah and Shannon's teacher reminisced about. How will this teacher answer these anxious students' question? How should she answer their question? How would I answer such a question?

Are we all hypocrites? Do we teach a brand of science that engages students, stating that it is 'real science', while fully knowing that science is typically not what we are having our students experience. There is a tension that every thoughtful science teacher must face. It is the tension between presenting to students both the routine and exciting aspects of science and the pedagogical necessity of keeping adolescents engaged and motivated. It is unfortunate that most of science can be characterised as routine. Thomas Kuhn (1962) made that very clear forty years ago in his description of 'normal science'. Unfortunately, adolescents are not patient enough to persist in the performance of repetitive tasks or those that do not capture their imagination. My students, and I suspect Jess, Sarah and Shannon, would have 'tuned out' long ago if they had experienced what I did when I did 'real science'. And, in a way, I may have 'tuned out' of 'real science' when I chose to become a teacher. Or did I?

Let us not forget that the individuals practising Kuhn's 'normal science' are individuals with Ph.D.s in science or at least individuals with an avid interest in science. They appreciate science so much that they gladly take the routine along with the rest. Professional scientists gladly spend most of their time performing routine tasks because they realise the necessity of these tasks for the development of those 'discoveries' that characterise the public's perception of science. These scientists, just like me, must have had one or more special experiences that 'turned them on' to science. For me it was my junior level animal physiology course. If I had not experienced the excitement of that class I would have most likely left the field and never considered working in that medical laboratory. I probably would have never considered teaching biology to high school students. I had grown to love biology and science in general.

We all know too well that if students 'tune out' the learning that could have 'hooked' them is lost. As educators we are constantly attending to much more than the cognitive development and achievements of our students. We must balance our concerns for subject-matter achievement with concerns for students' emotional and personal development. With respect to biology and science, I was also part salesperson. I wanted my students to learn the important ideas, principles and thinking skills associated with biology and science, but I also wanted them to develop an appreciation and positive affect towards science. Clearly, my goals and the goals of the teacher in the narrative extend well beyond just an accurate representation of 'true science'. And, if we are going to be at all successful we first have to get and maintain our students' attention. Consequently, we often distort the balance between the routine procedures of science and its more motivational aspects.

Am I suggesting that what we do instructionally is dishonest? Definitely not! What I am saying is that the supposed 'routine' aspects of science, the aspects reminisced about in the narrative, are typically boring and routine to the beginner. For, after you have been 'hooked', your appreciation and love of science make the activities that appear 'routine' and boring to the casual observer as interesting as the publicised discoveries. I have had students like Jess, Sarah and Shannon and I have been asked questions similar to the one they have posed. My answer typically emphasised the 'sexy' and intriguing aspects of science. Sure, I spoke about tasks that were less than dramatic. I wanted my students to know that brilliant discoveries were not the norm. But I would always keep in mind that my students were just beginning to develop a deep appreciation for science. Why let them 'tune out' before they had a chance to decide for themselves? Our task as teachers is much more complex than simply attending to subject–matter knowledge. We work with developing minds and fragile affect every day. All endeavours and disciplines involve activities that are motivating only to those who are enamoured with the topic at hand. Science is no different. Consequently, successful science teachers often focus a disproportionate amount of time on the more motivational aspects of their disciplines. We are not misrepresenting science, only emphasising the interesting and motivational. Our initial task is to invite students in and to hopefully develop the motivation for future learning. In a sense our long–term goal is to make the 'routine' as interesting as Kuhn's 'extraordinary science'.

Should school science be the same as real science? Should initial study of science totally represent the activities of the profession? In my opinion such a match would be developmentally inappropriate.

★   ★   ★

Both/and perspectives on the nature of science

Kenneth Tobin, University of Pennsylvania

Dear Vaille:
'What's it really like, working in science?' Jess asked. 'Is it the same as what we do at school?' Go ahead and tell her, Vaille. Tell Jess and her classmates how you experienced science from the inside. Be authentic. It is clear that the science you practised often fell short of what you regard as ideal. Explain the paradoxes, how your research on leukaemia was to benefit mankind, yet it involved practices with mice that you and most of us would not relish. In fact, from your telling of it, I was ashamed and fearful that the mice might be suffering needlessly. Nowadays there are stringent procedures to be followed when scientists experiment with living organisms. Would procedures like those you described be tolerated in science labs today? I am afraid you will answer me in the affirmative. Obviously you felt strongly enough about what you were required to do to make a career change. Tell your students why you decided to become a science teacher. Your accounts might stimulate some of them to consider science teaching as a career. Every year at Penn we get several former scientists who want to be teachers. Some aspect of their participation in science convinces them of the need for a career change, to teach others about science. Tell your students that there are aspects of science you did not enjoy and why you decided instead to educate others about science. Students can benefit from knowing about the human aspects of science and scientists. Too often they complete high school science without speaking to a scientist let alone a female scientist who questions some of the premises and practices of science. This is a rare opportunity you should not pass up.

Towards the end of the story you address your participation as a woman in science. The institution of science has not encouraged women as central participants and your examples are illustrative of your marginal status, characterised by lack of tenure, relatively low salary and little opportunity for your values to shape activities, priorities and working conditions. You, like so many women, appear to have been a peripheral participant in a community of scientists comprised mainly of white males. The account of your participation in at-risk activities is a stark reminder that women's bodies have traditionally been sites for struggle and oppression in many of society's niches. But to many it will come as a shock that a prestigious institution such as science is not open to all comers. As a part of a science education programme all students can build an awareness of the under-representation of women in science and what that means for those who aspire to become scientists. All students would no doubt benefit from discussions and deeper inquiry about the roles of women in science, the culture of science and the potential and desirability of recruiting participants from groups, such as women, who presently are under-represented in science. Making changes as an insider might appeal to some of the females contemplating further studies and careers in science. However, from the outside, and from your accounts from the inside as well, a career in science may not be perceived as viable for females.

Presently I am undertaking research in urban schools in which nearly all students are African American from conditions of poverty. Teaching science to these students raises issues similar to those you address in this chapter. African Americans are under-represented in science, an institution that was instrumental in propagating racist 'facts' about their alleged inferiority and that unscrupulously afforded unethical experiments built around the scientific theories of Darwin, Mendel and eugenics (Stepan and Gilman, 1993). Numerous studies endeavoured to show that blacks were inferior to whites. Bad science led to bad policies and practices. For example, African Americans with an IQ of less than 100 were offered financial incentives to be sterilised. Also, in research that continued until 1972, African American men with syphilis were told they had 'bad blood' and were left untreated so that medical scientists could learn more about the progression of the disease. Justification for the study was that 'The men's status did not warrant ethical debate. They were subjects, not patients; clinical material, not sick people' (Jones, 1981, p. 179).

In this chapter you paint a bleak picture of your experiences within science. Your tales are no doubt the tip of an iceberg of similar experiences that would have us shaking our heads in shame. Even today there are far too many instances of questionable ethics in science. However, many of the advances in science are wondrous and grounded in solid ethics. When we consider science teaching and learning it does not make sense to present science as monolithic and as *either* good *or* bad. Science is *both* good *and* bad depending upon where we focus. Use of a both/and ontology allows us to render visible and learn about the multiple faces of science and encourage all students (especially from under-represented groups) to participate. For too long science has been dominated by a perspective that is Eurocentric, white, male and middle class. Ways of thinking that deviated from the dominant perspective were regarded as deficient and discourses that were not scientific could not challenge the powerful voice of science. Science educators have a critical role in catalysing changes to recruit diverse participants into science and support new ethics, ways of making sense and practices.

I cannot help but wonder how some of the great master teachers, such as Socrates (Cooper, 1997), might have responded to Jess, Shannon and Sarah. I do not imagine Socrates would have instructed them directly on the topic or purported to know either the truth about science or what it might be like for a woman to participate as a scientist. I am certain he would ask incisive questions to motivate your students to examine the adequacy of their own perspectives and arrive at deeper understandings of the nature of science and the possibilities for pursuing successful careers in biomedical science. Does science always make the world a better place? How might you identify those branches of science that would allow you to use what you know to improve the lives of people? I can imagine a Socratic dialogue in which your role is to raise salient questions to elicit divergent thinking and associated responses from your students. Just as Socrates did, you might use an interactive dialogue to present what you know as a context for questions you want students to ponder (be careful, Vaille, Socrates was sentenced to death for his subversion of the Gods!). I envision a scenario in which points and counter-points emerge from interactive activities in which students are invited to ask questions, state their disagreements and present perspectives on any issue they wish to address. Accordingly, their emergent understandings would not be dominated by your perspective alone, but would reflect their active participation in an interactive dialogue that incorporated multiple perspectives.

Finally, you address the extent to which school science is a viable representation of science. I do not think it possible to make a strong statement that is inclusive of all contexts in which science education is practised. However, based on decades of research in several countries, it is clear to me that in many (and perhaps most) instances school science is not an authentic representation of science. Given what I have said previously about the many faces of science education I am not about to insist that all science courses can or should take a particular form. What I do advocate is that science be taught in ways that provide students with opportunities to understand its interfaces with society and to actively examine the roles of people in science, including those from communities in which they live. If students adopt a critical inquiry into the nature and practice of science they might well learn that groups are marginalised and that power imbalances distort the ideals that are so often represented as heroic accounts in textbook science. We should be so bold as science educators to critique the fabric of science while celebrating its accomplishments and deprecating its unethical practices. Incorporating a both/and perspective into the science curriculum is consistent with a form of science education that is adaptive to changing times and potentially transformative in serving personkind.

★   ★   ★

Editors' synthesis

While the story by Vaille Dawson is not about teaching the nature of science *per se*, the events described highlight several issues about how science should be represented in school. Dawson calls on her experience in both science and science education to decide what advice to offer three students considering a career in science. In recounting this episode, she raises two questions that lie at the heart of this chapter – what is the nature of science? and how can school studies reflect the nature of science?

Dawson's story and the accompanying commentaries provide further examples of the dualist character of the debate about the nature of science. One aspect of this debate concerns the worthiness of science – whether it is inherently good or bad. All three commentators offer examples of science subject to ethical transgressions, sexist and racist practices and boring routine. Dawson, for example, describes a range of experiences working in medical research, including using live animals for cancer research. In retrospect, she wonders about the ethical justifications for such work. Tobin, in his commentary, points to examples of where unethical, racist scientific practice led to government-endorsed policies discriminating against African Americans. Dawson also recalls her uncertain career prospects as a female at the margins of the scientific enterprise, reliant on her (predominantly male) colleagues for support, recognition and funding. Lederman remembers that the most exciting part of his work as a medical technician was joking over coffee about who would do blood and who would do urine analyses.

Each of the foregoing examples points to science as a flawed enterprise. And yet, as Tobin argues, it would be a mistake to think about science as '*either* good *or* bad. Science is *both* good *and* bad depending upon where we focus.' He suggests that while many past (and present) research practices might be called into question, there is much to be thankful for in the 'wondrous' scientific advances of the past century. The routine (and sometimes ethically debatable) tasks that Dawson and Lederman describe need to be balanced against 'breakthrough' discoveries in medical science. Worthy advances in leukaemia research, for example, have been built on some disturbing practices involving injecting live animals with cancerous cells. While some women struggle to find a place in science, so do some men, as Lederman's chequered career as a medical technician and a 'soft money' scientist illustrates. Science, it would appear, is neither 'monolithic' (to use Tobin's term), nor 'dualistic'. Rather it is a complex, human activity, full of trade-offs, paradoxes and dilemmas.

Given this complexity, it is little wonder that Dawson is troubled by her response to the questions asked by Jess, Sarah and Shannon. How can school studies reflect the nature of science? Lederman's response to this question focuses on the 'tension between presenting to students both the routine and exciting aspects of science and the pedagogical necessity of keeping adolescents engaged and motivated'. According to Lederman, school science is not the same as 'real science'. Wary of the dangers of switching students off science by engaging in routine activities, he proposes that teachers should 'focus a disproportionate amount of time on the more motivational aspects of their disciplines'. The role of the teacher, according to Lederman, is not to 'totally represent the activities of the profession'. In essence, Lederman proposes telling a 'white lie' to 'invite students in' so that they may become involved and develop further interest in a scientific vocation.

Tobin approaches the question from a different standpoint. He advises Dawson to explain to her students how she experienced science from the inside – the good side of her contact with science as well as the bad side – to tell the truth, to be 'authentic'. Tobin suggests the use of a Socratic dialogue between teacher and students revolving initially around 'incisive questions' to enable the students to articulate their own experiences as participants and consumers of science. Later, the students could question the teacher about her career moves in biomedical science and in science education. Tobin envisages an interactive dialogue where 'points and counter-points emerge from interactive activities in which students are invited to ask questions, state their disagreements and present perspectives on any issue they wish to address'. In promoting such discussion about the nature of science, Tobin proposes that we should be aiming to 'critique the fabric of science while celebrating its accomplishments and deprecating its unethical practices'.

Dawson offered the story, *What is science really like?*, as a 'provocation'. In the conclusion to her commentary, she acknowledges that there are many positives about working in a scientific environment and many outstanding scientific achievements. And yet, the questions she raises about how to represent the different faces of science are also valid. It is a difficult thing to balance stories about good and bad science, about ethical and unethical practice and have students experience both the routine and the extraordinary. In Dawson's school, for example, many views of science apparently co-exist and compete. Her laudable attempts to teach an inquiry-based human biology course, where questions about the nature of science are encouraged, are set against the formidable constraints of a traditional, textbook-oriented school curriculum dominated by external examinations. Working within and around these constraints, deciding what is 'developmentally appropriate' (Lederman), maintaining a 'both/and perspective' (Tobin), motivating students and engaging in an interactive dialogue about the nature of science are all part of the difficult but important work of encouraging students to become active participants in, and critical consumers of, science.

References

Allchin, D. (1998). Values in science and science education. In B. J. Fraser and K. G. Tobin (eds), *International handbook of science education* (pp. 1,083–1,092). Dordrecht, The Netherlands: Kluwer.

Brickhouse, N. (1998). Feminism(s) and science education. In B.J. Fraser and K.G. Tobin (eds), *International handbook of science education* (pp. 1,067–1,081). Dordrecht, The Netherlands: Kluwer.

Cooper, J. M. (ed.) (1997). *Plato: Complete works.* Indianapolis, IN: Hackett Publishing Company.

Duschl, R. (1994). Research on the history and philosophy of science. In D. Gabel (ed.), *Handbook on science teaching and learning* (pp. 443–465). Washington, DC: Macmillan.

Harding, S. (1991). *Whose science? Whose knowledge?* Ithaca, NY: Cornell University Press.

—— (1998). *Is science multicultural?* Bloomington, IN: Indiana University Press.

Jones, J. (1981). *Bad blood: The Tuskegee syphilis experiment: A tragedy of race and medicine.* New York: The Free Press.

Kuhn, T. (1962). *The structure of scientific revolutions.* Chicago, IL: University of Chicago Press.

Longino, H. (1990). *Science as social knowledge: Values and objectivity in scientific inquiry.* Princeton, NY: Princeton University Press.

Longino, H. and Doell, R. (1983). Body, bias and behaviour: A comparative analysis of reasoning in two areas of biological science. *Signs*, 9, 206–207.

Matthews, M. (1998). The nature of science and science teaching. In B. J. Fraser and K. G. Tobin (eds), *International handbook of science education* (pp. 981–999). Dordrecht, The Netherlands: Kluwer.

McComas, W. (ed.) (1998). *The nature of science in science education: Rationales and strategies.* Dordrecht, The Netherlands: Kluwer.

National Research Council (1996). *National Science Education Standards.* Washington, DC: National Academy Press.

Stepan, N. L. (1996). Race and gender: The role of analogy in science. In E. F. Keller and H. E. Longino (eds), *Feminism and science* (pp. 121–136). Oxford: Oxford University Press.

Stepan, N. L. and Gilman, S. L. (1993). Appropriating the idioms of science: The rejection of scientific racism. In S. Harding (ed.), *The 'racial' economy of science: Toward a democratic future* (pp. 72–103). Bloomington, IN: Indiana University Press.

Stinner, A. and Williams, H. (1998). History and philosophy of science in the science curriculum. In B.J. Fraser and K. G. Tobin (eds), *International handbook of science education* (pp. 1,027–1,045). Dordrecht, The Netherlands: Kluwer.

Wertheim, M. (1995). *Pythagoras' trousers: God, physics and the gender wars*. New York: W.W. Norton & Company.

Chapter 2

The laws of science

Contributions by David Geelan,
Marie Larochelle and Jay L Lemke

Editors' introduction

There is a deep and enduring tension between personal experience and the formal representation of scientific knowledge in school science classrooms. Students have ample personal experience of the physical properties school science seeks to explain: they know that balls rolled along a flat surface slow down and stop after a while; they know that the location of tadpoles underwater is not quite what it seems from above the water. Researchers interested in children's knowledge of science and cognitive change have explored ways in which students can work through their preconceptions (or misconceptions) about the knowledge of science (see Duit and Treagust, 1998). The tension between students' common-sense knowledge and the formal knowledge of science remains, however, because of the language science uses to represent important and long-settled knowledge. Scientific knowledge is represented in specialised vocabulary, syntax and genre structures, quite different from the language of common sense. As Martin (1993) has argued, science cannot be understood in the student's 'own words' because science 'has evolved a special language in order to interpret the world in its own, not in common sense terms' (Martin, 1993, p. 200).

In school science, the tension between personal experience and formal knowledge is heightened by the representation of long-settled knowledge as 'laws'. Textbook accounts obscure the long process from the first formulation of ideas to the point of orthodoxy (Sutton, 1996). For example, the law of refraction students encounter in their Grade 12 physics textbooks obscures the history of the idea now characterised as Snell's Law. Students learn to make calculations about refraction without any sense of who Snell was (a Dutch mathematician), when he worked on refraction (about 1621), where he first published it (he never did), when it became a basic building block of the theory of optics (more than eighty years later), or whose authority backed the elevation of Snell's algorithm to the status of a law (Huygens and Descartes). Through school science, knowledge that was once provisional and contestable is experienced by students as having far greater authority than their personal experience. As one of the students quoted by Désautels and Larochelle (1989) put it, '*A law is something you can't deny. A law is a law. … You obey a law*' (Désautels and Larochelle, 1989, p. 117, emphasis in the original).

In this chapter, the tension between scientific laws and personal experience is illustrated by a story written by David Geelan. Geelan describes his difficulty when confronted by student disbelief in Newton's First Law of Motion. Students' personal experience – that objects always tend to slow down – fits more closely an Aristotelian impetus theory of motion than a Newtonian theory of motion. He wonders how he can make more of students' experience in teaching the laws of physics. Geelan's story and commentary are followed by comments from Marie Larochelle and Jay Lemke.

Newton's Zeroth Law

David Geelan

'But it doesn't!' Every class has one – that critical voice, put there to keep us honest. In our philosophic moments we claim that their questions are valuable, and that we're glad they're there. But I was tired.

Friday, just after lunch. The five boys in this Grade 11 physics class have just come in from a sweaty game of football. They're hot, they're itchy and you really don't want to go too close. The three girls choose seats as far away as possible. It's too hot to work and nobody – least of all me – is really in the mood to wrestle with Newton's laws. After all, Newton was just sitting under a shady apple tree in cool old England when he made this stuff up for our devilment. The sun's slanting in through one of the west windows, and the Grade 9s broke the blind last week.

And on top of all this, Neil is refusing to make life easier. We're discussing Newton's First Law of Motion. I've written it up on the board, in the form that I think flows the best: 'An object remains in a state of rest, or of uniform motion in a straight line, unless acted upon by an unbalanced external force.' 'But it doesn't' interjects Neil. 'The first part is OK – if something's not moving, you have to have a force to make it move. But if something is moving, it's eventually gonna slow down and stop.'

'No,' I explain (patiently considering how I feel), 'that's because there are forces acting that we don't notice. When things are moving they often have friction forces, from air resistance or whatever. That's what slows them down.'

'Yeah, but the whole point is that Newton's Law isn't right, cos if something is moving it *will* slow down. So why make up a law that says it won't? What's a law like that good for?'

'OK then,' I say, 'think about what happens in outer space, where there are no forces like friction and wind resistance. Out there, an object will continue in the same straight line forever.'

'But how do we know that?' pipes up Kelly. 'We've never been to outer space.' James joins in: 'Yeah, and you're always telling us that science is about trying to explain our own experiences – in our experience, things always slow down and stop after a while. So Newton's Law is no good for explaining our experiences.'

'Lots of stuff in physics is like that though', says Phillip. 'It took ages for the scientists to even work out whether light's a particle or a wave, 'cos you can't see it or feel it or anything.' 'Yeah, they still don't know', says Jill. 'And there's other things in science – like atoms and molecules – that you can't experience: so what's the use?'

This seems almost like open revolt – are they going to give up on school science completely? I'm just about to launch into a whole set of complex vector diagrams, pointing out the usefulness of Newtonian physics, and the deadly errors of Aristotelian approaches. But then I don't. The students wait for a few moments, while I think. They're not all looking at me, and they're probably all thinking about going home. And it's still hot. But I'm thinking harder than I have for a long time.

I try to teach in ways that use my students' personal experiences as the raw material of what they learn. In fact, I believe that unless what I'm teaching helps them to develop plausible, workable explanations of their own experiences, then all they'll really be doing is accumulating inert 'facts' to hand back to me as required. And that would be a waste of my time and theirs. What I *really* tried to do in this lesson, I realise with some dismay, was get them to accept Newton's laws *because I said so*. I also believe very strongly that school science is for everyone, not just the few who will go on to tertiary study in science. So although I need to support the prospective scientists in my class, if what I'm teaching is guided totally by that then it's wasted time for probably 90 per cent of the students. Putting these two elements of my own value framework together, I'm forced to consider whether, in fact, James is absolutely right: Newton's First Law of Motion is useless and a waste of time for this class.

I have no doubt that the Newtonian revolution was enormously important historically and philosophically. Neither do I doubt that, if you're designing an aeroplane or a building, Newton's laws are very useful indeed. But for explaining the kids' normal, everyday experiences like rolling a skateboard along a car park, Aristotle's impetus theory *just works better*. And, that being the case, it's extremely difficult, from a science-for-all value position, to defend teaching Newtonian physics at the secondary school.

'I'll need some time to think about your point, but I think it's well taken', I say to the class. 'Perhaps we can investigate ways that Newton's laws *might* be useful. Um ... well, if you go on to do physics at university you'll need to do this stuff.' I hate this, even as I say it: I used to hate it when I was a student. If something has no intrinsic value for me now, but just the chance of being useful at some later time, why should I put energy into learning it now – I'll learn it then, if I need to! And I see the students having the same reaction.

I want to address the concerns of these students. They're good kids, and they're asking because they're genuinely puzzled, not just to be difficult. There *is* a gap between what I'm preaching – experience-based science for all – and what I'm teaching. So what should change – the students, the science or my educational values?

Teacher commentary

David Geelan

From my perspective (by no means the only possible one) this is 'really' a story about what it means to teach science, why we do it, and what value the science taught in schools has for our students.

Although the knowledge and information that we want to teach our students has great intrinsic value, is important to our culture, supports our technology and all that good stuff, it really has little or no personal relevance for the vast majority of our students. Sure, those who will go on to university physics or chemistry will find knowledge of Newton's Laws and atomic theory useful. But what of those who go on to become nurses, secretaries, welders, bus drivers, doctors or English teachers? These bodies of knowledge are essentially completely useless for explaining the events and processes of our lives. How, then, do we justify their prominent place in school curricula?

The way we teach science is strongly influenced by our own views on what science *is* (and is not). Although it has become fashionable to state in the preambles to our curriculum documents that science is both a body of knowledge and a set of processes, skills and attitudes, it is the former that tends to enormously dominate the curricula that follow. And students are (naturally) strongly influenced by this bias – they see science as a mountain of facts and theories to be memorised, rather than as a mode of life, an approach to living which is made up of values and ideas and interests and explanations.

But it's more even than that. Constructivist approaches to teaching and learning, which are becoming increasingly influential in science education, suggest that students construct their knowledge of scientific laws on the basis of their own experiences. Yet large bodies of the existing science syllabi are simply incapable of being experienced! Atomic theory cannot be directly experienced, only posited on the basis of rather abstract measurements and relationships. Neither can the nature of light. In other words, these are sophisticated, highly abstract models, designed to answer sophisticated, highly abstract questions. One thing they don't do at all well is answer simple, everyday questions. Ironically, this is because they're too simple! – they don't take into account all of the richness and complexity of 'real life'.

I'm still teaching science, and I'm still wrestling with these questions. I'm sure plenty of other science teachers think about this too. Or at least, I hope so. Some of the things I see from time to time make me wonder whether most science teachers are so 'married' to the content we've been teaching for so long that these questions just don't occur to them. (Perhaps non-science teachers in middle and elementary schools are actually coping better with these issues.) As one example, when efforts are made to integrate science with other learning areas to form integrated curricula, the question which is almost invariably asked is 'How can we fit the existing knowledge base of school science into the integrated units?' It's almost never 'What facets of science – skills and attitudes as well as facts and ideas – are necessary and integral to the study of this topic?' In other words, the science is taken as given, and all else must be bent to fit around it. Why is the unit theme, or better, the interests and needs of the students, not taken as given, and the science chosen to complement that? Surely this is how science is applied in life?

I can think of two ways we can address this problem, and I'm not sure which I prefer – perhaps a blend of both has the greatest potential to support students' science learning. One is to teach the same theories, but to cut back dramatically on the width of the curriculum in order to increase its depth. If we were able to devote serious time to each theory or idea, then we could teach Newton's First Law with sufficient sophistication – including notions of friction and so on – so that it *does* explain students' experiences. That is to say, avoid over-simplifying: teach the traditional science, but do it *right*. The other is more radical: if Aristotle's impetus theory of motion explains our everyday experiences better than Newton's or Einstein's schemes, then we ought to teach it. After all, I was trying to teach Newtonian physics, which is itself nearly a century out of date. Aristotle would be taught, not as a historical curiosity for ridicule or background, but as a viable, useful model for understanding what happens around us. To a science teacher this sounds almost heretical, but if we're serious about our constructivist teaching innovations and about science for all students, then perhaps the science must come to the students, rather than vice versa.

★   ★   ★

From picture to window

Marie Larochelle,[1] Université Laval and CIRADE (Centre Interdisciplinaire de Recherche sur l' Apprentissage et le Développement en Education)

To be consistent with the opinion advocated in this text, my commentary should be seen for what it is: a point of view that has been *inspired* by David Geelan's narrative and which has obviously been developed in keeping with my own set of sociodiscursive habits and resources. I do not claim in any way to have made an interpretation that is either exhaustive or authoritative; indeed, there may be some room for doubting its relevance altogether. To be sure, I know what he means by those endless, sluggish classes of a Friday afternoon, bathed in an occasionally 'heady' mix of exhalations. And I know all too well that overwhelming feeling of absurdity that comes from attempting to impose knowledge of dubious immediate practicality (i.e. knowledge that may one day 'come in handy') on students. But I must admit I am far from seeing eye to eye with David Geelan as to the social and cultural underpinnings from which the perspective and meaning of his story derive. However, a certain perspectivism (that I in turn would suggest taking towards the dilemma he has described) is of a piece with the type of reception I would urge for my remarks. In order to pursue the conversation he has initiated on a number of problematical subjects, I think it important to view the following commentary as just one possible *positioned* commentary among others.

The portrait of a dilemma

In a book aptly entitled *Les muets parlent aux sourds* (trans.: When the mute speak to the deaf), the social psychologist Suzanne Mollo used the statements provided by children on the subject of school to examine the practices involved in the socialisation into the world of school knowledge. It is a multifarious profile of 'tooling' (or the 'technologies of power', according to Foucault) that emerges. Whether the process is one of disciplining bodies, instituting knowledge as a field of objects rather than as a set of activities, standardising cognitive and discursive codes, or superimposing a status of pupil on that of child, the results are twofold: schoolchildren are constrained to muteness, teachers to deafness; thus, thanks to an ever-so-gradual education in conformity, the entire process – and indeed the reproduction of this process – appears to go forward unimpeded. When, finally, the children are provided the opportunity to speak, during an activity in which they are called on to imagine the end of a poem featuring a bird, schoolchildren, a teacher and the recitation of multiplication tables,[2] it is a veritable chorus of monologues that gushes forth, as though the children had in turn become deaf to one another.

Fortunately indeed, the mechanics of this process are less than foolproof, as has been marvellously illustrated in the reflexive ordering that David Geelan offers of his experiences and, in particular, of the questions haunting him as he reflected on what he says, does and has others do. Once having placed Newton's Zeroth Law on the day's agenda of study, he then found himself in a particularly awkward situation. For, previous to this course, the students had, after a fashion, devised their own law on the movement of bodies, and they now *justifiably* ruled Newton's position as being inadmissible. What is a teacher to do when, like David Geelan, he or she is disinclined to use techniques of domestication; when, rather, he or she is concerned with making science accessible, with fostering receptiveness among students towards other potentialities, other ways of viewing the world and taking one's place within it. What is a teacher to do when he or she is convinced that students are not suffering from a cognitive deficit but do in fact know something different from what he or she would like them to know; or, again, when he or she is aware of the vacuousness of using strategies designed to compel conformity or relying on the argument that such knowledge may one day 'come in handy'? Is one necessarily faced with the dilemma formulated in the conclusion of Geelan's story: 'So what should change – the students, the science or my educational values?'

From a world of objects to a world of subjects

Undoubtedly, more than one tack may be taken to this type of questioning. The approach I would like to discuss with the author may be likened to a 'pocket-size' epistemology,[3] one that may be plugged in as necessary, and which consists in laying out, in symmetrical fashion, the terms of a question that, as in the case of the above-mentioned question, come laden with ethical issues.

For example, in David Geelan's concluding question, we are confronted, as it were, with two worlds: on the one hand, there is a world of subjects ('students and my educational values') – hence, a world of tensions, conflicts and negotiations, as was eloquently illustrated in the classroom episode; on the other, a world of objects ('science') – in other words, a world of abstract, reified and hence unaccountable powers. And as with other such unaccountable powers that appear out of nowhere, such as 'society' and 'morality' (Fourez, 1992), they lend themselves poorly to any negotiation of meaning. The episode narrated by David Geelan provides a telling illustration of this point: by refusing this world of objects, students make mediation an arduous affair, and thus provoke the teacher to resort to a strategy that he otherwise disavows – i.e. use of the argument that 'such knowledge may one day come in handy'.

And yet, if an effort is made to re-humanise this world of objects – in other words, if this world is re-placed within culture by means of connecting it to the human and social projects that have produced it – then the dilemma is not so much likely to be solved as made potentially more 'manageable'. For all in all, the confrontation that now emerges no longer opposes groups of subjects *and* a description of the world (which, moreover, is often presented as *the* description of the world). Instead, it emerges *between* groups of 'describers of the world' (students, scientists, teacher) who are at that point free to occupy centre stage, and bring into play their ideas and principles – their anchoring in short, thereby engendering discussion and indeed the testing of their respective descriptions.

In other words, by reformulating this question according to the terms of this perspective, we will then be dealing with a process of negotiation between students' experiential commitments, scientists' epistemological commitments and teachers' educational commitments. Of course, it may be objected that by taking such an approach, I have simply shifted the angle of approach. I would concur with this view to a degree, but I would also point out that this shift also legitimises connections that are unlikely to emerge under the initial formulation. Take, for example the 'science-for-all' value position advocated by David Geelan and that may be understood as stemming from a desire to place science within culture. As initially formulated, this question contains a double bind: how, in fact, can one claim to place within culture a world of objects that is presented, precisely, as escaping all limitations deriving from this order? In the second, admittedly more polemical formulation, the place of science in culture is duly recognised, because science is embodied and presented as an activity performed by social actors – i.e. those who ply the knowledge trade.

In short, the second formulation leads to an entirely different question, one which makes it possible to conceive of science in social terms but as well to highlight the fact that, as with students' knowledge, scholarly knowledge does not simply emerge out of nowhere. On the contrary, scholarly knowledge is emblematic of those who have developed it, representing as it does their epistemological postures, social positions and alliances, as well as a particular zeitgeist. To borrow from von Foerster's cogent dictum, 'the logic of the world is the logic of the description of the world' (in Segal, 1986, p. 4); in other words, it is the logic of the observer who performs the description according to the *reflexive monitoring* of his or her own sociocognitive experiences, and in keeping with a position of membership in a sociodiscursive community whose commitments and narratives he or she shares, at least partially.

However, by reintegrating the observer into his or her own description, teaching amounts to much more than relativisation of various points of view. Indeed, teaching means seeking out the necessary relationships between a given point of view and an observer's choices and decisions, and then grasping how, by the same token, these choices are a product of his or her way of reflecting on and working out the reasons, values, ideologies and representations that are assumed to be reasonable within his or her community of practice. Such an approach obviously conveys a form of ideology. However, as Fourez has also pointed out, the issue has never been one of attempting to eliminate all ideology (an ideological project in itself, to be sure), or of glossing over relationships of power. The issue, actually, involves locating the ideas and values which we wish to promote in school, in addition to those, precisely, we wish to avoid.

Thus, I would describe the relevance of this 'pocket-size' epistemology for the present case as follows: by refashioning a position of symmetry between the terms of a question, what has until that time appeared as *immobilised* can now instead be *mobilised*. To borrow a metaphor from Bauman (1989, p. vii), this epistemology entails moving from an image of science as though the latter constituted a picture on the wall – i.e. one which is 'neatly framed, to set the painting apart from the wallpaper and emphasise how different it [is] from the rest of the furnishings' – to an image of science as resembling a window, through which it is possible to glimpse a world which is not so distant from our own – i.e. a world of tensions, conflicts and negotiations.

★   ★   ★

Science and experience

Jay L. Lemke, City University of New York

'Newton's law is no good for explaining our experiences', says a student in this sunbaked Australian classroom, and his teacher worries whether Newton's laws mightn't be just a bit out of step with an experience-based approach to science for all. Of course they are. Newton's approach to dynamics was more like Euclid's approach to geometry than like his own experimental treatises on optics; it was formalistic and deductive. He took no empirical prisoners and, famously, 'framed no hypotheses' – by which he probably meant to say that he was not just guessing at generalisations from experimental results. For Newton, what mattered was irrefutable, logical, mathematical certainty; what he could prove. His 'laws' are more like Euclid's axioms than like our modern notions of scientific generalisations. And his methods of argument were hardly meant 'for all' in his day, or, realistically, in ours.

Experience-based approaches to science teaching often misrepresent the role of theory. Pragmatic cultures like those in Australia, the US, or the UK seem to favour empiricism: theory is seen as nothing more than the summary and generalisation of what experience and experimentation show. It is represented as the end-product of empirical research. It's also acknowledged as a practical tool for setting up experiments and estimating the sizes of various effects, in a rather engineering-minded way. But it is not presented as Newton, or Einstein, knew it: a parallel reality that can be explored in its own terms, a realm of the imagination where we can leap ahead of all possible experiments and generate impossible possibilities (time dilation, anti-matter, black holes, quarks) that time and again have been found to have exact parallels in the world of experimental reality. For many of us the excitement of science does not come from endless hours in the laboratory collecting data-points, nor does it come only from those rare moments when something is seen or measured that was totally unexpected or that confirms for the first time what theory had already imagined. It comes from the creative possibilities of theoretical speculation, and the power of theoretical tools to take us where no mind has gone before.

When tax money is collected to support science education, the big payers are looking for a handsome return: a sufficient number of competent technicians, engineers and R&D people to do the ordinary work of science. There is not such a big market for scientific visionaries and speculators. When the community of professional scientists shapes its image, the picture mostly reflects the large numbers of experimental scientists whose chief values are carefulness and caution. These scientists present themselves as people who stick close to their data and whose modest generalisations can be trusted for public policy and financial investment purposes. Not many adolescents find this image particularly exciting. Frankly, not a lot of us adults do either.

When nose-to-the-lab-bench science is combined with minimal doses of highly abstract concepts (like Newton's 'laws'), there may be some fun to be found in fooling around in the lab, or even in getting a 'right' answer, but there is precious little to stir the soul and fire the imagination, or produce genuine emotional engagement and personal identification with science. The abstractions are just add-ons, another burden to carry to and from the lab or the examination. Almost no one sees these abstract concepts for what they are: stray cogs and gears broken loose from the great imaginative engines of theoretical science.

There is great neglect of the affective dimension of human learning in our theories of science education: of joy and desire, imagination and caring. We do not often enough consider what gets people excited about scientific work or scientific ideas, or what sorts of personal dispositions lead people to enjoy abstract and critical reasoning in the service of scientific imagination. What images of science and scientists can our students identify with emotionally and viscerally? What is admirable or heroic about science? And where is that in our curriculum? When we talk of 'experienced-based' approaches to science, are we thinking only of the experiences we arrange for students to have, and neglecting all their other experiences, those that determine what they will devote their best efforts to?

When we do consider these matters, are we competent to bridge the gender gap our culture promotes in the attitudes of male and female students? The images and metaphors, examples and ideals that excite the guys (adventure, danger, power) may leave many young women thinking the male attitude is not really very serious about life. And what matters to women? Helping others, healing the ecosystem, strengthening the web of social relationships and mutual support? Of what importance in these value systems are Newton's 'laws' or other abstractions that can't be experienced directly? As Jill says, 'so what's the use?' What good can we do with them?

Experience-based science education too often concerns itself only with establishing truth, and not with placing truth either in the service of doing good or in the service of seeking out new human possibilities. Our curricula show students the way we think things are, but not why this matters. If students are already interested, already curious about something, there's no problem. But what gets us interested in something to begin with? What values and feelings, what sense of who we are and what we want to do and be shape our interests? Why not a values-based science education?

I am not looking for new and trickier ways to justify the old curriculum. I don't want to propose how we ought to adapt the teaching of Newton's First Law to the values and emerging identities of a diverse range of students. If this scientific principle is as useful as we claim, most value- and interest-driven paths of inquiry will engage with it sooner or later. I first encountered it when a book I was reading on General Relativity mentioned it as a sort of primitive version of the principle of motion along geodesic curves in space-time (yes, I read Einstein before Newton, and it was less confusing that way). I read that book because of an interest in cosmology, which grew out of an interest in first astronomy and then astrophysics and stellar evolution. My love of astronomy started from wonder at the stars, abetted by early gifts of a toy planetarium and (after endless asking) a small telescope. I could bring the night sky into my bedroom after school; I could view things in the sky that had been invisible to me before. I could expand and deepen my wonder at the stars and imagine universes of possibilities. And so I was led from nature to science (and science fiction), and briefly passed by Newton's First Law on my way through much more modern and exciting scientific theories.

I had my nose rubbed in Newton's laws in high school PSSC Physics and again in college Physics 131. I never did find Newton intellectually exciting, even though I earned a Ph.D. in theoretical physics. (I might some day return to Newton out of an interest in the history of ideas, however; so there's still hope!) Newton was quite irrelevant to my scientific self-education; what mattered were the topics I was interested in. What I had to learn to satisfy my curiosity along the way (algebra, tensor calculus, the Greek alphabet, partial derivatives, neutrino physics), I learned with relish because it helped to get me where I wanted to go. I can't really say that any of the required courses I had to take turned out to be the least bit useful to my later work, except for fulfilling requirements. What was useful were the years of experience in finding out what I wanted to know.

I got most of that experience in libraries, not in classrooms or laboratories. My explorations of scientific theory were done by reading, thinking, doing mathematical derivations (rarely numerical calculations), and writing my conclusions for (originally) imaginary audiences. I came to understand some of those theories quite deeply, without ever taking a single relevant data-point, without ever having a first-hand experience to which any of them were particularly relevant. Most scientific theories of the twentieth century are simply not relevant either to everyday experience or to most of what it is possible to experience in a meaningful way in a school science lab. Their relevance even to what one 'experiences' in a research lab is pretty indirect. As a teenager I did observe particle beam experiments at some major research facilities; what I saw was impressively big, but any connection to the theories I was learning about was as strictly in my imagination as were the visualisations I concocted while reading my books or the diagrams I sketched while doing my derivations.

There is a place for lab experiences in school science, as there is for drawing connections to students' out-of-school experiences. Their place is in opening gateways for students to newfound interests in this or that topic in science. Their role is in enabling students to make a link, to identify, to engage some part of themselves with something in science. These links are unpredictable and individual; they depend on the whole prior history of students' lives, on their attitudes, values and interests, their images of themselves and their dreams for their futures. Some students will in this way become excited by the ideas or activities of science and pursue them with our help, or with someone else's. If this desire for science is kindled early enough, and supported long enough and well enough, many students will find their paths of inquiry passing through a wide range of scientific ideas. Some of them may even stop and think a while about Newton's First Law. But whether they do or not, they will be getting the true benefits we often claim for a good scientific education but which no required curriculum can 'deliver'.

★   ★   ★

Editors' synthesis

David Geelan's story describes a situation familiar to many teachers: a long, slow Friday afternoon and a disengaged group of students combining to challenge the teachers' beliefs about what can and should be achieved in school science. Larochelle and Lemke, in different ways, express some sympathy for the situation in which Geelan found himself. Larochelle knows the 'feeling of absurdity that comes from attempting to impose knowledge of dubious immediate practicality', and Lemke agrees that teaching Newton's laws is 'a bit out of step with an experience-based approach to science for all'. Neither of the commentators, however, shares Geelan's enthusiasm for what he calls experience-based science.

At issue for both of the commentators are the easy assumptions that science educators make about the meaning of 'experience'. Larochelle contests the uneven treatment of experience in the world of subjects, represented by the classroom, and the world of objects, represented by the fixed laws of science. The experience of the subjects is brought fully into play in this story: the effect of the heat on the teacher and the students, the girls' separation from the boys, and the students' unwillingness to suspend their common-sense knowledge in favour of the immutable laws of physics. The experience of the objects in this story, Newton's Laws, is obscured by their presentation in the fixed and final formulation of 'states of rest', 'uniform motion' and 'external unbalanced forces'. As Larochelle argues, one of the ways to open up the possibilities for learning science is to problematise this world of objects, revealing science to be an activity performed by social actors who carry forward a variety of epistemological commitments in their mediation of experience.

Lemke contests the narrow, pragmatic frame within which science educators position experience and the priority they give to the experience they arrange for students over the experience students have in encountering the theoretical and imaginative world of science. Much of the current work in science deals, as Lemke and Geelan say, with phenomena that cannot be experienced 'in a meaningful way in a school science lab'. In place of staged empirical encounters, Lemke argues for supporting students to make links between science and their passions, interests and values. Students, he says, need experience of the parallel reality of theory, where the leaps of imagination enable abstract encounters with 'possible experiments and ... impossible possibilities'.

Both commentators share Geelan's concern about justifying the teaching of 'knowledge that may one day come in handy', and they are both concerned to reconceptualise 'experience' in school science. One possibility is to reposition science as a form of experience, epistemologically symmetrical to students' experience. Another possibility is to contest the priority of lab-bench facsimiles of experience over direct experience of scientific theory through reading, thinking and imagining. The challenge for teachers of science is to locate the person in the experience of science: the person who passionately wants to know and the person who shares in jointly constructing the meaning we call science.

Notes

1   I (Larochelle) would like to thank Donald Kellough, the translator of this commentary text, who once again has negotiated the passage between the French and English language games with panache.
2   The poem, 'Page d'écriture', is by Jacques Prévert.
3   Morf's expression (personal communication, 1992).

References

Bauman, Z. (1989). *Modernity and the Holocaust*. Ithaca, NY: Cornell University Press.
Désautels, J. and Larochelle, M. (1989) *Qu'est-ce que le savoir scientifique? Points de vue d'adolescents et d'adolescentes*. Quebec: Laval University Press.

Duit, R. and Treagust, D. F. (1998). Learning in science: From behaviourism towards social constructivism and beyond. In B. F. Fraser and K. G. Tobin (eds), *International handbook of science education* (pp. 3–25). Dordrecht, NL: Kluwer.

Fourez, G. (1992). *Éduquer. Écoles, éthiques, sociétés.* Bruxelles: De Boeck.

Martin, J. R. (1993). Literacy in science: Learning to handle text as technology. In M. A. K. Halliday and J. R. Martin, *Writing science: Literacy and discursive power* (pp. 106–202). London: Falmer Press.

Mollo, S. (1975). *Les muets parlent aux sourds. Les discours de l'enfant sur l'école.* Tournai, Belgique: Casterman.

Segal, L. (1986). *The dream of reality. Heinz von Foerster's constructivism.* New York: Norton.

Sutton, C. R. (1996). Beliefs about science and beliefs about language. *International Journal of Science Education*, 18 (1), 1–18.

Chapter 3

Laboratories

Contributions by Bevan McGuiness,
Wolff-Michael Roth and Penny J. Gilmer

Editors' introduction

The laboratory is a commonplace of science and school science. For more than a century, the laboratory has been uniquely associated with the pursuit of school science. The science curriculum is infused with images of students conducting rigorous laboratory-based experiments, mimicking the behaviour of real scientists in real scientific laboratories. 'Hands-on' has become a catch cry for science education, particularly over the past forty years, driving curriculum development (and facilities management) in the developed and developing worlds. And yet, notwithstanding the central place of the laboratory in school science, there is a growing corpus of research which calls into question both its value and effectiveness, and its connection to the enterprise of science (Hegarty-Hazel, 1990; Hodson, 1993; Lazarowitz and Tamir, 1994; Milne and Taylor, 1998; Tobin, 1990).

Two major critiques of school science laboratories have emerged in recent times. The first critique draws attention to the mismatch between the high ideals of laboratory-based inquiry and the reality of most 'cookbook' style practical work, with its emphasis on skill development and confirmation of predetermined conclusions (Hodson, 1993). The presumption that the school science laboratory is a place for genuine inquiry is largely a myth (Hodson, 1990; Milne and Taylor, 1998). Much of what goes on under the guise of experimentation is routinised and more concerned with technique and data than discourse. Assessments typically reflect an image of laboratory work as a closed rather than an open-ended enterprise. Genuine experimentation is rare, often confined to extra-curricular science activity such as science fairs. Given this state of affairs, many commentators are now calling for more 'authentic' forms of laboratory work and assessment, emphasising intellectual and problem-solving skills, a much reduced emphasis on technical skill-based bench work (Arzi, 1998) and an expanded definition of the term laboratory to incorporate recent advances in information technology, and data collection and processing.

A second and related critique of laboratory work centres on the assumption that students can mimic in some way what happens in 'real' science laboratories. Many scholars have observed that science in 'real' laboratories is conducted within a social milieu of interpretation, justification and argumentation. Scientific positions are 'constituted by the researchers' paradigmatic affinities which contribute to frame a phenomenon, to define the operating conditions under which its observation is carried out' (Désautels and Larochelle, 1998, p. 118) and to determine how data are to be treated (Woolgar, 1990). These positions are socially derived and argued within particular communities of scholars, in accordance with sets of beliefs, rules and assumptions. By contrast, school students typically act from an individualistic perspective, believing that objects or phenomena offer up observations to the observer, that data speak for themselves, and that observations and data form the basis for theory building or modification (Désautels and Larochelle, 1998). Indeed, in the absence of an interpretative frame, students appear ill equipped to mimic the mature and complex patterns of social behaviour of 'real' scientists.

Taken together, these two critiques – about the mismatch between goals and realities, and about the difference between school science and 'real' science – provide a complex set of issues for teachers and others who wish to reform the school science laboratory. These issues include how to imagine a form of laboratory work which is 'authentic' in a world where students lack the social and cognitive resources to mimic the scientific endeavour, how to move the emphasis from an individualistic view of science towards science as a social practice, and how to shift from a culture of right answers to a culture of interpretation, negotiation and justification. These issues form the backdrop to the story that follows. In *Titrations, titrations*, Bevan McGuiness recounts his experience in teaching the technique of titration to a group of Grade 11 senior chemistry students. In doing so, he raises questions about the relevance of the activity and the type of learning taking place. The story is followed by his own commentary on the activity and commentaries by Wolff-Michael Roth and Penny Gilmer.

Titrations, titrations

Bevan McGuiness

Teaching senior chemistry can be a mixed blessing sometimes. There are times when you just have to slog through lengthy theoretical sections, such as atomic theory and electron configurations, where there simply aren't any easily performed experiments available. And then there are times when there is a whole series of intricate and demanding experiments. Such a time is titration time. It comes along every year at the same stage of the course, when we dust off the burettes, find the volumetric flasks and introduce the students to the joys of titres, aliquots and equivalence-points.

I remember one year, I had an excellent class. They were motivated, quick to grasp concepts and eager to excel. So naturally when it came time for the titration section, I was keenly anticipating the way in which they would approach their work. In preparation, I found some of my laboratory note-books from my university days and made sure of the intricacies. If any class I had was likely to ever stretch my understanding of a technique, it would be this one. So I practised, I spoke to the laboratory technicians and asked them to check that all the burettes they provided were of the new type with the teflon taps that would not fall out unexpectedly and generally made a nuisance of myself around the laboratory workshop.

In class I prepared the students by directing them to the appropriate sections in their textbooks so that when they came to class they would be well prepared for the experiment. We talked in advance about the idea of experimental uncertainty and how it could be reduced by the use of precise apparatus, and we discussed the difference between accuracy and precision. In all I thought them well prepared for the, what I considered, fun ahead.

At last the day arrived. I remember it clearly. It was warm and sunny, the students came in just after lunch-time and they were all a bit hot and sweaty. Immediately they came in I called their attention to the demonstration titration I had set up. Carefully I went through the steps. I demonstrated the technique that my teacher had shown me when I had been in high school.

First of all, I went through the use of the pipette, showing the manipulation of the two different types of pipette fillers and discussing the reasons for not pipetting by mouth. Then I put the conical flask under the burette and with my right hand swirling the flask, I put my left hand around the burette and carefully opened the tap to allow the low concentration acid dribble out into the swirling flask. It was at this stage that I remembered that I had not put in any indicator, so I played my favourite game of 'spot the deliberate mistake' and challenged the students to identify what I had forgotten. It was gratifying to have several students volunteer the correct answer. Carefully, I added the appropriate indicator, demonstrating the technique of adding it to the aliquot of alkali.

It was great, I did three titrations and got them to within 0.5 ml of each other. At the third the students even gave me a little round of applause. We then discussed the use of error analysis to correctly record the results. This last exercise slowed down the interest of the class as the realities of the complexities of percentage errors dawned upon them. By the time all of this had been covered, the period came to an end. I farewelled my class with cheerful cries of 'See you tomorrow' and reflected on a very successful demonstration lesson.

The next day when the students started their own titrations I had second thoughts about the success of the demonstration. At the outset, the students made basic errors in their pipetting techniques. Then they insisted on making the actual titration a two-student job, with one swirling the conical flask and the other operating the tap. I watched in disbelief as I walked around the room. Finally I could take it no more, and called them all to stop what they were doing and pay attention to the front of the room. Once again, I went through the whole procedure, demonstrating and explaining as I carried out another titration, and once again, I sent them back to their desks to try the technique. This time they performed a bit better, but still there were errors. Oh, well, there is always tomorrow.

Tomorrow came and the students tried once more to master the technique of titrating. It is worth pointing out at this stage that we were working through a series of experiments. The first was to prepare a standard solution, then to use that to standardise another solution. This standardised solution was then to be used to calculate the concentrations of two or three commercial products. Naturally, a certain amount of time had been allocated to this set of practical work, an amount that is, on paper, quite generous. Of course, it was becoming apparent that this class would run over time. But, as always, I chose to ignore that in preference to finishing the work.

The work continued on the following day, the one following that, and on for several days. During that time, the students' skills improved and their titrations became more and more accurate, and more precise. Once this had occurred, it was time to discuss error analysis. Typically, this elicited groans of complaint, indeed disbelief when the complexities involved became apparent. This class was no exception, and there came the predictable 'Oh no' and 'You're kidding' and even a few 'I don't get this at all' remarks. But, being good students, they buckled down and made the effort to learn the mathematical manipulations necessary to deal with percentage errors and experimental uncertainties.

However, after all these difficulties, we struggled on through together. I say 'together' seriously as it felt that I became a part of the class, joining in with their struggle with this long and demanding period of their studies. We had worked hard and we had come to the stage where the titration technique had been successfully tackled and, dare I say it, mastered.

Finally, the time came when we faced the last hurdle, the end of unit test. Somewhat nervously, I collected the test papers from my colleague who had written it. Walking to the class, I read through it and felt comfortable. As tests went, this was a fair, if predictable, one. There were three nice titration calculations and even a few multiple-choice questions based on titration technique. That pleased me, considering how much work we had put in on the technical side of the course.

However, when I marked the tests, I was shattered. Apart from the predictable few students who would succeed at anything, the marks were very poor. Indeed they were appalling. I couldn't believe it. Hadn't we spent more time than normal? Hadn't I personally spent literally hours going over and over again the whole titration system?

The answer, when it came, should not have been a surprise. I asked one of the mid-range ability students (you know the type, he averaged a C, but on a good day pushed it up to a B, a good lad who tried hard and gave his best) what had happened.

'What happened, Bill? We spent heaps of time on titrations and you all bombed badly on the test. What's the story?' I asked him.

'Yeah, but we spent all the time on the skills, the experiments. The test was all on calculations about titrations. We all studied up on the techniques, you know, all the stuff you taught us. We didn't think too much about the calculations', he said, a little bitterly.

'But I told you all that the whole thing was about the calculations at the end. I said that', I protested.

'Oh yeah, you did. But we spent all that time on the pracs. So we thought that was the big thing.'

As he walked away, carrying his test paper with the 29% grade in red on the front page, I was forced to reflect that maybe I did indeed have to think, perhaps re-think, my priorities in teaching chemistry.

Teacher commentary

Bevan McGuiness

Whenever we teach students we take on a wide range of tasks and problems. The task of teaching chemistry is no different in that it has its own peculiar brand of problems. One of the major problem areas that is highlighted in this everyday story of a commonplace event is that of assessment. When we assess students, what exactly are we assessing? And, even more significantly in this story, do our ideas of assessment always coincide with those of our students?

In this story, I had spent a noticeably long time with this particular class going over the practice of the titration analysis technique. Whilst this was of itself not unusual, it is a difficult section involving as it does new techniques as well as new concepts, and we spent more time than normal discussing the theory behind the practical considerations. As a consequence of this, the students assumed that the upcoming test would reflect this time allocation which is, in all fairness, a reasonable assumption. Something which I didn't mention in the story was that at the beginning of the course, I gave the students a full assessment outline which detailed not only the allocation of marks but also relative weightings of each assessment item. They therefore should have known that the test was going to be primarily calculation-based, rather than practically based. But they did not make that step and were thus disappointed with the test when it came.

Another point about the testing of titrations, and indeed any practical work, is the question of how to best assess it. Clearly in the test I gave, the work was assessed on a theoretical basis, with most emphasis on the calculation side of the work. There were some questions, simple ones to be sure, on the technique of titration but the bulk of the test was about the work that follows from a successfully completed experiment. When we assess a practical section of a course such as chemistry, what are we actually assessing? If we test them with a pen-and-paper test, are we assessing the student's practical ability or their literacy? Is it possible for a student to pass a pen-and-paper test on an experimental technique without having done the experiment? In my experience it is possible for this to happen.

There are at least two different ways of assessing practical work, both of which I have since used. One method is to use a specifically designed written test based explicitly on the actual processes of the experiment. Such a test is a useful tool for discerning if a student can remember the steps involved in carrying out a titration, and then completing the calculations associated with such a procedure. It does not however give any information as to whether the student has the skills to personally carry out the equipment manipulations necessary.

Another assessment tool that can be used is the practical test where a student is given a set of equipment, or access to a wide range of equipment, and a problem to solve. Such a test as this gives the student the opportunity to use the equipment to solve the given problem. This test will enable the teacher to watch students carry out an experiment and then check their calculations based on their results.

As is usual with a senior teaching programme, the major problem with an assessment tool like this one is the perennial one of time. It takes time to set up a test, time to set up the equipment and solutions necessary and time to carry out the test. Unlike a normal test, the time constraint issue comes up for comment. If the test is to be testing the student's practical ability, then why must there be a limited time? In industry, whilst there are certainly rigorous time constraints, they are unlikely to be as short as a standard high school period. And similarly, would we be testing their actual ability, or just how much they can do in a short period of time?

Clearly, the assessment tool I used was inappropriate for the work we had done, but how to assess something as complex as titration is not an easy area to address. Another issue which I raise as a possibly peripheral point is that the other class who sat the same test as my class performed much better. The time my class had spent on the practical work the other class had spent solving problems, and the other class had seen a couple of demonstration titrations. As a consequence of this time spent on activity, the students in my class were disadvantaged in their final grade.

When I thought about this story, considering writing this commentary, it occurred to me to ring some chemical analysis companies. I asked the chemists working at eight such companies whether they actually used titrations in the course of their normal duties. The responses were mixed, with five companies saying that titrations were a normal, regular part of their analysis, two saying they were never used at all, and the last company said that titrations could be used on irregular occasions, if nothing else would do the job. The general impression I gained from talking to these chemists in the workplace was that the titration technique would never totally disappear, but it was gradually being replaced by new techniques. One chemist said that they use the ideas and techniques of titrations, but not with 'burettes and stuff', they use dosimeters. Also there was a distinct feeling that titrations belonged to 'classical chemistry', to be replaced as soon as another technique could be developed to do the same job.

However, at present, titrations are an important part of chemical analysis in the industry. This is an aspect that I have since incorporated in my own teaching of this part of the course. Now whenever I introduce this topic, I emphasise the overall importance of the technique in industry. With some of the information I gained from some of the companies I spoke to, I can describe actual analyses done in industry so as to put the experiments into a real-life context.

★   ★   ★

Phenomenology, knowledgeability and authentic science

Wolff-Michael Roth, University of Victoria

Titrations, titrations raises many serious questions that many teachers and science educators fail to adequately address. Why do we ask students to engage in laboratory activities? What is the relationship between moving some equipment around and the canonical discursive practices students develop? What is the purpose of the activities in which students engage? and What is the relationship between these activities and the activities of scientists? and What is the relationship between the activities in which students engage in class and those they engage in during tests? In other words, to what extent do tests assess what students have learned? I begin with a reflection on the phenomenology of knowing and learning and continue to a description of authentic scientific practices.

Learning from laboratories (and demonstrations)

The most fundamental question to ask is what students are expected to learn when they engage in laboratory activities or watch demonstrations. Science education ideology and common lore holds that 'hands on' (or, more recently, 'hands-on, minds-on') helps students to learn the canonical theoretical discourses and practices of science. However, there is virtually no research that shows how and in which ways manipulating some equipment or apparatus should change someone's understanding of theoretical frameworks of science. What evidence do we have that doing a titration (even 'correctly') helps students to learn any chemistry? It has been argued that the claims about the value of traditional laboratory activities are largely unexamined and constitute a 'powerful, myth-making rhetoric' (Hodson, 1990, p. 34); school laboratory activities are largely ill conceived, confused and unproductive in that many students learn little of or about science and do not engage in doing science. To understand why this may be so, we need to take a learner's point of view on curricular activities; that is, we need to view science laboratory activities (labs or demos) from the perspective of someone who does not yet know the science these activities are intended to teach. Let us take a look at a phenomenological view on cognition.

We live in a world that we take for granted without continuously expressing how the world looks to us (Heidegger, 1977). The world is a background to our daily activities. However, when asked, we begin to focus to individuate objects and events, that is, we make some of the vague background more salient and therefore 'foreground' some aspects. However, what we foreground depends on the situation and the horizon of past experiences which we bring to the situation. What we know strongly influences what and how we make salient and therefore what structural properties are that we attend to. Given the great differences between the experiences of teachers and students – or even more pronounced, between students and scientists – it is therefore not surprising that when students look at the world they structure it differently (Roth, 1995, 1996). My research showed that physics students ordered their laboratory experiences and constructed regularities in ways that were not compatible with the theory that the teacher wanted to teach (Roth et al., 1997a); and during demonstrations, students made salient aspects that were irrelevant, and even contradictory, to the laws which the teacher wanted to explain by drawing on the demonstrations as resources (Roth et al., 1997b).

These comments make it quite clear that it is therefore unreasonable to expect students to construct the same laws and theories that it took scientists

2,000 years to construct. That is, 'discovery' is largely a myth. Furthermore, students cannot just be shown some demonstration and told some structure in order for them to understand the theoretical framework of the science. The view I sketched here also provides a different frame for understanding how we might want to look at 'knowledge' and 'knowing', and therefore at teaching and learning. From a phenomenological perspective, we are always already in a world shot through with meaning. From birth on, we participate in activities which constitute the way things are for the community (Heidegger, 1977). The social and material worlds we experience are sensible because of the way we co-participate, acting in and interacting with these worlds. Such co-participation in ongoing, situated and structured activity produces knowledgeability which is 'routinely in a state of change rather than stasis, in the medium of socially, culturally and historically ongoing systems of activity, involving people who are related in multiple and heterogeneous ways' (Lave, 1993, p. 17). Lave further points out that social locations, interests, reasons and subjective possibilities of co-participants are different, and co-participants therefore engage in contingent improvisation to negotiate particular situation definitions. The production of failure is as much a part of such routine collective activity as the production of average, ordinary knowledgeability.

This is a very activity-centred view of knowing and learning. As we change our participation, we learn. But as we change our participation, the world we experience also changes. Learning is therefore constituted by changing participation in a changing world. This therefore also changes how we might look at teaching. Teaching no longer is the transfer of information but has to be conceptualised in terms of the opportunities we can set up that afford students possibilities to change their participation in a changing world (Lave, 1996). Because we participate with others, intelligibility of discourse and action are first and foremost social. Our activities, and in fact the world as we see it, make sense because we already share it within a community. That is, the consensual nature of scientists' practices arises from co-participation in accountably doing science.[1]

When we use this phenomenological perspective to reflect on the titration episode we begin to ask how students' activities are part of a larger whole that contextualises what they are doing. We also ask how students' changing participation in shaking the flasks and opening and closing the tap may change their participation in calculation activities. If there is little in common between participating in titration activities and doing paper-and-pencil tests, one needs to question, 'What is the value of doing titrations?' Once we decide that we want students to participate in titrating, our evaluations of their competence should be during the practice of doing titrations. Why isolate learners from the resources they have in normal activity to test them in artificial contexts and ways that give little information about competence in normal activity? Finally, and this leads us into the next section, students are asked to get the titration activities right – although they may have never co-participated in the authentic practices of titration – not to make their titrations accountable to others.

Errors and correctness in authentic science

Science educators need to ask themselves how the activities they plan for their students reflect scientific knowledge and science as practice. In my view, most science teaching today misrepresents the nature of science and interferes with rather than scaffolds students' participation in authentic practice. My own understanding of science and scientific practice comes from having worked in a research laboratory and from doing, with my graduate students, ethnographic and cognitive research on scientists' (and software engineers') everyday work. In contrast to professional science, school science activities such as the one described in *Titrations, titrations* have 'correct' answers held by someone, usually the teacher. Whatever students do is measured against these answers.[2] On the other hand, in everyday science we most often do not know anything like a 'correct' answer. Whether some data point or a series of data points corresponds to a signal or a noise depends on the theoretical framework which researchers bring to their work and on the reproducibility of the data series (e.g. Garfinkel *et al.*, 1981; Woolgar, 1990). Frequently, scientists engage in collective interpretation sessions during which they use processes of argumentation – at least one scientist plays the advocate for the data and another the devil's advocate – to construct some sense of whether the data correspond to a signal or noise (Amann and Knorr-Cetina, 1988). For this reason, students frequently find themselves in a quandary as to the laboratory experiments they conduct or demonstrations teachers present because, as they are to learn the theory, they do not have the tools to decide whether what they see is the signal or simply some noise not to be attended to (Roth *et al.*, 1997a, 1997b).

Scientists, as a community, have developed a range of practices that assist in making visible signals that do not seem signals at all (Roth and McGinn, 1997). Let us take a look at an example.[3] In Figure 3.1 (top), I represented an artificial but plausible curve of experimental data. Normally, these data may be taken as indicating *one* peak. However, if a researcher has a hunch that there are 'really' two peaks that she should expect, she might want to estimate the bandwidth of her data collection apparatus and model it mathematically. Using a mathematical process of 'unfolding', she could then 'recover' the 'true' peaks to look like the bottom graph in Figure 3.1.[4]

In a similar way, our scientist may have collected the data plotted in the top graph of Figure 3.2. Again, if she has a hunch that there really should be a phenomenon and therefore a signal instead of the virtually straight line, she may want to use a technique that is sensitive to changes. She could therefore manipulate the data she collected employing a (mathematical) derivative operator, or by using electronic means that are sensitive to changes. Such

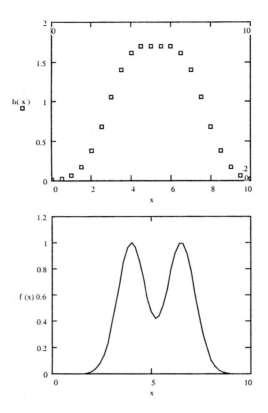

Figure 3.1   The top graph may represent the actual data collected by a
scientist. If the scientist assumes that the 'real' data are overlaid by
the bandwidth of the instrument used to collect the data, they can
engage in a process of 'unfolding' the data with a 'reasonable'
apparatus function. Such an unfolding may then yield the 'real'
function f(x) in the lower panel.

procedures, used with the data in top graph of Figure 3.2 would then give her
the data as they are plotted in the bottom graph.

The point is that scientists develop in the course of their work a range of
practices that allow them to bring together their expectations (theory) and
the data they collect. These practices are reasonable within the community
and are used to make accountable their actions. What the 'real' data are – one
or two peaks in Figure 3.1 or the top or bottom graph in Figure 3.2 –
depends on the theoretical baggage our scientist brought to the experiment,
both the theory of nature and the theory of apparatus. Separating the signal
that theory predicts from other influences is a highly situated and contingent
achievement and depends on the researcher's experimental background and

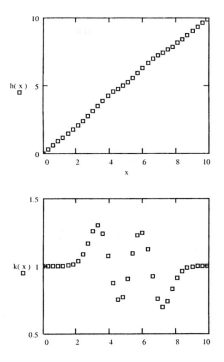

Figure 3.2   Top. A graph, h(x), of artificial but reasonable experimental data. Bottom. If the researcher assumes that there is a 'real' signal, she may want to use electronic means (at the level of data collection) or mathematical means (with the raw data) to produce the derivative k(x) of the original graph.

theoretical understandings of the domain and possibly hunches about what the phenomena could reasonably – that is, defensibly and accountably – look like. Whether the data are 'real' and correspond to a phenomenon depends on the researcher's competence in making the experiment and her analysis accountable within her own research community. Whether the wiggles on the original graph in Figure 3.2 (top) are due to experimental error or whether they in fact can be used to disclose some phenomenon cannot be established beforehand, but has to be embedded within a range of practices that allow scientists to make their accounts credible. In this process, even questions such as whether a second run can be considered the same (and therefore a candidate for assessing confirmation or disconfirmation of the first) or whether it was in some aspect different are embedded within the contingencies of scientists' laboratory work.

In contrast, the kind of laboratory work that students did in the titration story is predictable from the very beginning. Here, we do not deal with 'discovery' work but with the nitty-gritty of technicians' work, which, though exacting, reveals little of the exhilarating experience of the discovery sciences and the ways and means by which scientists construct the knowledge that we later come to accept as 'truths'. Students learn little about scientists' purposes for using precision in titration, about making their actions accountable to research co-participants and to the research community at large. Given these stories about 'real' science, how can anyone expect students to get it right on the first time? How could they be able to separate signal from noise? How should they know which is the signal that is relevant to the phenomenon at hand?

As a community, science educators and science teachers need to change our thinking about teaching and learning. At the moment, students and teachers focus on grades. What we need to do is change teaching practices to make them compatible with the learning perspective espoused in these reflections. As a community, we need to bring about co-participation in sensible and plausible activity and the production of ordinary knowledgeability in chemistry (and other sciences); we need to bring about contexts with a primary purpose of learning rather than grading; and we need to bring about contexts in which producing reasonable accounts guides students' laboratory activity rather than getting some purported 'right' answer.

★   ★   ★

Assessment and students' interest: connecting to learning

Penny J. Gilmer, Florida State University

Considering forms of assessment

Bevan McGuiness listened to his student respond to his question about why the students did so poorly on the unit examination on titrations, 'Oh yeah, you did [emphasise the calculations at the end]. But we spent all that time on the pracs. So we thought that was the big thing.'

As teachers we must remember that both the method we choose to assess our students' learning and what we emphasise during class time drive the students' learning. Bevan chose to assess his students' learning by an end-of-the-unit examination on titrations that emphasised the ends (i.e. the final calculations and error analysis) but not the means to the learning (the practicalities of preparing a standard buffer, titrating the base, and using that standardised base to determine the concentrations of unknown commercial acids). Bevan's students spent many class periods learning the process skills of conducting titrations but only the final day of the unit calculating the concentrations of some commercial acids and doing the error analysis.

Capturing our students' interest

A teacher needs to capture the students' interest for the student to learn the complexities of titrations including, as Bevan wants, the 'joys of titres, aliquots and equivalence-points' and of the error analysis. For instance, Bevan's students might be interested to know that there are natural indicators in certain plants called anthocyanin dyes that give geraniums, raspberries, strawberries and blackberries their red colour. Poppies get their red colour from a cyanidin dye that is red when in acidic conditions but blue with basic conditions. It is actually the sap of the plant that controls the pH of the flower, so poppies' sap is acidic leading to red flowers and cornflowers' sap is basic, giving blue flowers. These natural dyes are used sometimes in foods, as people discovered that some of the artificial red dyes caused cancer in laboratory animals (Oxtoby et al., 1994). Ideas like this might get Bevan's students to see the relevance of chemistry and why it interests people. The power of chemistry is that it can explain so much of the world.

Sharing personal experiences in chemistry

I always try to give some practical experience from my life as a chemist on how the topic under study has been important in my career. For instance, with titrations, when working on my doctorate in biochemistry at the University of California, Berkeley, my research contributed towards an understanding of the mechanism of action of a particular transaminase enzyme as it formed a covalent bond with one of two substrates. The person who had studied this enzyme previously had reported that there were *two* active sites per tetrameric protein (i.e. two binding sites for the substrate to this enzyme with four identical protein chains per intact unit). Not intending to observe anything different than what was reported previously, I titrated the enzyme with the substrate, quantitating it by using a visible colour change that occurred on binding. From my very first experiment I found that my data indicated that there were *four* binding sites per tetramer (Gilmer et al., 1977), and it took me a year's worth of experiments to convince my directing professor that the literature was wrong. This story always impresses students that science is an incremental process of understanding and that it is rigorous. However, I also share with my students how good I felt when my major professor did a titration himself of the same enzyme but with another substrate that he was studying, and he confirmed my report of *four* binding sites per tetramer.

Using the Internet

Another thing that might have helped Bevan's students see the importance and practicality of determining the concentrations of the commercial acid products would have been to encourage his students to look on the Internet for practical applications of doing titrations. His students might have even selected a commercial product that they wanted to titrate.

Alternately, Bevan's students might have become interested to determine the amount of acid in acidic rainfall isolated from different locales within their country. The students would become motivated to do a standard titration first to develop their methods, so that they could test unknowns that could be more meaningful to them. When testing the samples of acid rain, instead of having a fully outlined procedure, students would have to think about how to conduct the experiment so the results would be meaningful and reproducible. Bevan's students would come to know science as it is done, with its frustrations and rewards. They could take ownership of their own data. They could also interact with students around the world who are conducting similar studies through Project GLOBE on the Internet at <http://www.globe.gov>

For a chapter on acids and bases in a biochemistry course that I recently taught at university level, students became interested in the practical applications of buffers through searches on the Internet. My students found that buffers are used in electrophoresis of DNA to determine gene sequences and in feed for cattle, to increase the mass of beef.

Using portfolios in assessing students' learning

Bevan might have included within his assessment, not only his traditional end-of-the-unit written test, but also alternative assessment such as his students' learning of their Internet project. Since many students still do not know how to use search engines on the Internet, Bevan would have had to teach them how to do that. When students are given freedom to explore, they will innovate and find all sorts of things that the teacher did not realise beforehand. This means that the teacher must be a learner too, be open to learning from his/her own students, but at the same time also be critical and questioning of what the students proclaim.

I find in my own class activities that if I have the students work in collaborative groups, it helps the students learn, as they must use the language of the discipline, as they try to explain to each other what it is that they know as they teach each other. Students all come to the classroom with their own prior knowledge and experiences (Glasersfeld, 1989). Each student can share understandings with peers in the classroom. Students can learn from each other as well as from the teacher.

For Bevan's assessment of what his students contributed and learned, each student could write an entry into a portfolio which contains evidence of the student's learning (Collins, 1992). I have found it helpful to guide the students in their writing by having them follow a written rubric of what the students should include. For instance, my most recent five-point rubric (which is always evolving) for individual students' electronic portfolios included:

- *Sharing accurate understanding of the science content* (helping both the student to utilise the discourse of science and the teacher to realise students' misconceptions)
- *Using good grammar and spelling to communicate learning* (helping the student to communicate more clearly)
- *Reflecting on prior learning and current learning* (helping the student link what he/she already had learned to new learning; students also realise through reflection what helps and inhibits their learning)
- *Referencing where the student learned additional material* (from a website, book or newspaper article that the student has found that facilitated learning)
- *Asking a good question that the student still has in his/her mind at the end of the student's research* (giving the teacher a window into the student's mind to see how far each student is in his/her learning)

It takes time for the teacher to read what the students have written and to respond individually. However, doing this allows the teacher to start to connect to his/her students' learning, to find out what the students know and don't know while still teaching the unit. As the teacher does this and reflects on his/her teaching, the feedback the teacher receives influences the teaching later in the week. Instead of finding out at the end of the unit what the students do not know, the teacher finds out while there still is an opportunity to change emphases, clear up misconceptions and enhance learning in the classroom. This is the first step towards conducting action research in your own classroom. Action research in elementary (Spiegel *et al.*, 1995), middle (McDonald and Gilmer, 1997) and high school (Yerrick, 1998) settings can provide teachers at all levels with visions of how to improve science teaching and learning in their own classrooms.

★   ★   ★

Editors' synthesis

Perhaps more than most laboratory activity, titration technique in school chemistry has been raised to the status of high art (or science). In some parts of the world, serious state and national competitions are held for school students to demonstrate their titrations skill. This emphasis on perfecting the technique appears as the overriding focus of the lesson described in *Titrations, titrations* (the word 'technique' appears eighteen times in McGuiness' story and commentary). The zeal with which this teacher pursues titration technique will, no doubt, be familiar to those who have taught senior chemistry. However, given the critiques of laboratory work offered at the beginning of the chapter, we are left to wonder how this kind of activity might rate as 'authentic' science. Several angles on this issue are provided by the commentators.

The first angle is that the science laboratory needs to proceed in an atmosphere of accountability rather than rightness. As Roth suggests, 'we need to bring about contexts in which producing reasonable accounts guides students' laboratory activity rather than getting some purported "right" answer'. This is a complex business, as Roth points out, as knowledgeability develops from a culture of co-participation in 'ongoing, situated and structured activity'. Roth draws parallels with images of scientists at work. His observations of the complex social milieu of conducting science is confirmed by Gilmer's account of her doctoral research in biochemistry. Apart from doing endless titrations, one of Gilmer's major tasks was to convince her directing professor that the literature was wrong. Authentic school science, according to these commentators, develops within a context of persuasion, negotiation and argumentation.

Secondly, the titration activity needs to be considered in relation to its scientific, problem-solving context. The importance of capturing student interest is raised by Gilmer in her discussion of the value of studying plant dyes, commercial acid products and acid rain. However, capturing interest is a tricky business as Gilmer's own experience can testify. Her own research on the properties of a particular transaminase enzyme clearly captured her interest at the time, but would likely have been of little interest to more than a few others. Clearly, though, authenticity contains important elements of relevance and interest to the individuals concerned.

A third angle considered by our commentators is that the activity needs to tap into 'real world' resources and techniques. As McGuiness observes, while burettes may still be used in some chemistry laboratories, they are rapidly being replaced by more modern tools. Gilmer canvasses some of the possibilities of using the web to explore some of the practical applications of titration chemistry. Other possibilities include the use of computer simulations. As the respondents to McGuiness' straw poll indicated, it is not the ideas behind titrations that are being superseded but the equipment and the particular skills for using that equipment. Authenticity, it would appear, involves approaching scientific problems using a range of resources and techniques.

The final angle concerns the relationship of the activity to the assessment practices. All three commentators draw attention to mismatch between the activity in the story (with its emphasis on process) and the assessment (with its emphasis on calculations). While McGuiness offers several possibilities for rectifying this situation including a practical test where students are given 'access to a wide range of equipment, and a problem to solve', he still hints at the need to check the students' answers. Roth proposes that assessment should be conducted in normal rather than artificial contexts, based on the notion of explaining to others rather than getting right answers. In Gilmer's commentary, she suggests that assessment be based around the means to learning (such as the practicalities of preparing a standard buffer) rather than the ends (the final calculations). She also explores some of the possibilities for using portfolios (including electronic portfolios) to tap into students' understandings. Authentic laboratory work, it would seem, needs to be matched by authentic assessments.

These four angles on authenticity – about social context, relevance, resources and assessment – provide some ways of interpreting the events in the story, *Titrations, titrations*, and some ideas about how to move forward. It would appear that it is not necessarily titrations (or even technique) which is the issue in this story but the social, intellectual and cognitive milieu within which this laboratory activity is located. It is entirely possible that titrations (and technique) can be part of authentic scientific practice, as Gilmer's own research experience can attest. However, Gilmer's experience was part of a scientific, rather than a school science, endeavour, with different norms of conduct. The challenge for McGuiness and his fellow science teachers is to find ways of assisting students to develop parallel norms of behaviour, to marshal the social and cognitive resources to conduct authentic laboratory work.

Notes

1   Etymologically, words such as *communicate, community, consensual* and *collaborate* derive their first syllable from the Latin cum, meaning 'with'. Communication and community therefore always and already presume our being with others, allowing us to share, have something in *common, consent* and *collaborate*.

2   There is research that shows that even the best-trained teachers sometimes assume they have the right answer which leads to the interesting situation that students' tests are compared to standards that are not in agreement with the scientific canon (e.g. Roth *et al.*, 1997b; Roth *et al.*, 1996).

3   During my M.Sc. research, I (Roth) saw many such graphs being collected from experiments in which electrons were made to interact with gaseous matter. The data collected by the astronomers in Garfinkel *et al.* (1981) could be of this nature.

4   To produce these data, I (Roth) took the reverse direction. Beginning with the 'real' function, I folded it ('covered it up') with an apparatus function. Interested readers may obtain the actual calculation by writing to me.

References

Amann, K. and Knorr–Cetina, K. D. (1988). The fixation of (visual) evidence. *Human Studies*, 11, 133–169.

Arzi, H. J. (1998). Enhancing science education through laboratory environments: More than walls, benches and widgets. In B. J. Fraser and K. G. Tobin (eds), *International handbook of science education* (pp. 595–608). Dordrecht, The Netherlands: Kluwer.

Collins, A. (1992). Portfolios for science education: Issues in purpose, structure and authenticity. *Science Education*, 76, 451–463.

Désautels, J. and Larochelle, M. (1998). The epistemology of students: The 'thingified' nature of scientific knowledge. In B. J. Fraser and K. G. Tobin (eds), *International handbook of science education* (pp. 115–126). Dordrecht, The Netherlands: Kluwer.

Garfinkel, H., Lynch, M. and Livingston, E. (1981). The work of a discovering science construed with materials from the optically discovered pulsar. *Philosophy of the Social Sciences*, 11, 131–158.

Gilmer, P. J., McIntire, W. S. and Kirsch, J. F. (1977). Pyridoxamine-pyruvate transaminase: I. Determination of the active site stoichiometry and the pH dependence of the dissociation constant for 5-deoxypyridoxal. *Biochemistry*, 16, 5,241–5,246.

Glasersfeld, E. von (1989). Cognition, construction of knowledge, and teaching. *Synthèse*, 80, 121–140.

Hegarty-Hazel, E. (ed.) (1990). *The student laboratory and the science curriculum*. London: Routledge.

Heidegger, M. (1977). *Sein und zeit* [Being and time]. Tübingen, Germany: Max Niemeyer.

Hodson, D. (1990). A critical look at practical work in school science. *School Science Review*, 70, 33–40.

—— (1993). Re-thinking old ways: Towards a more critical approach to practical work in school science. *Studies in Science Education*, 22, 85–142.

Lave, J. (1993). The practice of learning. In S. Chaiklin and J. Lave (eds), *Understanding practice: Perspectives on activity and context* (pp. 3–32). Cambridge: Cambridge University Press.

—— (1996). Teaching, as learning, in practice. *Mind, Culture, and Activity*, 3, 149–164.

Lazarowitz, R. and Tamir, P. (1994). Research on using laboratory instruction in science. In D. L. Gabel (ed.), *Handbook of research on science teaching and learning* (pp. 94–128). New York: Macmillan.

McDonald, J. B. and Gilmer, P. J. (eds) (1997). *Science in the elementary school classroom: Portraits of action research* [Monograph]. Tallahassee, FL: SouthEastern Regional Vision for Education; available On-line: <http://www.serve.org/Eisenhower/FEAT.html>

Milne, C. and Taylor, P.C. (1998). Between a myth and a hard place: Situating school science in a climate of critical cultural reform. In W. W. Cobern (ed.), *Socio-cultural perspectives on science education: An international dialogue* (pp. 25–48). Dordrecht, The Netherlands: Kluwer.

Oxtoby, D. W., Nachtrieb, N. H. and Freeman, W. A. (1994). *Chemistry: Science of change*. Philadelphia, PA: Saunders College Publishing.

Roth, W.-M. (1995). Affordances of computers in teacher–student interactions: The case of Interactive Physics™. *Journal of Research in Science Teaching*, 32, 329–347.

—— (1996). Art and artifact of children's designing: A situated cognition perspective. *The Journal of the Learning Sciences*, 5, 129–166.

Roth, W.-M. and McGinn, M. K. (1997). Graphing: A cognitive ability or cultural practice? *Science Education*, 81, 91–106.

Roth, W.-M., McRobbie, C. and Lucas, K. B. (1996, April). Students' talk about circular motion within and across contexts and teacher awareness. Paper presented at the annual conference of the American Educational Research Association, New York, NY.

Roth, W.-M., McRobbie, C., Lucas, K. B. and Boutonné, S. (1997a). The local production of order in traditional science laboratories: A phenomenological analysis. *Learning and Instruction*, 7, 107–136.

—— (1997b). Why do students fail to learn from demonstrations? A social practice perspective on learning in physics. *Journal of Research in Science Teaching*, 34, 509–533.

Spiegel, S. A., Collins, A. and Lappert, J. (eds) (1995). *Action research: Perspectives from teachers' classrooms* [Monograph]. Tallahassee, FL: SouthEastern Regional Vision for Education.

Tobin, K. (1990). Research on science laboratory activities: In pursuit of better questions and answers to improve learning. *School Science and Mathematics*, 90, 403–418.

Woolgar, S. (1990). Time and documents in researcher interaction: Some ways of making out what is happening in experimental science. In M. Lynch and S. Woolgar (eds), *Representation in scientific practice* (pp. 123–152). Cambridge, MA: MIT Press.

Yerrick, R. (1998). Reconstructing classroom facts: Transforming lower track science classrooms. *Journal of Science Teacher Education*, 9, 241–270.

Part II

Dilemmas about difference

Chapter 4

Gender

*Contributions by Wendy Giles, Peter Leach,
J. Randy McGinnis and Deborah J. Tippins*

Editors' introduction

Gender matters in science. At the deepest level, the conceptual structure of science is built on the basis of sex distinctions. Linnaeus, for example, imported traditional sex hierarchies into his hierarchical distinctions between the class of a plant and the orders of plants in that class. The class of plant, higher up the taxonomy, is identified on the basis of the number of male organs and the order, lower down the taxonomy, is identified on the basis of the number of female organs (Schiebinger, 1993). Historically, science has taken for granted such masculine epistemologies and the practice of science predominantly has been a male domain (Harding, 1991). The consequence of these historical patterns is that fewer women than men enter science and even fewer women occupy senior science posts in universities and other research institutions (Osbourne, 1994). When women do enter science they choose the 'soft' biological sciences more often than the 'hard' physical sciences, focusing on science that helps people, animals and the earth (Baker and Leary, 1995).

Gender differences are also played out in school science education. In many countries girls choose less science and are less likely to choose the physical sciences (Rennie *et al.*, 1991). In their science textbooks, women and girls continue to be presented in passive roles (Potter and Rosser, 1992). In class, teachers of both sexes interact more frequently with boys (Crossman, 1987; Jones, 1990) and girls have less access to laboratory equipment (Tobin, 1988). In tests and examinations, especially in physics, female students are likely to encounter assessment items set in the 'real world' contexts of weapons and warfare (Parker and Rennie, 1998).

Against such structured patterns of disadvantage for girls in science, researchers have worked to identify gender equity strategies for the classroom. In her review of equity issues in science education, Baker (1998), for example, identifies a series of equity strategies reported as successful by other researchers. These include using small group or cooperative learning strategies (Scantlebury and Kahle, 1993), structured engagement patterns to reduce dominance of boys in classroom discussion (Baker, 1988), discussions that use students' ideas as a starting point and do not require students to come up with a right answer (Corey *et al.*, 1993), experiments that require groups of students to work towards a common goal (Martinez, 1992), and real-world contexts that are more inclusive of females' interests (Rennie and Parker, 1993).

Several of the gender equity strategies identified by Baker appear in *A crash course*, the story that begins this chapter. Wendy Giles, a researcher, describes the opportunities offered to a group of girls and a group of boys in a Grade 8 physical science practical class. The teacher, Peter Leach, is introduced by Giles as 'sensitive to gender issues in his teaching strategies'. Despite this sensitivity, the opportunities on offer in his science class are taken up unequally by groups of boys and groups of girls. In the commentaries that follow *A crash course*, Giles describes her reaction to the lesson, Peter Leach comments on his intentions, and Deborah Tippins and Randy McGinnis offer their readings of the gender issues that emerge in the description of the lesson.

A crash course

Wendy Giles

As part of a research project, I was observing students during their transition from primary school to secondary school. Elizabeth was one of the students I had chosen. As a primary school student, she had expressed a great interest in science and wanted to become a nurse because she wanted to help people, and because she had spent a lot of time in hospital as a small child. She was finding science at high school better than she expected because most lessons involved some sort of activity, and she found the teacher approachable and easy to get along with.

Elizabeth's science teacher in her first year of high school, Mr Peter Leach, was young and enthusiastic. He promoted a relaxed atmosphere in his classroom as he believed that students learned best in a non-threatening environment. He was well aware of recent developments in science education, and was sensitive to gender issues in his teaching strategies. Therefore, in most of his lessons, he attempted to place the concepts and activities in a context which would be meaningful for the students. He encouraged group problem-solving and relied more on hands-on activities than working from the textbook.

On this particular day towards the end of the first term, Mr Leach allowed the students to form their own groups for the activity. Elizabeth chose to work with three other girls with whom she had been sitting. She listened attentively while the teacher outlined the procedures to be followed. Involving the students in the discussion, Mr Leach began by talking about car accidents and the effect they can have on the occupants of the car. Speed, seat belts and head rests were all mentioned in the lead up to the activity. Each group was provided with a trolley (the car), a ramp and some plasticine which was to represent a person. The car, with the 'person' placed at the front, was to be rolled down the ramp and crashed into a wood barrier so that the effects of the collision on the person could be observed. Students were asked to measure how far from the barrier the plasticine dummy came to rest after the collision. The activity was to be repeated using different starting points on the ramp.

A group of boys next to Elizabeth began immediately to roll their car down the ramp before they had placed the person in the car. It took them a while to get organised and record the results. They were making a lot of noise and shouting with excitement at every collision.

'Oh, what a beauty! Did you see that?'

'Let me push it this time.'

'Push it harder. What do we do with this plasticine?'

'Dunno.'

'Push it again!'

In contrast, Elizabeth and her friends spent a long time making the plasticine into a human figure which was as realistic as possible. The instructions on the activity sheet included the ratio of arms, legs and head by weight. The girls discussed the construction of their person, and weighed the portions carefully.

'You make the head like this – with your finger to make it hollow.'

'Where's the match to join it with? Don't mess it up!'

'Can we give it hair? It has to sit down on the trolley, so the legs have to bend.'

They were very involved in the context. It was almost as if they did not want to try out the activity although they watched the nearby boys' group with apparent interest. Elizabeth's group did not make one test run with their car.

Mr Leach walked around the room. He observed each group carefully, but did not intervene in the activities at any point. Every group except Elizabeth's had recorded some results from their experiment. Finally, Mr Leach indicated that there was no more time available for the first part of the experiment, and explained that the next stage required two cars, so groups had to combine. Elizabeth's group joined with the nearby boys' group. One car was placed 30 centimetres in front of the ramp, and the other one was rolled one metre down the ramp to hit the stationary car. Students were to observe the effects of the collision on the occupants of both cars. At first, Elizabeth argued with one of the boys over the use of the ruler.

'It has to be from a metre.'

'Let me do that! Give me the ruler.'

'No, I can do it.'

Elizabeth proceeded to mark the spot. Then, the boys rolled the cars and the girls observed and recorded. The only equipment handled by the girls in the group during this activity was the ruler until it was time to pack up when they all helped. During the class discussion of the results, it was clear that Elizabeth's group was the only one not to have results from the first stage. They seemed content to use the results of the boys' group to write up the experiment.

Observer commentary

Wendy Giles

Generally, gender-inclusive practices within the classroom either address the interests and strengths of girls, or provide opportunities for activities which girls tend not to engage in outside the school. These strategies are also beneficial to boys because they aid their development in these areas. Encouraging, or even allowing single-sex groups to operate within the classroom seems to be a strategy which should encourage girls to participate more in manipulating materials and experimenting. The small groups are conducive to peer discussions and cooperative problem-solving. In the lesson described here, the problem had been placed in a meaningful social context. Therefore, it would appear that the girls in the class should benefit from this type of lesson.

However, the close proximity of the somewhat disruptive boys' group seemed to have a negative effect on the girls. If the whole class had been female, then perhaps the girls would have felt less constrained to only observe and record. If the boys had their own class as well, maybe they would have realised that in the end, their activity was meaningless unless they followed the rules and recorded some results. The arguments for and against single-sex science classes have been well documented. Girls show more favourable attitudes and participation rates in single-sex classes, although achievement is largely unaltered. Boys tend to behave in more disruptive ways in all-boys classes, and seem to prefer mixed-sex groups. Girls prefer single-sex classes. But using single-sex groups within a mixed class does not necessarily mean that the same advantages or disadvantages will apply. The incident in Elizabeth's class illustrates that point.

Other aspects of girls' preferred learning styles are illustrated here. They tend to prefer longer periods of time to solve problems. Elizabeth's group conscientiously followed the instructions in making their dummy out of plasticine, only to be penalised because time was up. The boys' group, which rushed into the activity without following the instructions, were perceived to have completed the activity more satisfactorily. If this lesson had been part of an integrated programme covering a number of curriculum areas, then the pressure to finish the task within a set time would have been lessened, and perhaps the groups which had been more thorough would have achieved the best results. Integrated programmes have been suggested as beneficial to early adolescents in the middle school years, as well as being one strategy for a more inclusive curriculum. Allowing sufficient time for the activity to be completed properly would have prevented any one group from being disadvantaged.

When the groups joined together for the final experiment, the boys dominated, even though Elizabeth attempted to assert herself. The girls were relegated to observers and recorders. At this point, the teacher could have intervened to distribute tasks within the group more equitably. It was puzzling to note that he did not interfere, even though it is obvious that he was aware of the situation.

Teacher commentary

Peter Leach

Students were required to investigate the effects of collisions and sudden stopping at a variety of speeds. The trolleys were cars and the plasticine dummies were supposed to represent people. Many students would have experienced one or both of these situations before but probably would not have thought about what happened and why. Hopefully, this activity allowed the students to view the results of car accidents and consider the reasons for head rests and seat belts.

After discussing the topic as a whole group to set the context, students were given freedom to work through the tasks at their own pace within the constraints of the lesson time and materials. I consciously allowed groups to form voluntarily, all were single sex, and a maximum membership of four. Friendship groups work on the assumption that group dynamics already exist and that students will feel more comfortable in these groups. Tensions and dominance, which can occur in mixed-sex groups, are also avoided. I was interested to note that when groups had to combine, Elizabeth and her group chose to combine with the boys. Social interaction was probably more the driving force than the need to complete the activities.

In addition to the specific science objectives, I was keen to give the students (Elizabeth included) as much freedom as possible to 'play' with the materials and experiment with group dynamics. Playing with materials increases confidence in manipulating and experimenting with different things as well as encouraging curiosity. Experimenting with group dynamics (consciously or otherwise) allows the students to find their most rewarding way of operating. In this situation, Elizabeth's group were doing exactly this.

Intervention by me would have not allowed this experimentation and development to take place. The non-completion of the activity is also part of the learning process, that is, how does a group combine the need to achieve certain things as well as interact socially? Groups must be able to work relatively independently of teachers if the members are to progress cognitively. The teacher then is in the position to be able to become part of a group, be part of members' learning.

The results of the interactions within Elizabeth's group and the collaboration with the group of boys is illustrative of early experiences of group work and mixed-sex groups. Elizabeth's group were yet to develop a more productive group dynamic that enabled them to complete activities as well as socially interact. The mixed-sex group illustrated many of the concerns people have as to the effectiveness of group work. The social constructions and expectations encourage the domination of group situations by the loudest person(s), these usually being male. Females are expected and prepared to sit back and observe, collect results and use second-hand data. Single-sex classes do not suffer similar fates. Males are forced to work more cooperatively and females are given the opportunity to experience *all* facets of the investigative process, not just recording. Confidence must benefit as a result. This development in confidence may be apparent in the differences between activities completed by Elizabeth's group and others. The 'reluctance' to attempt the activity, and preparedness to watch the boys refer back to the stereotypical male–female roles. Other girls' groups who were not adjacent to a boys' group may have been more confident to try, experiment and manipulate.

Group membership in that class has changed since that lesson, but the majority of groups remain single sex. These changes reflect changing peer affinities. Elizabeth's group has become smaller and, interestingly, includes one of the boys from the group mentioned. The third member of the group is still one of the original group. The rest have shifted away to form other single-sex groups.

★   ★   ★

Managing inquiry

Deborah J. Tippins, University of Georgia

As I initially read this case, I realised that I was seeing it through my 'gender equity' alert glasses. As soon as I read the 'crash' topic, I thought 'a-ha', a typical male topic involving violence. As I pondered this case I wondered, why am I thinking 'crash' is a male topic? After all, most people are generally curious about car crashes. Of course, I think it's clear that the teacher, who claims to be gender sensitive, in actuality is not. I realised, however, that there were issues in this case that went beyond questions of gender equity. At the heart of this case are questions of what constitutes effective science inquiry and to what extent cooperative grouping and hands-on strategies facilitate science learning.

The laboratory investigation portrayed in this case has the potential for inquiry. However, the investigation needed to be organised in a different way and facilitated by the teacher. In organising the activity, the teacher had students 'self-select' cooperative learning groups, resulting in groups segregated by gender. While this type of grouping does not have to pose a problem, in this case the girls' group accepted a regulated position with respect to involvement in the lab's activities. It was apparent that the girls were content using the boys' data and ultimately accepted their marginalised roles as secretaries. Since it seems like this pattern of participation might be repetitive, the teacher should consider using different patterns of grouping. Issues of grouping such as the one illustrated in this case raise ethical considerations: how can the teacher honour students' group choices but at the same time nurture diversity?

During the activity, both boys and girls spent the majority of class time exploring tangents only somewhat related to the concept of inertia. The context of the activity provided a situation where boys had a tendency to be distracted by crashing the cars. At the same time, the girls' attention to construction of the plasticine dummy reinforced concepts of proportion rather than inertia. Over time, this pattern of involvement could become an undermining situation for both groups of students. In order to minimise the potential for this to happen, laboratory activities should be designed to provide more open forms of inquiry, and the teacher should develop his role as a facilitator rather than observer.

As a precursor to the laboratory activity, the teacher outlined procedures and introduced a discussion emphasising the importance of seat belts and head rests in accident prevention. Perhaps a more inductive form of inquiry would emphasise the importance of group discussions during and after the activity rather than beforehand. Similarly, the procedures for the activity might also have been more open-ended in nature. The detailed directions for building a realistic plasticine dummy served as a trivial distraction for the girls, and only reinforced the inordinate amount of time and attention given to the details of proportion.

In this laboratory, the teachers' role was one of passive observer rather than active facilitator as he 'observed each group carefully, but did not intervene... at any point'. As a facilitator, the teacher could intervene at various points to interject questions, respond to student queries, keep students focused on the science concepts central to the activity and act as an enabler for active participation of girls in the laboratory. While the teacher in this case did promote a non-threatening learning environment, students may need more feedback as well as an explicit indication of the extent to which the teacher is 'approachable'.

This case illustrates many different aspects of science teaching and learning. On the one hand, the case illustrates the value of accurate measurement in scientific inquiry. By contrast, the case also highlights the importance of affective dimensions of the learning environment such as tolerance, perception and fairness. For further insight, my questions to the teacher in this case are:

1   Are you aware of Elizabeth's interest in nursing?
2   Did you notice the girls' lack of confidence and the boys' over-confidence?
3   How would you describe the nature of the learning taking place in this activity?

★   ★   ★

Standpoints and the cycle of inequity

J. Randy McGinnis, University of Maryland

In this Australian secondary science classroom, girls and boys are engaged in a participatory investigation using manipulatives to model the effects of collision on a person. Directing the learning environment is their male science teacher, Mr Leach. The lesson is distinguished by the use of small learning groups, problem-based instruction, the analysis of relevant phenomena based on student-collected data, and the social construction of scientific knowledge. This is an exemplary science lesson – or is it? Enter the scene a female science education researcher who reports what she sees, and what could initially appear as exemplary science teaching practice becomes problematic. Exemplary practice takes on a new dimension as the focus of the report on the lesson is the impact of the male science teacher's teaching on a subset of the students, a female student (Elizabeth) and her all-female small learning group. The impact of the teacher's actions, including his non-actions, on all of his students now becomes the focus of our thinking.

Subsidiary, but intractably linked in our thinking, is the nagging issue of the sex difference between the male teacher, his female students and the female science education researcher. The sole informant of Mr Leach's science lesson is a woman. Her focus in the classroom observation is a girl (Elizabeth) whom she has been observing during her transition from primary to secondary school. One wonders what is the role of the gender status of the researcher in this situation? Would a male science education researcher have reported a similar observation? The positionality of the female science education researcher (Wendy Giles), the voice in this report of science teaching practice, becomes a second focus of our thinking.

As a male science methods professor who teaches classes consisting predominately of females, I have made it my concern to search out and study the literature on gender equity. I have spent much time documenting and reporting my own efforts as a male to promote gender-inclusive education in my own practices (McGinnis *et al.*, 1997; McGinnis and Pearsall, 1998). It is my belief that only through a deconstruction of science teaching practices, the deleterious impact of the sex difference (expressed in socially constructed gender roles) between the male teacher and his female students will science learning ultimately be ameliorated. Furthermore, drawing on research conducted by Byrne (1993) and by Shepardson and Pizzini (1992), I believe that girls in science learning can suffer from gender bias from teachers of both sexes which negatively affect their attitudes, beliefs, participation and achievement in science. Revealingly, Shepardson and Pizzini found that some female teachers perceived boys as more cognitively intellectual in their science abilities than girls, and that they perceived girls as more cognitively procedural than boys. This gender bias by teachers can be especially powerful when coupled with cultures that socialise girls to be dependent and boys to be independent at early ages (Mann, 1994).

In thinking about Mr Leach's teaching actions, it is informative to note that the female science education researcher reports that 'he was well aware of recent developments in science education, and he was sensitive to gender issues in his teaching strategies'. His acceptance during the first portion of the lesson of Elizabeth's preference of learning in a small group consisting of all girls is consistent with research conducted by Rennie and Parker (1987) on grouping by sex in science classrooms. Rennie and Parker found that girls in mixed-sex groups had fewer opportunities for hands-on experiences in science lessons than did the boys. Therefore, Mr Leach's allowance of single-sex small learning groups during the portion of his lesson that required use of the manipulatives reflected a '[sensitivity] to gender issues in his teaching strategies'. However, his lack of anticipation of the girls' and boys' difference in interest and their perception of a learning task in this science lesson is inconsistent with more recent gender research by Murphy (1994). In a similar instance of science teaching practice, Murphy observed that girls spent most of the lessons' allotted time on planning and designing an investigation rather than carrying out the full array of procedures as the boys did. The implication was that teachers needed to either provide more time for both girls and boys to complete an investigation or to artfully intervene and encourage girls to attend to the rest of the activity's procedures. In this lesson, Mr Leach did neither. Instead, his lack of intervention during the small group time as Elizabeth's all-female group focused exclusively on the construction of a plasticine figure suggests other factors at play in his thinking. For example, it is tempting to conjecture that Mr Leach's commitment to promoting a 'relaxed atmosphere in his classroom' through the establishment of a 'non-threatening environment' restricted his ability to redirect the girls' attention towards carrying out the full procedure or the boys' need to more accurately construct a model of a person. (Alternatively, I do wonder if he considered allowing more time for the lesson to validate the girls' attention to the accurate construction of the plasticine figure?)

Conversely, combining Elizabeth's all-girl group with the all-boy group during the latter part of the lesson belies the conclusion that Mr Leach was informed sufficiently 'of recent developments in science education' in research on gender or cooperative learning strategies. Slavin (1990) found in an extensive review of cooperative learning studies that cooperative learning is effective when there is a clear expectation of individual accountability for all members of the group. The use of a group task structure which fosters the contribution of each student in various roles over time is highly recommended. Mr Leach did not evidence that he was aware of the need to promote this. A reading of the gender-inclusive literature on teacher–learner interactions and expectations (see, for example, Kahle and Meece, 1994; Roychoudhury *et al.*, 1995; Sadker and Sadker, 1994) clearly shows that, on the whole, males are favoured in science lessons by their teachers at all levels while females are discouraged. In particular, girls are likely to receive fewer verbal and social encouragement cues from the teacher than the boys to answer science questions, contribute to science discussions and persist at experimenting. In Mr Leach's lesson that Wendy Giles reports, this inequitable situation is heartbreakingly instantiated. Instead of Elizabeth and her female group being actively encouraged by the male science teacher to take on active roles in sciencing, the girls predictably took on the roles of observers, recorders and equipment packers while the boys 'rolled the cars' and collected data. The result is that the girls were relegated to the status of 'voluntary minorities', carrying the cultural baggage of docile, dependent helpers (Tobin, 1996) during the second portion of the lesson. While this status determination was not probably the overt intent of Mr Leach's and the learners' actions, that is what the female science education researcher observed and reported as the enactment of the curriculum in Elizabeth's science class.

Finally, I would like to discuss the role of the gender of the science education researcher in reporting this instance of science classroom practice in a lesson taught by a male teacher. Many readers of this report may wonder if it is fair that Wendy Giles' focus in the classroom was on a subset of the male teacher's students, Elizabeth and the girls in her learning group, instead of the class as a whole. To respond requires some consideration of the purpose of research and a statement of my personal beliefs. I hold the belief that educational research is a disciplined inquiry in which meaningful topics are studied (Cronbach and Suppes, 1969). The most meaningful topics to me are ones that bear on social justice. In this case, Wendy Giles' role as a researcher was as an observer (Creswell, 1994). Her stated research focus was on 'observing students during their transition from elementary school to secondary school. Elizabeth was one of the students I had chosen.' As a result of the participant selection, the researcher's report focus is centred on the small learning groups in which her case study participant (Elizabeth) learned science. Since, as I have briefly described, the gender research indicates that girls, in general, are differentially impacted by sexism (regardless of the teachers' sex) in the science classroom, it is most appropriate from a social justice perspective on educational research that the female researcher focuses on the girls. It is with this population that we need new understanding. Feminist theorists have long asserted that women hold a different standpoint than men due to the difference in the social experience of men and women (Harding, 1986). This female standpoint needs to be a prominent feature in research particularly in which the teacher is male and he teaches female students. It is apparent from reading Wendy Giles' report that while it is important that male science teachers are as committed as Mr Leach to fostering a 'non-threatening environment' in which 'concepts and activities [are placed] in a context which would be meaningful for students' more is required to assist females such as Elizabeth in achieving equity in science education. For most males, who have enjoyed privilege throughout their educational histories in science learning environments because of their sex, reports by science education researchers that document inequitable impact on female students are especially meaningful. Comfortable teaching practices, such as accepting that girls will not fully participate in all aspects of sciencing, need to be re-examined if the cycle of inequity in science teaching and learning for females is to be broken. The hope is that from this type of social justice research that studies the traditionally under-served, a new awareness will arise that will benefit how all students are taught science.

The hard work now is for Ms Giles to effectively communicate her observations with Mr Leach. My fervent wish is that Mr Leach, and all other science teachers, are open to this conversation.

★   ★   ★

Editors' synthesis

In principle, *A crash course* describes the kind of lesson that many science educators advocate. The broad strategies used by the teacher – cooperative learning, hands-on activities and a socially meaningful context for the science content – are widely regarded as appropriate for students in general and for female students in particular. As the story of *A crash course* unfolded it became clear that the activity structure, which ought to have been gender inclusive, served to reinforce students' performance of gender-stereotyped social roles. Three issues emerged in the commentaries on this story: context, intervention and standpoints.

Deborah Tippins opens her comments with the acknowledgement that she first read the story through her '"gender equity" alert glasses'. Seeing 'crash' she expected some kind of male violence in the treatment of the topic, but then realised that car crashes are of interest to people in general. Despite the historical preponderance of weapons and warfare contexts in school physical science, this teacher had gone to some lengths to set up a context that was hoped to be gender neutral. As he explained in his later commentary on the lesson, Mr Leach's intention was to help students consider the effect of car accidents on people and the reasons for fitting head rests and seat belts to cars. Despite this careful establishment of a gender-neutral context for learning, the single-sex friendship groups made what seems to be stereotypical use of the laboratory activity. Provided with the resources to imagine cars and people, the girls' group focused on the construction of a realistic human shape and the boys' group noisily enjoyed the collisions they created.

Tippins' objection to the lesson was not the potentially masculine topic, but to the way the teacher managed the students' inquiry. As she notes, in this lesson the consequence of single-sex groups is the girls' relegation to the passive role of the boys' secretaries. Single-sex groups need not necessarily marginalise girls, but the fact that they did so in this case alerts Tippins to the consequences of the teacher's decision not to intervene in the groups. Less observation, more facilitation and more focus on the science concepts during group work might have enabled the girls' group to overcome their gendered response to the laboratory activity. Randy McGinnis takes up the issue of intervention, arguing that Mr Leach's commitment to a non-threatening environment restricted his ability to redirect the girls towards completing the procedure and the boys towards accurately constructing a model of a person. Specifically with regard to gender differences, Mr Leach might have anticipated that the girls would spend more time on planning the investigation than would the boys. He might have provided more time for the activity, or intervened to ensure that the girls attended to all of the procedures in the activity. More broadly, he might have been more specific about the roles of each group member, and then intervened to ensure that the girls did not fall into the marginal role of observers, recorders and equipment packers.

A third issue identified by McGinnis concerns the standpoints adopted in writing and reading this case study. Wendy Giles' standpoint, as a female researcher with an interest in gender-inclusive classroom practices, gives priority to the experience of the girls in the class. From this standpoint she expresses disappointment that the teacher did not intervene to distribute tasks more equitably in the final experimental group. For Mr Leach, a male teacher who positions himself as providing opportunities for students to increase their confidence by playing with materials and experimenting with group dynamics, non-completion of the activity is part of a more extended process of learning to be independent of teachers. Although his commentary explicitly acknowledges that the girls' willingness to 'watch the boys' has its roots in 'stereotypical male–female roles', his classroom preferences do not seem to be framed by a concern for gender equity. This option is not open to either of the other commentators on this story. For McGinnis, male teachers' membership of a privileged group prevents them from noticing the consequences of laissez-faire teaching for a less privileged group. Girls' lack of participation in some aspects of science, he argues, must be recognised by male teachers if the cycle of inequality is to be broken.

References

Baker, D. (1988). Teaching for gender differences. *NARST News*, 30, 5–6.

—— (1998). Equity issues in science education. In B. J. Fraser and K. G. Tobin (eds), *International handbook of science education* (pp. 869–895). Dordrecht, The Netherlands: Kluwer.

Baker, D. and Leary, R. (1995). Letting girls speak out about science. *Journal of Research in Science Teaching*, 32, 3–28.

Byrne, E. M. (1993). *Women and science: The snark syndrome*. Washington, DC: The Falmer Press.

Corey, V., van Zee, E., Minstrell, J., Simpson, D. and Simpson, V. (1993). When girls talk: An examination of high school physics classes. Paper presented at the annual meeting of the National Association for Research in Science Teaching, Atlanta, GA.

Creswell, J. W. (1994). *Composing and writing qualitative and quantitative research*. Newbury Park, CA: Sage Publishing.

Cronbach, L. J. and Suppes, P. (1969). *Research for tomorrow's schools*. New York: Macmillan.

Crossman, M. (1987). Teachers' interactions with girls and boys in science lessons. In A. Kelly (ed.), *Science for girls?* Milton Keynes: Open University Press.

Harding, S. (1986). *The science question in feminism*. Ithaca, NY: Cornell University Press.

—— (1991). *Whose science? Whose knowledge? Thinking from women's lives*. Ithaca, NY: Cornell University Press.

Jones, M. (1990). Action zone theory: target students and science classroom interactions. *Journal of Research in Science Teaching*, 27, 651–660.

Kahle, J. B. and Meece, J. (1994). Research on gender issues in the classroom. In D. L. Gabel (ed.), *Handbook of research in science teaching and learning* (pp. 542–557). New York: Macmillan Publishing.

McGinnis, J. R. and Pearsall, M. (1998). Teaching elementary science methods to women: A male professor's experience from two perspectives. *Journal of Research in Science Teaching*, 35 (8), 919–949.

McGinnis, J. R., Tobin, K. and Koballa, T. R. (1997, March). Teaching science methods to women: three tales of men professors reflecting on their practices. Paper presented at the National Association for Research in Science Teaching, Oak Brook, Illinois (ERIC Document Reproduction Service No. ED406200).

Mann, J. (1994). *The difference: Growing up female in America*. New York: Warner Books.

Martinez, M. (1992). Interest enhancement to science experiments: Interactions with student gender. *Journal of Research in Science Teaching*, 31, 363–380.

Murphy, P. (1994). Gender differences in pupils' reaction to practical work. In R. Levinson (ed.), *Teaching science*. New York: Routledge.

Osbourne, M. (1994). Status of prospects of women in science in Europe. *Science*, 263, 389–431.

Parker, L. H. and Rennie, L. J. (1998). Equitable assessment strategies. In B. J. Fraser and K. G. Tobin (eds), *International handbook of science education* (pp. 897–910). Dordrecht, The Netherlands: Kluwer.

Potter, E. and Rosser, S. (1992). Factors in life science textbooks that may deter girls' interest in science. *Journal of Research in Science Teaching*, 29, 669–686.

Rennie, L. J. and Parker, L. H. (1987). Detecting and accounting for gender differences in mixed-sex and single-sex groupings in science lessons. *Educational Review*, 39 (1), 65–73.

—— (1993). Curriculum reform and choice of science: Consequences for balanced and equitable participation. *Journal of Research in Science Teaching*, 30, 1,017–1,028.

Rennie, L. J., Parker, L. H. and Hildebrand, G. (eds) (1991). *Action for equity: The second decade*. Perth, Australia: National Key Centre for School Science and Mathematics, Curtin University of Technology.

Roychoudhury, A., Tippins, D. and Nichols, S. E. (1995). Gender-inclusive science teaching: A feminist-constructivist approach. *Journal of Research in Science Teaching*, 32 (9), 897–924.

Sadker, M. and Sadker, D. (1994). *Failing at fairness: How American schools cheat girls*. New York: Charles Scribners Sons.

Scantlebury, K. and Kahle, J. B. (1993). The implementation of equitable teaching strategies by high school biology teachers. *Journal of Research in Science Teaching*, 30, 537–545.

Schiebinger, L. (1993). *Nature's body: Gender in the making of modern science*. Boston: Beacon Press.

Shepardson, D. P. and Pizzini, E. L. (1992). Gender bias in female elementary teachers' perceptions of the scientific ability of students. *Science Education*, 76 (2), 147–153.

Slavin, R. E. (1990). *Cooperative learning: Theory, research, and practice*. Englewood Cliffs, NJ: Prentice Hall.

Tobin, K. (1988). Differential engagement of males and females in high school science. *International Journal of Science Education*, 10, 239–252.

—— (1996). Gender equity and the enacted science curriculum. In L. Parker, L. Rennie and B. Fraser (eds), *Gender, science and mathematics: Shortening the shadow* (pp. 119–127). Boston: Kluwer.

Chapter 5

Equity

Contributions by Barry Krueger, Angela Barton and Léonie J. Rennie

Editors' introduction

Representation, according to Gallard and colleagues (1998), is the central issue of curriculum and equity. Representation is the public expression of our thoughts so that they can be inspected, scrutinised, criticised and shared with others (Eisner, 1993). The forms of representation used and valued by teachers influence how students come to understand and represent their own thoughts. Classroom organisation, selection of content and activities, student groupings, teacher instructions, body language, reward signals and assessment procedures are all examples of forms of representation. The problem is that in selecting equitable forms of representation teachers can only rely on their own realities (experiences and understandings) to decide what is important to attend to and what is not. Other classroom realities – such as those of the students – are largely inaccessible to the teacher. This inevitable mismatch between the teacher's reality and the various student realities leads to a set of dilemmas for the teacher in selecting equitable forms of representation.

We illustrate some of the equity dilemmas faced by teachers by referring to an earlier study (Wallace and Louden, 2000) of science teaching in a Grade 10 Australian classroom. In this study, we showed how the realities of the science classroom differ depending on your standpoint in the classroom. We focused particularly on a teacher, Ms Horton, and Karl and Punipa, two students in Ms Horton's class – a non-streamed group from a working-class neighbourhood. Karl was achieving marginal C grades in science and Punipa was a borderline A student. Karl's parents were of Maori origin and Punipa's parents from Cambodia. In describing this classroom – the forms of representation used by Ms Horton to provide a caring classroom, Karl's quietly disruptive behaviour and Punipa's focus on maximising her grades – it became clear that the experiences and aspirations of these three people did not always match, and often conflicted, with each other. Ms Horton's caring approach involved a cheerful and positive disposition, with a relaxed approach to teaching the science content. These forms of representation were comforting for Karl, who responded positively to Ms Horton's approach, but left Punipa – who was anxious to improve her grades – looking for more predictable, conventional and pressing forms of science instruction. Clearly, Ms Horton's interpretation of equity as caring advantaged some and disadvantaged others.

When we slow down and look at this science classroom from different perspectives, the troubling thing is that, in one form or another, all perspectives are true. It is troubling because the teacher, who sits in the middle of these multiple realities, can only attend to the one that is true for her. The forms of representation selected are based on her own experience, her own reality. Moreover, as Ms Horton rushes headlong through the classroom experience, it is difficult to access those alternative realities which exist simultaneously to her own. Knowledges about other realities are contradictory, partial, irreducible and can never be fully understood by the teacher (Ellsworth, 1992). In any event, she cannot easily balance the simultaneous and often competing demands of teaching in a caring way, while dealing with the complexity of problems presented by Karl, Punipa and the twenty-five other students in her class. As researchers we can show how complex these matters are, but Ms Horton is still there – it is she who is faced with the dilemma of selecting equitable forms of representation. Which (and whose) equity is attended to depends on the teacher's experience of, and understandings about, what is important and what is not.

These issues of representation and multiple realities set the context for the following story. In *All the batteries are gone*, Barry Krueger describes his experience teaching electricity to a Grade 9 general science class. The dilemma for the teacher is which (and whose) reality should he attend to – the reality of a group of girls falling behind the rest of the class, the reality of the boys pressing ahead with their investigations, the reality of a shortage of equipment or the reality of promoting a spirit of inquiry? And, given those realities, which forms of representation are most appropriate to achieve equity within the classroom? The story is followed by commentaries by Barry Krueger (about his own teaching), Angela Barton and Léonie Rennie.

All the batteries are gone

Barry Krueger

'None of them go on', exclaimed Laura as she pressed the switch.

Laura and Megan bent over their circuit, checking to see if it was assembled correctly. None of the bulbs glowed when they added the second light globe into their circuit.

'Try it again', suggested Megan, none too sure that it would make any difference. Once again Laura pressed the switch, and once again none of the bulbs lit.

'There can't be any current coming out of the battery', Laura concluded.

Megan nodded in agreement. I frowned with annoyance. My Grade 9 science class were working from the booklets that accompanied the newly purchased electrical kits. Had Laura held the switch down for several seconds longer she would have observed the filaments of the globes glow a faint red colour. I made a mental note to work through this experiment and find more suitable bulbs next time. Laura and Megan dutifully recorded their conclusion, unaware that a current, albeit a small current, was flowing.

Elsewhere the other groups were experiencing varying degrees of success. A few of the boys had already finished the activities on series and parallel circuits and they were testing fuses. It was a prudent move to purchase these kits, despite the teething problems I was having with their use. At least the students could complete the core activities at their own pace. I shuddered to think how I taught this unit in the past. The problem with the lock-step method that I used previously was that some groups would finish their work in fifteen minutes and others would never finish in the allocated time. It seemed that it was mainly the boys who finished early. They would then spend the remaining time messing about rather than continuing with their written work. Sometimes I packed activities up, not because the students had finished, but because those who had finished were too disruptive. This year, at least, all the students would be able to complete the core activities. Moreover, there were plenty of extension activities for those students who would finish early.

Holly and Simone came over to the bench where I was showing Laura and Megan what they should have observed. They waited, quietly, in the background.

'How are we supposed to know?' asked Megan with just a hint of frustration in her voice. 'We followed the instructions.'

I turned towards Holly and Simone, ignoring Megan's question.

'All the batteries are gone', complained Holly. 'We don't have a battery and we need another globe. Michael's got three', she continued, 'and he won't give us one.'

I wondered what Holly and Simone had been doing in the last fifteen minutes if they didn't have a battery. A similar situation had occurred in the previous lesson when several of the boys had taken more than their share of bulbs and there were not enough for the rest of the class. Today it was the batteries as well.

Michael's group had taken three batteries instead of the one they were allowed. Jason's group had also taken three batteries. Both groups were working quite industriously. Michael had realised, unlike Laura and Megan, that an extra battery would cause the two light bulbs connected in series to glow. His group were quite pleased with their discovery, and they grudgingly yielded one of their batteries to Holly and Simone.

Jason and Shane, on the other hand, were several activities ahead of Michael's group. They were busy entertaining the small group of boys that had gathered around their bench. Shane was demonstrating to them how a fuse works.

'And when you join up this wire you make a short circuit and the fuse blows', he explained as he joined the wires together. The fuse wire glowed red and then white hot for an instant before it melted. The boys were impressed.

Sidling up, I asked Shane, 'How's it going?'

The other boys returned to their benches.

'Do you really need both batteries in your circuit?' I asked without trying to sound too threatening. 'Can't you use one like the instructions say?'

'It doesn't work as well', Shane replied. 'We'll show you.'

I watched while Jason wound another piece of fuse wire around the terminals. Shane removed one of the batteries from their circuit. It looked as if they had blown three or four fuses already this lesson. I wondered how many more fuses they would have to blow before they would be satisfied. Shane pressed the switch and joined the wire to produce the short circuit. The light bulb went out straightaway and the fuse wire started to glow red, fusing after three or four seconds.

'See what I mean!' exclaimed Shane.

'It still works doesn't it?' I remarked as I smiled and pocketed their extra batteries.

'But not as well', murmured Shane.

I checked Jason's notebook. He had not used a ruler to draw his circuit diagrams and his observations were far too brief. Shane's book was no better.

'You need to give more detail here', I remarked. 'How will you remember what you have observed?' Looking around the class it seemed to me that the girls were engaged in both performing the activities and recording their results, whereas most of the boys were just experimenting. I asked Jason and Shane to spend the next 15 minutes writing down their observations and their conclusions thoroughly before continuing with the activities.

Returning to the front of the laboratory where several groups were waiting for my help, I noticed that Laura and Megan were having difficulty constructing their parallel circuit. They were starting to get behind the rest of the class. It would be much easier for me to construct their circuit for them and then leave them to make the observations. After all, there were other students waiting and I really didn't have the time to work through the circuit with Laura and Megan. Other groups had blown their bulbs and they had to be replaced, Gareth had a question and he had already been waiting for some time and I needed to check the progress of several other groups. Perhaps I could quickly make up the circuit for Laura and Megan...

Teacher commentary

Barry Krueger

I have always found it particularly difficult to teach electricity to my junior high school science classes. For example, if I'm not careful, whole-class discussions become monopolised by a few boys who tell exaggerated stories of their experiences and ask questions that would hardly enter the other students' minds. It is so easy to let these boys set the agenda for the lesson and to allow the other students, particularly the girls, to be excluded from the discussions. In a similar manner, students have been excluded from opportunities to learn from laboratory work because I have generally employed a lock-step approach and allowed the faster students to set the pace. The story that I have recounted describes my observations from one of a series of laboratory lessons in which I attempted to bring about more equitable opportunities for learning.

I was initially quite pleased with the design of the laboratory program. The students were busy working their way through the core activities at their own pace and there was ample extension work. The problems that I had encountered previously with some groups fooling about because they had finished their activities and with other groups failing to finish their activities were circumvented. It was in this sense that the programme was a resounding success. However, differences in opportunities to learn were still being perpetuated, but in less obvious ways.

Although I created space in the laboratory programme for all the students to finish the core activities, I could not programme for differences between the students in their skills and confidences. My experience tells me that more boys than girls have electronics kits at home, know which end of a battery is positive and are able to identify how to connect light bulbs into circuits. Consequently, many boys are more adept than girls at identifying faults in their circuits. I am sure that whereas Megan and Laura concluded that no current flowed in their circuit, the more experienced students manipulated their equipment until they observed the expected outcome. How were Megan and Laura to know? After all, they were following the instructions they were given. I wonder how many of the lesser experienced students, like Megan and Laura, were able to reach the desired conclusion.

It is not easy to supervise fifteen different groups working on their circuits given the never-ending problems of flat batteries, blown globes and loose connections. It seems that I always have to be in three places at once explaining instructions, helping students with their circuits or giving out extra equipment. Unknown to me, Holly and Simone were unable to work on their activities because several of the boys had taken more than their share of the resources. This simple management problem was overcome in the following lessons by ensuring that the batteries and the bulbs were packed inside the kits rather than given out separately.

However, the most insidious way that some students were excluded from learning lay in my different interactions with groups of students. Perhaps I'm being too hard on myself, but it is here that I feel I have failed. Whereas I stood back and allowed Shane's group to demonstrate their circuit to me, I intervened in Laura and Megan's group, took over their circuit and showed them what they were supposed to observe. Again, later in the lesson when they were having difficulties, I considered constructing their circuit for them. Whereas I allowed Shane's group to show me their expertise, I reinforced Laura and Megan's lack of expertise. I suppose that showing these girls what they should have observed, or constructing their circuit for them, would have been expedient if time was a concern, but it wasn't. The subtle message was one of creating dependence. This was hardly the type of outcome I desired. It is so easy to tell students what is wrong with their circuits, or even worse to fix their circuits for them, particularly when you unconsciously doubt their competence. Looking back now, it would have been far better to help Megan and Laura work their way through their circuit. I wonder how often we perpetuate differences between students in such subtle and insidious ways?

★   ★   ★

Feminist challenges to teaching electricity to all children

Angela Barton, Teachers College, Columbia University

Barry Krueger's story, *All the batteries are gone*, is a powerful reminder of the complex ways in which gender, experience, power and science intermingle in the science classroom. As I read his story, I was brought back to one of my own experiences with electricity in college physics. I was in a lecture hall with about 400 other engineering and science majors, and the professor was describing series circuits and electrical charges. At the start of the lesson, I thought I understood series circuits and electrical charges. However, when the professor put the capacitor in his example, I became really confused. I could not get beyond the capacitor to understand the example. I felt frustrated, too afraid to raise my hand to ask what a capacitor was. After all, I remembered hearing about capacitors in middle and high school science. At the end of class I put aside my embarrassment and asked the man sitting next to me, 'what is a capacitor?' He laughed for a minute, and then very generously explained to me how it worked. Although, I have to admit it took me a few more years to actually figure out capacitors, I was surprised at this man's knowledge. I asked where he learned what it was, because I certainly could not find such a detailed description in our text. Without hesitation, he told me that as a child he mucked about with electrical supplies in his family's garage. 'Ohhh', I thought. 'That explains it.'

I begin my response to Krueger's story with a story of my own because it highlights three interrelated layers of issues we need to address in our science classrooms. First, although I grew up in a family that supported the belief that 'I could be whoever I wanted to be when I grew up', and although I was encouraged to explore the natural and physical worlds as a child, I never created – or was given – opportunity to explore electricity and electrical supplies as a child. The closest I ever came to this was dissecting the family phone (which caused me to be grounded for a month because I couldn't put it back together)! As a child, I never thought that *not* playing with electrical supplies would put me behind in school, and in particular in my science studies. Yet, my lowest science grades – and my lowest science confidence – crept into the limelight over and over again when we did things with electricity: middle school physical science, high school physics and college physics.

Thus the first layer of issues involves looking at the opportunities that girls have to acquire actional knowledge in the physical sciences such that they could equal the males in achievement and participation. This suggests that out-of-school experiences are important. From a gendered standpoint, feminists remind us that the ways in which we are often socialised at home shape the 'knowledge' we bring to school (Rosser, 1997). In Krueger's story, the boys were 'way ahead' of the girls in the electricity unit. Although I am sure that not all boys had experiences with electricity supplies outside of schools and all girls did not, it is probably the case that more boys than girls have had these experiences, and that this has had an effect on how comfortable they feel manipulating the science materials in school.

As teachers, we have to remember that the effect of out-of-school experiences on school knowledge is not just a gender issue (Barton, 1998). Although not raised in this story, we also have to consider other factors that influence the kinds and amounts of resources to which children have access. It is often the case that children living in urban poverty have fewer resources, especially fewer material resources such as batteries and bulbs. Therefore, like Krueger did, we need to provide all of our students the time and the space to muck about with these kinds of materials in science class to help build confidence, familiarity and experiential knowledge among all students.

The second issue has to do with a critique of the science that the children are learning and the possible effect this may have on what and how they learn. Feminists have critiqued science for being based on androcentric foundations, where the androcentric foundations permeate the social structure of science, its applications and methodologies (Barton, 1998). For example, science has prided itself on a rigorous method of study that separates the knower from the known and that values objective, externalist understandings of the physical and natural worlds. In the same light, feminists have argued that we need to expand this androcentric basis of science, especially in the science classroom, and that we can do this by valuing women's experiences and women's ways of knowing such as caring, cooperation and connection. In the case of the batteries, the girls were clearly being given an opportunity to play with the batteries, and this is important. They were also given the opportunity to explore collaboratively in single-sex groups, and this may be important as well. However, I wonder if the girls would have engaged more intensely in the project if it was somehow tied to their needs and interests rather than positioned as a separate activity with the sole goal of learning the science. As teachers we need to remember that learning and doing science does not occur in a social vacuum; that it is contextual. This last point complicates my first point because it suggests that in addition to providing girls with experiences outside of those they might experience in our gendered society, we also need to provide these opportunities in ways that are socially and culturally congruent with the students (Lee and Fradd, 1998).

The third layer invokes relations of power, gender and knowledge in the science classroom. Again I return to my opening story. As a college student majoring in chemistry at a predominantly male institution, I was embarrassed, perhaps afraid, to ask the physics professor what a capacitor was. I was afraid of interrupting his lecture. I was afraid to admit my 'not-knowing', especially in front of my peers in the classroom. I, like many girls are socialised to do, was also afraid to step outside of my role as 'good student' (Barton, 1998). Yet, as Krueger's story shows us, stepping outside the role of 'good student' actually helps one become a good scientist. For example, the girls in this story enact the part of the good student: they followed instructions, took only the required amounts of material as well as detailed notes, and stayed within the parameters of the assigned task. The boys, on the other hand, by resisting the role of the good student, were honing their inquiry skills and were on their way to becoming good scientists. They deviated from the task at hand and developed their own experiments, they questioned the role of the different variables, they demonstrated their findings, and they questioned the standardised knowledge of science as presented by texts, tests and other institutional structures. As illustrated by the boys, there was plenty of 'space' for them to move beyond the prescribed activity to test out their own hypotheses and ideas – to do science. But, for some reason, the girls did not even seem to know that this was a possibility; they did not seem to know that it was allowable.

So, the question in terms of power, gender and knowledge in the science classroom arises: who gets rewarded? when? and, for what? Krueger clearly was sensitive to his students' needs – both girls and boys. He pushed the girls to explore on their own, and he reined the boys back into the assigned task. Yet, from a gendered standpoint, I suspect that the 'deviant' actions of the boys will privilege them in the science community in the long run.

Experience, knowledge and power are pervasive, entangled issues faced by science teachers intent on promoting inclusive spaces for students to immerse themselves in deep and intellectual ways with the natural and physical worlds. By reflecting and articulating these issues in rich contextual ways, Krueger has created an intricate piece. Barry Krueger shows us all how complicated it is for teachers to manage these issues alongside of more traditional concerns in science education. Yet, it is stories, like this one, that will help us all move closer to inclusive science education.

★   ★   ★

Business as usual?

Léonie J. Rennie, Curtin University of Technology

Boys grab the equipment and don't share; they race ahead, experimenting beyond the instructions, often wasting or spoiling resources; they are reluctant to write up their notes, and what notes they do write are untidy and incomplete. Yet they seem to understand more than the girls. Shane knows how to blow 'fuses', showing off to the other boys. Michael realises, unlike Laura and Megan, that the two bulbs glow with an extra battery in the circuit. The girls are slow; they follow instructions but have difficulty constructing their circuits; they record their observations dutifully; they get behind.

The teacher begins to despair. He wants everyone to be involved. He can see advantages in students doing their own activities at their own pace, but is torn between the benefits of this and the need for some pacing to ensure that a few students (the girls?) don't fall behind. He is tempted to make the circuit for Laura and Megan to save them time but also seems to realise that this will deny them the opportunity to learn from the experience of doing it themselves. What is the teacher to do?

Krueger has characterised this dilemma as one about gender. Certainly he has given us some stereotypical stuff by pointing to differences in behaviour and the pedagogical problems that arise in a way that focuses on gender. The boys work fast, the girls are slow. The boys spend time experimenting creatively, the girls spend time following instructions slavishly. The boys write sloppy notes, if at all, the girls record neatly, even if they are unsuccessful. But does the author mean that this happens all of the time for *all* boys? and *all* girls? Probably not. Probably there are slower boys who work neatly and faster girls who don't; boys who bungle their circuits and girls who get them right first time.

This idea of 'all boys' and 'all girls' is at the heart of the some of the things we characterise as gender problems. It is most likely that, even in this class, there is more variation among the girls and among the boys than there is between girls as a group and boys as a group. Certainly this is true in most groups. For example, Hyde (1981) re-examined the 'well-established' gender differences described in the famous Maccoby and Jacklin (1974) review and found that they were, in fact, tiny. Median effect sizes were 0.24 for verbal ability and 0.43 for quantitative ability. Hyde's superimposed distribution graphs illustrate clearly the huge overlap between males and females on these measures. In their review of gender differences in motivational orientations towards achievement in school science, Steinkamp and Maehr (1984) use a similar graph of the superimposed male and female distributions of motivational orientation to show how the extensive overlap suggests that the statistically significant difference between the means (which represented an effect size of about 0.3) has little practical significance. Despite the age of these studies, we find that difference, rather than similarity, is the focus of most studies relating to gender, and it colours our thinking.

We can take participation in physics courses as another example – one of the most consistent patterns we refer to as reflecting gender difference. On average, there is a greater proportion of boys in a particular cohort than girls who choose to enrol for physics. Often we interpret this as a difference in interest in physics. Yet the difference in physics interest is greater among boys, and among girls, than it is between boys and girls. We find it is so easy to focus on the boys as a group, and on the girls as a group, that it is a simple step to look at between-group differences as a way of deciding students' needs and how we might deal with them. We find it easy to think of students in stereotypical ways, expecting gendered patterns of behaviour based on our own classroom experiences of what is typical for boys and for girls.

Let us go back to the classroom in the narrative. What if it were Holly and Simone who had taken extra batteries and were entertaining a small group of girls with a fuse-blowing demonstration? What if it were Jason and Shane who waited quietly in the background to tell the teacher that some girls had taken extra batteries and wouldn't share? What if it were Megan and Holly who had untidy, incomplete notes and were skipping ahead with the activities? Would this seem strange? Would we be surprised? If so, it is because it is a pattern counter to our stereotyped view of who is likely to do what in classrooms. Do we really want the girls to be more like the boys? or the boys to be more like the girls? If so, we are privileging one group over another on the basis of their sex. It is a way of making sex a determinant of who succeeds in science. Surely we want both boys and girls to succeed, to share, to explore beyond the instructions but to conserve resources and record their observations!

Perhaps we can re-characterise the problem, by ignoring for a moment that it was some boys who didn't share, and some girls who got behind. What other solutions might there be to this teacher's problems?

If not sharing equipment is a problem, then a more generous allocation of resources might help, because everyone would have as many batteries and bulbs as they needed. If it is a problem that some students are not getting through all of the required core activities, then less content to cover in the curriculum would help by creating more time for the slower workers to get the core activities completed. If another problem is the teacher being stretched too thin, with so many students needing his attention, then smaller classes is a solution. Then the teacher would have time to help anyone in need and to monitor the performance of every student to ensure progress. Of course, there are impediments to all of these solutions, particularly with regard to cost. Smaller class sizes require many more classrooms and much more money for teachers' salaries, more resources means additional cost, more equipment to manage and probably more waste. And how much content is crammed into science courses is often out of the hands of the classroom teacher.

There are no easy solutions. If there were, we would have found them by now. But my point is that there are other ways to look at the issue. The kinds of problems described in this narrative would be alleviated by any of the solutions I have suggested. Searching for a solution based on gender is the avenue least likely to be profitable and probably also the least equitable. In the standards-focused curricula being adopted around the world, there is only one basis for equity. Students must be treated according to their needs. Sometimes their needs are associated with a social grouping, like gender, culture, or religion, but often not. Further, these social variables are entwined and intersect in multiple, often unpredictable ways. Dealing with them all is not easy. Dealing with just one of them, gender, may sometimes help, but not always.

I don't see a gendered solution to the problems in the narrative. Drawing our attention to the fact that mostly boys do this and mostly girls do that enhances and recreates the gender divide. I think more progress might be made if students are recognised as individuals, considering their behaviour in terms of their individual interests, experiences and needs. Some students (not all boys) might need help in learning to share resources, some students (not all girls) might need help in learning to construct circuits. Instead of focusing on students as girls or boys, we could look at them as individuals, needing to learn in their own way and at their own pace. Perhaps the trade-off, at least in the short term, is a spread-out classroom in terms of where students are up to, and greater strain on the teacher to manage resources and procedures. But if every student is task-oriented and working well, isn't that a step forward?

★　　　★　　　★

Editor's synthesis

The case story, *All the batteries are gone*, and the accompanying commentaries raise several layers of issues about equity and the teaching of science. At first reading, the story appears to be a clear case of the gendered nature of science classrooms. Krueger's framing of the story and his own reflections lead to the conclusion that many of the curriculum representations depicted in the story are biased against the girls and in favour of the boys. The subject matter, the opportunities to compete for resources, the teacher's different responses to the girls vs the boys all point towards 'boy'- rather than 'girl-friendly' science. Krueger, for example, speaks of the low likelihood that girls will encounter circuits at home, of the problems with boys taking more than their share of the resources and of the dangers of 'creating dependence' among the girls. Barton agrees and responds to the issues raised in the case by highlighting the need to increase opportunities for girls (and boys) to acquire actional knowledge, re-examine the androcentric foundations of science and change power relations in science classrooms.

An alternative interpretation is provided by Rennie who points to the dangers of reading too much into the gender issue. She says that, in common with many other gender studies, this case focuses on 'difference, rather than similarity ... and it colours our thinking'. Such thinking, according to Rennie, draws 'our attention to the fact that mostly boys do this and mostly girls do that [and] enhances and recreates the gender divide'. She continues, 'searching for a solution based on gender is the avenue least likely to be profitable and probably also the least equitable'. Rennie argues that a more fruitful (and equitable) pathway is to think of students as individuals with their own experiences, interests and needs. She proposes several strategies that might assist the teacher to cater for all students, boys as well as girls – the slower, neater, less adventurous students and the faster, more adventurous students. These strategies include reducing class size, cutting back on course content and making more resources available in the classroom.

Notwithstanding these different readings, both Barton and Rennie agree that the issues raised by the case are complex and difficult. Rennie, for example, points to the difficulty for the teacher of having to deal with social variables that 'are entwined and intersect in multiple, often unpredictable ways'. Teachers are caught, according to Barton, between the need to provide students with new experiences, and doing so in ways that are socially and culturally congruent. 'Experience, knowledge and power', argues Barton, 'are pervasive, entangled issues faced by science teachers intent on promoting inclusive spaces for students to immerse themselves in deep and intellectual ways with the natural and physical worlds.'

These comments by Barton and Rennie bring us back to the dilemma raised at the beginning of the chapter. What is the teacher to do, when there are so many realities in the classroom? Krueger finds himself caught in the middle. By choosing to focus on girls' experiences, for example, he may well disadvantage the boys. If, like Ms Horton, he were to focus on the low achievers in his class, he could well be doing a disservice to the higher achievers. The teacher can only act on that which is known to him, and that can only ever be a partial view based on his own experience. However, Krueger's writings about his teaching, his openness to new ideas, and his preparedness to try different strategies to cater for all students, sets an example for others to follow. For only through a diversity of experiences and deeper understandings can teachers expand their representational repertoire, thus creating more possibilities for creating inclusive science classrooms.

References

Barton, A. C. (1998). *Feminist science education*. New York: Teachers College Press.

Eisner, E. (1993). Forms of understanding and the future of educational research. *Educational Researcher*, 22 (7), 5–11.

Ellsworth, E. (1992). Why doesn't this feel empowering? Working through the repressive myths of critical pedagogy. In C. Luke and J. Gore (eds), *Feminisms and critical pedagogy*. New York: Routledge.

Gallard, A., Viggiano, E., Graham, S., Stewart, G. and Vigliano, M. (1998). The learning of voluntary and involuntary minorities in science classrooms. In B. J. Fraser and K. G. Tobin (eds), *International handbook of science education* (pp. 941–953). Dordrecht, The Netherlands: Kluwer.

Hyde, J. G. (1981). How large are cognitive gender differences? *American Psychologist*, 36, 892–901.

Lee, O. and Fradd, S. (1998). Science for all, including students from non-English-language backgrounds. *Educational Researcher*, 27 (4), 12–21.

Maccoby, E. E. and Jacklin, C. N. (1974). *The psychology of sex differences*. Stanford, CA: Stanford University Press.

Rosser, S. (1997). *Re-engineering female friendly science*. New York: Teachers College Press.

Steinkamp, M. W. and Maehr, M. L. (1984). Gender differences in motivational orientations toward achievement in school science: A quantitative synthesis. *American Educational Research Journal*, 21, 39–59.

Wallace, J. and Louden, W. (2000). *Teachers' learning: Stories of science education*. Dordrecht, The Netherlands: Kluwer.

Chapter 6

Culture and ethnicity

Contributions by Deborah J. Tippins,
Sharon E. Nichols, Mary Monroe Atwater
and Glen S. Aikenhead

Editors' introduction

One of the key contributions of constructivism to science education is the understanding that learners make their own sense of the world and the curriculum, beginning with what they already believe. What students believe depends, among many other things, on the cultural context in which they live. From one cultural group to the next, there are differences in the taken-for-granted understandings of science and the physical world. Differences between western and indigenous ways of learning science, for example, have been documented for Aboriginal people in Australia (Christie, 1991), Maori in New Zealand (McKinley *et al.*, 1992) and Native Americans (Haukoos and Satterfield, 1986). For these and other people, cultural difference impacts on their opportunity to learn. Sometimes the issue may be with science itself, with the Whiggish assumption that western science is unproblematically the agent of human progress. Sometimes the issue may be with school science, with its preference for linearity, abstractness and specialised language. Sometimes the issue may be with the institution of school rather than the specifics of science. For students whose families have been marginalised and excluded from schooling and whose idea of the good life does not revolve around academic success, it is not always obvious that it makes sense to buy into the constraints and obligations of classrooms, homework and examinations.

These issues about science, the subject of science in schools and the structure of schools in general work together to reduce some social and cultural groups' opportunity to learn. For teachers, the consequences of cultural difference are often alarming. Lower than average performances of particular cultural groups are frequently reported. In the TIMMS study, for example, lower than average performances were reported for black and Hispanic students in the United States (Jakwerth, 1999) and Aboriginal students in Australia (Lokan, 1999). In addition to these performance differences of concern to all teachers, white and middle-class teachers frequently find students from different cultural groups hard to teach. Despite their best intentions, cultural diversity gets in the way of some teachers' attempts to interest students in school science.

In this chapter, Deborah Tippins and Sharon Nichols describe how Stacey Harmon attempts to bridge the gap and teach more culturally relevant science. Stacey is a composite of many teachers who have struggled with issues of diversity and their significance in the science classroom. Based on her belief that science should not be taught in isolation from culture, Stacey plans and implements a culturally relevant science lesson. When her Grade 9 physical science students fail to draw any meaningful conclusions about culture and science from the 'build and insulate an igloo' activity, Stacey begins to question the meaning of cultural relevancy. She engages in a conversation with 'critical friends' Deborah and Sherry, and modifies her approach to designing culturally relevant science lessons. The story is followed by commentaries from Mary Atwater and Glen Aikenhead.

Igloos and icebergs

Deborah J. Tippins and Sharon E. Nichols

Stacey is in her first year as a Grade 9 teacher at Monroe High School in Delland, a fast-growing suburban community punctuated by an emerging computer technologies industry and a lucrative business market. Stacey transferred to Delland after teaching for three years in her home town of Wilkerville, where she enjoyed the comforts of living in a small town. Her decision to move to Delland was prompted by an interest in meeting other young, single professionals. However, the move to Delland presented a sharp contrast to life in Wilkerville. She was placed at Monroe High School, an east side school which struggled to encourage student attendance and had the reputation of being the district's lowest 'low performance' school.

Stacey's first few months at Monroe were very distressing, as most of her students seemed to resent having to be at school. She found it difficult to balance the outbursts displayed by some of the students with the apathetic detachment of others. Each day as she drove by the low-income housing areas where most of her students lived, she found it difficult to understand why they lacked the motivation to escape such poor living situations. If they would only devote minimal attention and energy to their school studies, Stacey thought, they, too, could obtain jobs with the local technology companies. Most of the entry-level jobs required merely a two-year training certificate from the local community college. Stacey knew that unless students were motivated to learn and develop basic skills, they would never be considered for future employment. What could she do to help her students develop an interest in learning science?

In late autumn, Stacey had the opportunity to attend the state science teachers' association conference. Looking for ideas to help her address the

needs of her culturally diverse group of students, she attended a workshop entitled, 'Ice-capades: A multicultural approach to learning about heat energy.'
Teachers attending this session were challenged to use materials provided to
build a house which would prevent an ice cube from melting. Working with
combinations of foil, styrofoam and paper, Stacey and three other teachers
constructed a heat-resistant ice house. As they waited ten minutes, recording
changes in temperature inside and outside the ice house over time, the workshop facilitator discussed the application of concepts related to heat energy to
the design of Eskimo igloos. Stacey found the cooperative and hands-on
problem-solving approach used in the session very engaging. She felt that the
activity was an interesting example of how science concepts could be taught in
ways that were culturally relevant. She looked forward to using this activity, and
others like it, during her unit on heat energy next week.

The following week Stacey introduced the 'build and insulate an igloo' activity
just as she had experienced it at the conference. Her students were familiar with
working in cooperative groups and were fairly quick to organise themselves and
the materials. As in the teachers' workshop, Stacey used the ten minutes
required for testing out temperature change to present a short lecture about
igloo construction and Eskimo culture. While a few students were interested in
her presentation, the majority were preoccupied playing with the building pieces,
and ignored her attempts to interest them in Eskimo culture. Stacey soon began
to understand that her students thought the activity was silly, especially when
one of her Hispanic students, Emilio, shouted out, 'Gee, maybe I should get a
bunch of styrofoam to build an igloo at the housing project!' Disappointed that
the activity was not perceived as more meaningful, Stacey felt that somehow she
had missed the mark. She looked forward to sharing her frustrations with
Deborah and Sherry, science educators from the nearby university, who
were collaborators in Monroe High School/University partnership. At the after-
school partnership meeting, Stacey began to share her experience:

STACEY: I thought that the students would really benefit from seeing how phys-
    ical science is connected to a culture other than their own. With all the
    emphasis on 'teaching science for all' in the National Science Education
    Standards, I thought the igloo activity would be the perfect example for
    helping students see connections between physical science and culture.
SHERRY: Yeah, I would think students would be motivated by the opportunity to
    connect physical science with real life. But it's been my experience that
    students sometimes have difficulty relating science to other cultures
    because they know little about their own culture. Many students have never

given a thought to the role of science in their own culture. So it is not surprising, after all, that your students were unable to connect the example of heat energy in Eskimo culture.

STACEY: This whole question of what constitutes culturally relevant science is a difficult one to answer.

DEBORAH: One model that's really helped me understand the influence of culture on science teaching and learning is the 'iceberg metaphor'. The majority of an iceberg is below the surface of the water, with only the tip of the iceberg visible above the surface. This is not unlike our conceptions of the nature of culture. It is usually the ideas on the 'tip of the iceberg' that get emphasised when we consider the meaning of culturally relevant science – items such as the fine arts, games, music, dress, foods, etc., of different cultural groups. However, it is the ideas below the tip of the iceberg that are much more important in terms of influencing the teaching and learning of science – concepts such as approaches to problem-solving, incentives to work, conversational patterns, relationship to animals, conceptions of past and future, preference for competition or cooperation, ordering of time, patterns of group decision-making, arrangement of physical space, body language, notions about logic and validity and many more.

As Stacey walked out of the teachers' lounge after the partnership meeting, she saw a note posted on the bulletin board which announced: 'The city of Delland will sponsor the building of thirty homes during the month of May. These homes will be sold to qualified families who might otherwise never be able to afford owning a home. You are invited to donate your time and/or materials to the construction of these homes.' It struck Stacey that Emilio's comment had much to say about the meaning of culturally relevant science teaching and learning. Perhaps it was inappropriate to ask her students to relate to the lifestyles of those living far removed from their local situation. Maybe what was missing was an opportunity to teach students how to use science to deal with their own everyday situations. Following Emilio's suggestions, she might ask her students to examine their own housing and how to use science to better design homes that could keep them warm in the winter. Perhaps they could work with the local electric company to develop materials to better insulate their homes. Stacey was excited – the timing was great – she could use the housing ad to interest students in heat energy as it relates to their everyday experiences.

★   ★   ★

Culturally relevant science pedagogy: needing to understand the culture

Mary Monroe Atwater, University of Georgia

Some educators have proposed culturally relevant teaching as one approach to successfully teaching concepts to Black students and other students of colour (Atwater, 1995; Atwater and Brown, 1999; Foster, 1995; Gordon, 1982). According to Ladson-Billings (1994), culturally relevant pedagogy is an approach to learning and teaching that utilises cultural referents so that students develop knowledge, skills and attitudes and are empowered intellectually, socially, emotionally and politically. Teachers who effectively employ culturally relevant pedagogy have broad pedagogical understandings in the following three areas: conceptions of themselves and other individuals, conceptions of social relations and conception of knowledge. Grant and Ladson-Billings (1997) have further elaborated on these pedagogical understandings. As far as conceptions of themselves and others, teachers who are culturally relevant act in the following ways: (a) believe that all of their students are capable of academic success, (b) view their pedagogy as an art which is unpredictable and always evolving, (c) perceive themselves as members of a community, (d) view teaching as a way to give back to the community of their students and (e) believe that knowledge is pulled out of the student, not put in. Their ideas about social relationships include (a) maintaining fluid student–teacher relationships, (b) establishing and maintaining a connectedness with their students, (c) developing a community of learners among students and (d) favouring students learning collaboratively and being responsible for each other's learning. Finally, these teachers' conception of knowledge involves the following: (a) knowledge is shared, recycled and reconstructed, (b) knowledge must be critically analysed, (c) one must be passionate about knowledge and learning, (d) teachers must scaffold or build bridges to enhance learning and (e) assessment and evaluation must be multifaceted and must integrate multiple forms of excellence. In order to be a culturally relevant teacher, one must consider one's underlying beliefs and ideologies about learning and teaching.

With this theoretical background, the analysis of the case entitled *Igloos and icebergs* can commence. Stacey, a first-year Grade 9 teacher at Monroe High School, has left her hometown where she taught for three years so that she will be able to meet young, eligible single professionals. The reader knows very little about Stacey's culture, ethnicity or race. What one does know is that Stacey is teaching students whose culture is very different from hers. In addition, Stacey is aware that she is being unsuccessful in teaching her students science. She attends a workshop on culturally relevant science teaching and decides to utilise the activity in her classroom. Of course, Stacey's students do not respond as the teachers did in the workshop. She is very disappointed and does recall a statement that Emilio shouted: 'Gee, maybe I should get a bunch of styrofoam for the igloo at the housing project!' At this point, both the school personnel and Stacey have an obligation to familiarise Stacey with the cultures of the students in the school. In addition, Stacey should have immediately attempted to connect with a successful teacher in the school. Stacey did drive through the housing project and concluded that her students should be motivated to learn because of their parents' or guardians' poverty. However, Stacey has failed to use the knowledge she possesses to connect with her science students. Originally, she probably was more interested in teaching science than teaching students science.

After the workshop, Stacey should have developed her own understanding of what is culturally relevant pedagogy. It appears that she believed that a teacher takes a science activity without any modification and uses it in a classroom of students without considering the students' culture and the connections the activity has to the students' lives. Her approach is not culturally relevant pedagogy. In no way has Stacey reflected on her own beliefs and ideologies about science learning and teaching. She has assumed that since her beliefs and ideas worked well in her home town, they will work well in Delland.

Upon her reflection of the results of her failed effort at culturally relevant pedagogy and a note that she saw posted, Stacey begins to reflect on her own beliefs and ideas about science learning and teaching. She is now going to ask her students to study their own dwelling places and determine better designs for their homes based on ideas about thermal energy, heat, conduction and insulation. Stacey is now beginning to understand what culturally relevant pedagogy is. It should be noted that Stacey did contact two university professors who helped her to begin to understand culturally relevant pedagogy.

Stacey is still a long way from being a culturally relevant science teacher. She is probably unaware of her own culture and racial identity; hence, she will have a very difficult time understanding her students' cultures and racial identities. She has not developed a very strong relationship between her students and herself. The reader does not know if Stacey believes that science knowledge should empower her students to change the world in which they live if they so desire. Hence, the reader has no idea how passionate Stacey is about science learning and teaching. Will Stacey ever develop to the point that she views science teaching as giving back to the communities of her students? And of course, the question still remains: will Stacey be successful in her second attempt at culturally relevant pedagogy?

★   ★   ★

Whose culture? What culture?

Glen S. Aikenhead, University of Saskatchewan

> Based on her belief that science should not be taught in isolation from culture, Stacey plans and implements [what she thought was] a culturally relevant science lesson.

Within a transmission orientation to school curriculum, relevance is often defined by the discipline expert or by the dominant culture. Stacey attempts to liberate herself from this solely transmission orientation by taking on a transactional orientation. Sadly she fails. As Deborah Tippins and Sharon Nichols point out, relevance must be defined by the *students'* culture, so students can interact with the curriculum in a familiar context. On three occasions Stacey unwittingly expresses a type of colonising attitude: when she assumes that her Eurocentric view of relevance could be imposed upon her students, when she cannot understand why her students lacked the motivation to escape their 'poor' living situation, and when she socially constructs Alaska Natives with her Eurocentric label 'Eskimo'.

But much more, school science will forever be taught in isolation from culture until we recognise that science is itself a culture (Pickering, 1992). Science is characterised by a community of scientists who share 'norms, values, beliefs, expectations and conventional actions' (a standard anthropological definition of culture; Phelan *et al.*, 1991). Only when we approach science instruction as a cross-cultural event for most students – an event requiring them to move between their own culture and the culture of science – can we begin to address the cultural isolation of school science (Aikenhead, 1996). Stacey is wrong to try to help 'students see connections between physical science and culture'. Instead we need to help our students see the connections between the *culture* of physical science and the *indigenous culture* of our students' own identities.

Stacey rightly concluded that it was inappropriate at that time for her to ask her students to relate to people (Alaskan Natives) so far removed. However, Stacey should have also concluded that physical scientists are similarly distant (in terms of culture) from most of her students. This cultural perspective on science would have opened up new ways for her to ask students to relate to physical science (Aikenhead, 1996; Jegede and Aikenhead, 1999).

Using the metaphor of an iceberg, Deborah explains the superficiality of Stacey's lesson by pointing out that we should not isolate artifacts from a culture (e.g. igloos), but we should consider a whole range of subtle features of students' cultural identities. Instead of tokenism, we also need to validate students' indigenous knowledge about nature that strengthens their self-identities (Aikenhead, 1997).

It would help if we set aside colonising attitudes and assimilative practices inherent in simplistic constructivist approaches to science teaching advanced by many reforms to science education. Alternatively, in a cross-cultural approach, students will have access to learning the culture of science without necessarily replacing their indigenous beliefs about nature. Students will *add* new contexts to their cognitive schemata in which science concepts logically fit (Aikenhead and Jegede, 1999). In this cross-cultural approach, science beliefs can be compared and contrasted with indigenous beliefs as coming from *two different cultures*, each with their own predominant worldviews, ideologies, epistemologies, language conventions, norms, values, etc. An anthropological simile may help to clarify the type of learning intended here. Students will be like anthropologists – learning science to be literate but not to take on the culture of science as their own. Anthropologists are not assimilated into the cultures they study, but they become adept at acting appropriately within those cultures.

Science for practical action

Stacey's science activities (designing warmer igloos, and designing better homes in 'the projects') are actually *technology design* activities. A conventional goal of science is to develop new knowledge for the sake of knowledge, while the conventional goal of technology is to solve problems in response to human and social needs (Layton *et al.*, 1993). At the end of the narrative story, Stacey concludes that she will ask her students to use school science content to better design homes. Yet again she commits the 'igloo faux pas' by not realising that the culture of science is different from the culture of technology design and that science content can seldom be transmitted (applied) directly to technology design (Collingridge, 1989).

Layton and colleagues' (1993) in-depth case study about people insulating their homes showed how the science of thermodynamics was of little or no use for practical action. 'It is clear that the requirement to understand science on science's terms … is challenged in fundamental ways by the findings from the case studies' (p. 124). Engineers have known for years that people must transform science concepts into context-specific concepts before practical action can draw upon science.

Stacey needs to learn how to 'deconstruct and reconstruct scientific knowledge to achieve its articulation with practical action' (Layton *et al.*, 1993, p. 128). This is not only a challenge to Stacey, but to all of us who espouse cultural relevance. One promising avenue to success is a *cross-cultural* approach to teaching in which deconstructing and reconstructing from one culture to another becomes a natural, almost intuitive, process (Aikenhead, 1997). It mirrors, for example, studying Spanish in an immersion fashion for the purpose of acting appropriately in a Spanish culture, as opposed to memorising Spanish to pass a grammar examination – a process called playing

Fatima's rules (Jegede and Aikenhead, 1999; Larson, 1995). Fatima's rules advise us not to read the textbook but to memorise the bold-faced words and phrases. Fatima's rules can include such coping mechanisms as 'silence, accommodation, ingratiation, evasiveness, and manipulation' (Atwater, 1996, p. 823).

Politics of school science

The challenge for Stacey, and for the whole reform movement as well, involves rethinking the ideology of school science. Loughran and Derry (1997) investigated students' reactions to one science teacher's concerted effort to teach for deconstructing and reconstructing ('deep understanding'). The researchers caught students playing Fatima's rules for reasons that related to the culture of public schools:

> The need to develop a deep understanding of the subject may not have been viewed by them [the students] as being particularly important as progression through the schooling system could be achieved without it. ... They had learnt how to learn sufficiently well to succeed in school without expending excessive time or effort.
>
> (p. 935)

Their teacher lamented, 'No matter how well I think I teach a topic, the students only seem to learn what they need to pass the test, then, after the test, they forget it all anyway' (p. 925). Tobin and McRobbie (1997, p. 366) documented a teacher's complicity in Fatima's rules: 'There was a close fit between the goals of Mr. Jacobs and those of the students and satisfaction with the emphasis on memorisation of facts and procedures to obtain the correct answers needed for success on tests and examinations.' Costa (1997) synthesised the work of Larson (1995) and Tobin and McRobbie (1997) with her own classroom research and concluded:

> Mr Ellis' students, like those of Mr London and Mr Jacobs, are not working on chemistry; they are working to get through chemistry. The subject does not matter. As a result, students negotiate treaties regarding the kind of work they will do in class. Their work is not so much productive as it is political. They do not need to be productive – as in learning chemistry. They only need to be political – as in being credited for working in chemistry.
>
> (p. 1,020)

When playing Fatima's rules, teachers both transmit a curriculum and screen students for post-secondary institutions.

For a large majority of students, school science is experienced as an attempt to assimilate or screen them politically. Most students exhibit creativity and intransigence in their quest to circumvent assimilation and avoid expending unnecessary effort. Culturally relevant science, on the other hand, requires students to cross cultural borders into the culture of science, and to negotiate scientific and technological meanings in the context of their everyday culture (influenced as it is by science and technology).

★   ★   ★

Editors' synthesis

What counts as culturally relevant science? Is it just a matter of linking standard science content with culture-specific applications of this content? Or are there deeper matters at risk when teachers attempt to teach school science across the borderlands of home language and culture, race and social class? *Igloos and icebergs* describes a dilemma familiar to many teachers working with students in diverse communities. Stacey identifies – no doubt correctly – cultural difference as one of the reasons she is having difficulty engaging her students, but she is unclear about what aspects of culture she should focus on to make her lessons more relevant. When she speaks with Deborah and Sherry after school, Deborah suggests that she attend to deeper features of culture, the features that are beneath the waterline of the cultural iceberg.

Mary Atwater takes up some of these beneath-the-waterline issues in her commentary. She draws attention to three aspects of culturally relevant pedagogy: teachers' conceptions of themselves and other individuals, their conceptions of social relations and their conception of knowledge. As Atwater explains, Stacey shows no awareness of her own racial and cultural identity and without this awareness is likely to have difficulty understanding her students' identities. Secondly, the narrative provides no evidence that Stacey understands the impact of social relations on teaching. She was disappointed that her students did not share her own belief in education as a key to social mobility, and did not yet have the skills to build a classroom characterised by community and collaboration. With regard to Grant and Ladson-Billings' third test of culturally relevant pedagogy, Atwater notes that Stacey is beginning to understand that she may have to rethink her assumptions about what is to be taught and learned if she is to build a bridge between school science and her students' cultures.

Aikenhead's response, however, shows how easy it is for white teachers to adopt the attitude of the coloniser when they attempt to register cultural difference. Although she has the best intentions in mind, in this story Stacey's attempt to bridge between her own culture and that of her students is built on culturally shaky foundations. Artifacts of culture such as igloos – along with music, dress and food – cannot be understood in isolation from their cultural context. Moreover, Stacey makes a terrible colonial *faux pas* in naming Alaska Natives as Eskimos. Thirdly, Stacey fails to see the cross-cultural dimensions of the whole enterprise of science education. As Aikenhead says, for all but a few students, learning school science requires cross-cultural communication from their home culture to the culture of science. The culture of physical scientists, he says, is far distant from students' indigenous cultures. In order to enter into the culture of school science, students need to understand its norms, values and practices. Most often, students do not make this cross-cultural journey in school science. Instead, they play by Fatima's rules, pursuing what will be tested rather than the deep structure of discipline knowledge.

In Stacey's account, of course, students do not even play by Fatima's rules. As she characterises them, the students are apathetic and resentful. In her move from culturally comfortable Wilkerville to culturally alien Delland, Stacey has encountered students who make only minimal efforts to meet her expectations. Her problem is familiar to generations of teachers and teacher educators, but her well-meaning attempt to make science more engaging to her students barely touches the deep cultural issues that divide her from her students.

References

Aikenhead, G. S. (1996). Science education: Border crossing into the subculture of science. *Studies in Science Education*, 27, 1–52.

—— (1997). Toward a First Nations cross-cultural science and technology curriculum. *Science Education*, 81, 217–238.

Aikenhead, G. S. and Jegede, O. J. (1999). Cross-cultural science education: A cognitive explanation of a cultural phenomenon. *Journal of Research in Science Teaching*, 36 (3), 269–287.

Atwater, M. M. (1995). The multicultural science classroom part II: Assisting all students with science acquisition. *The Science Teacher*, 62 (4), 42–45.

—— (1996). Social constructivism: Infusion into the multicultural science education research agenda. *Journal of Research in Science Teaching*, 33, 821–837.

Atwater, M. M. and Brown, M. L. (1999). Inclusive reform: Including all students in the science education reform movement. *The Science Teacher*, 66 (3), 44–48.

Christie, M. J. (1991). Aboriginal science for the ecologically sustainable future. *Australian Science Teachers Journal*, 37 (1), 26–31.

Collingridge, D. (1989). Incremental decision making in technological innovations: What role for science? *Science, Technology and Human Values*, 14, 141–162.

Costa, V. B. (1997). How teacher and students study 'all that matters' in high school chemistry. *International Journal of Science Education*, 19, 1,005–1,023.

Foster, M. (1995). African American teachers and culturally relevant pedagogy. In J. A. Banks (ed.), *Handbook of research on multicultural education* (pp. 570–581). New York: Macmillan.

Gordon, B. (1982). Toward a theory of knowledge acquisition for Black children. *Journal of Education*, 64 (1), 90–108.

Grant, C. A. and Ladson-Billings, G. (1997). *Dictionary of multicultural education*. Phoenix, AZ: Oryx.

Haukoos, G. and Satterfield, R. (1986). Learning styles of minority students and their application to developing a culturally sensitive classroom. *Community/Junior College Quarterly*, 10, 193–201.

Jakwerth, P. (1999) TIMMS performance assessment results: United States. *Studies in Educational Evaluation*, 25 (3), 277–281.

Jegede, O. J. and Aikenhead, G. S. (1999). Transcending cultural borders: Implications for science teaching. *Research in Science and Technological Education*, 17 (1), 45–67.

Ladson-Billings, G. (1994). *The dreamkeepers: Successful teachers for African American children*. San Francisco: Jossey-Bass.

Larson, J. O. (1995, April). Fatima's rules and other elements of an unintended chemistry curriculum. Paper presented at the American Educational Research Association annual meeting, San Francisco.

Layton, D., Jenkins, E., Macgill, S. and Davey, A. (1993). *Inarticulate science?* Driffield, East Yorkshire, UK: Studies in Education.

Lokan, J. (1999). Equity issues in testing: The case of TIMMS performance. *Studies in Educational Evaluation*, 25 (3), 297–314.

Loughran, J. and Derry, N. (1997). Researching teaching for understanding: The students' perspective. *International Journal of Science Education*, 19, 925–938.

McKinley, E., Waiti, P. and Bell, B. (1992). Language, culture and science education. *International Journal of Science Education*, 14, 579–594.

Phelan, P., Davidson, A. and Cao, H. (1991). Students' multiple worlds: Negotiating the boundaries of family, peer, and school cultures. *Anthropology and Education Quarterly*, 22, 224–250.

Pickering, A. (ed.) (1992). *Science as practice and culture*. Chicago: University of Chicago Press.

Tobin, K. and McRobbie, C. (1997). Beliefs about the nature of science and the enacted science curriculum. *Science and Education*, 6, 355–371.

Chapter 7

Power

Contributions by Karen McNamee, Ken Atwood,
Nel Noddings and Peter C. Taylor

Editors' introduction

Who has the power in classrooms? In 1932, Willard Waller wrote, 'Children are certainly defenseless against the machinery with which the adult world is able to enforce its decisions: the result of the battle [between teachers and students] is foreordained' (p. 196). Seventy years on, the assumptions behind Waller's statement continue to be powerful organising referents for schools and classrooms. Many commonplace school activities – such as instruction, assessment, student discipline and teacher appraisal – are based around the assumption of teacher power and student acquiescence. This asymmetrical notion of power in classrooms is commonly accepted (and expected) by the participants of schooling and also enshrined in legislation. The teacher is required by law to maintain a safe and orderly environment and held to be professionally responsible for student engagement and learning. Power, under this conception, is treated as an object or property that a person can own. One person (typically the teacher) has the power over another (typically the student) and is therefore responsible for all that happens in the classroom. It follows that power cannot be shared, that if the teacher loses the battle with students, she has somehow forfeited the authority to teach.

In more recent years, many scholars have problematised the prevailing view of power in classrooms (Ellsworth, 1992; Gore, 1993; Ropers-Huilman, 1998). Building directly on Foucault's idea that power is a system that nobody owns, 'exercised from innumerable points, in the interplay of nonegalitarian and mobile relations' (1978, p. 94), these scholars have described power in relational terms. Under this conception, power is not a property but rather a dynamic flux that thrives within social relations. Here the formal authority vested in the teacher is seen separately from the informal power relations in the classroom. Power relations are constructed interactively and the teacher's agenda is one of many competing agendas. This conception avoids the dualism of powerful/powerless suggested by hierarchical notions of power. Rather it suggests that no one person has unequivocal power and individuals can be both powerful and powerless at the same time (Davies and Hunt, 1994).

Alongside these debates about the nature of power in classrooms, there is a growing movement promoting notions of equality in schools. With roots in democratic schooling (Dewey, 1966/1916), critical pedagogy (Giroux, 1988; Shor and Freire, 1987) and feminism (Ellsworth, 1992; Gore, 1993), the equality movement seeks to distribute power more evenly among the participants of schooling. Two major schools of thought can be seen in this movement, one based around notions of empowerment/emancipation (Habermas, 1972; McLaren, 1989) and the other around relationships/emotions (Boler, 1999; Noddings, 1984). The empowerment/emancipation school holds that it is the teacher's role to actively and consciously use her authority to empower students and transform existing social inequalities and injustices. The relationships/emotions school conceptualises the teacher's role as one of caring, of promoting a dialogue in a safe setting where participants can connect and are aware of each other's well-being and ideological differences (Noddings, 1998).

While the emphasis in both these schools is on power *with* rather than power *over* (Kreisberg, 1992), advocates of equality in classrooms remain conflicted about the teacher's role in the exercise of power, leaving largely unquestioned the assumption that the teacher knows what is best for students (Burbules, 1986; Gore, 1993). The notion of empowerment, for example, suggests that it is the teacher's role to give power, to confer power, to enable the use of power, and the student's role to receive power, to become empowered. In caring for students, teachers may be exercising what Boler (1999) calls pastoral power, another form of social and emotional control over students. While the intent in both schools is to share and empower, the exercise of that intent may result in yet another (though far more subtle) form of the dominance of teacher over students described by Waller seventy years ago.

These conflicting notions of power lie side by side in the classroom, presenting the teacher with an enduring paradox. On the one hand, the teacher feels (and is held) directly responsible for students' learning. On the other hand, the teacher looks for ways of connecting with students, of maximising their involvement with, and responsibility for, their own learning. Finding the balance between freedom and authority – between power with and power over – is perhaps the central paradox of teaching (Lather, 1986; Shor and Freire, 1987). The teacher is both powerful and powerless at the same time as she treads a difficult line. This paradox about the operation of power in classrooms forms a theoretical frame for reading this chapter. A practical illustration of the paradox is presented in the following story, *More than murder*, by Karen McNamee. In the story, McNamee recounts a dramatic episode in a Grade 11 biology class where she forcefully exercised her authority over a group of students whom she determined had disrupted a laboratory exercise on scientific observation. The story is followed by commentaries from the teacher, Ken Atwood her academic colleague, and Nel Noddings and Peter Taylor.

More than murder

Karen McNamee

My first Grade 11 biology practical lesson in the second week of first semester was always going to be a challenge. I was faced with a class of thirty-four unknown faces and unfortunately, as this was my first year at this school, my reputation as a teacher who only accepts high standards of behaviour was untried. Prior to this lesson, I had not experienced any specific behavioural problems, but there were a number of 'trouble makers' who seemed to be testing me out. Also, I had been told by other teachers that it was not unusual for students to enter Grade 11 with little experience of practical work in science since, in Grades 9 and 10, the students are too 'ratty'. Regardless of this, I remained determined to attempt practical work. I was very conscious of the risks involved when conducting practical lessons with such a large number of students. To be successful and safe, careful planning, strict safety measures, and cooperation on the part of the students were required.

I planned what I thought was an exciting practical lesson which focused on observing characteristics of eight different types of living things. Each specimen was located in a 'station', and students, working in groups of four, rotated between the stations every five minutes. At each station, the students were required to note their observations on a record sheet.

After an initial explanation of the task to the class, and the few minutes of chaos that seems to be inevitable as students divide into groups and approach their initial stations, everyone seemed to be working busily. I was in constant demand and moved between groups to answer questions. About half way through the lesson, I asked in a relaxed tone:

'How is it all going? Any problems with your observation for the previous station?'

They giggled. Their giggles were met with a questioning look. 'It wasn't moving very much, Miss', said one student.

'I wonder why not', I replied.

'Maybe it's dead.'

I kept cool. 'It wasn't dead before, so what's going on?' They giggled some more. Smiling and trying to look nonchalant, I set a trap. 'So you used the gas on him, hey?'

'Yeah, Miss. It shouldn't have been sniffing that stuff.'

I had them. I turned my smile into a hard scowl. 'So you mean to tell me that you used the gas without being told? You deliberately killed one of the living specimens and you have ruined that part of the prac for everyone else in this class?'

'Yes, Miss', came the subdued reply from one student. The other students of the group kept silent.

I walked purposefully to the front of the class and wrote a note detailing the crimes, to the school's deputy principal. I requested that the four students involved be withdrawn from my class and not be returned until they supplied me with a written apology. I also suggested that these students be encouraged to consider other subject choices as they were 'obviously not serious about studying biology and the class was already over-crowded'.

To make a big impact on the rest of the class, I called for the class's attention. I restated my expectations of classroom behaviour and described the incident that had just occurred. Next, with as much drama as I could muster, I pointed out that 'in my class, not following instructions is totally unacceptable and will not be tolerated'. Then, finally, the four perpetrators were banished from my class to the office. In silence, they walked from the room, with thirty of their peers watching.

By the end of lunch that day, news of the incident had spread around the school. 'Mrs X expelled 4 people for mucking up in a prac.' From this point on, the behaviour of that Grade 11 biology class during practical work was exemplary. Dear little cockroach, rest in peace.

Teacher commentary

Karen McNamee

In this class I was in a difficult and potentially dangerous situation. The laboratory was overcrowded and I was inundated with student enquiries. Constant surveillance of all students was impossible. The students were unaccustomed to participating in laboratory practical work. They were also unaccustomed to my expectations for behaviour which were designed to maintain a safe environment for all. Regardless of my attempts to clearly spell out appropriate standards of behaviour, the four students involved in the incident outlined in this case, through their unauthorised use of gas and the general tampering with equipment, demonstrated behaviour that was clearly unacceptable. Further, they seemed to have no understanding of the potentially serious and dangerous consequences of their actions. They also clearly displayed little respect for the live specimens used in this exercise and acted in a wilful and destructive manner towards them. Given the context of this case — that the practical exercises were conducted in crowded conditions with inexperienced students – I was concerned that, if this incident went untreated, there could be every possibility of similar or more serious incidents arising in the future. Such incidents could result in the destruction of equipment, injury to those involved and to others, all of which are the responsibility of the teacher.

I believe that such a dramatic response on my part was warranted, especially as I believed it would help to prevent future, potentially worse problems. Withdrawal of the 'perpetrators' from the class situation in such a dramatic way highlighted to all students the seriousness of the incident and the central issue of the case: the inappropriateness of unsafe behaviour in the laboratory. The action taken served to make the students more aware of the importance of appropriate behaviour and the need to follow instructions. Essentially, in this case, I was motivated by the desire to prevent future problems and acted to 'nip them in the bud'.

I also hoped that by referring the four students responsible for the incident to the deputy principal, I would serve to draw the attention of the administration to the dangerous situation created largely by the excessive class size. I was optimistic that the administration would act to reduce the class size, to create a safer environment.

For teachers working in similar circumstances, and for myself in the future, students should first be provided with simple, safe laboratory experiences to minimise the potential safety risks. Then, the complexity of the practical experiences could be gradually increased as the students demonstrated appropriate behaviours, developed their practical skills, and an atmosphere of trust is created. Finally, inappropriate laboratory behaviour should never be treated lightly, and safety should never be compromised.

Colleague commentary

Ken Atwood

Power, or rather contestation for dominance within the classroom, would seem to be the central issue of this case. It details the feelings and perceptions of a teacher who seems to feel unsure initially of her place within the relations of power of the classroom, and actions taken by the teacher to identify clearly to the class that she occupies the dominant, central power position.

It should be noted that in this case there seems to be a bid to portray the incident of the 'murdered' cockroach as an attempt by a group of four boys to challenge the dominance of the teacher. The co-option of terms like 'murder' suggests that the teacher sensed some premeditation in the act and constructed a scenario in which she was ultimately to be the victim.

It is important to realise that the actual motivation on the part of the students is essentially irrelevant here. The students may have had no conscious intention of disrupting the practical exercise, challenging the teacher or trying to exert some type of dominance within the classroom. They may have just considered it to be fun to kill a cockroach – although this should still remain a concern for two reasons: killing a specimen when the subject of the practical exercise was to observe living characteristics; and the unauthorised use of gas in a situation which could be characterised as a concern for occupational health and safety. Nevertheless, we can infer from the case that the teacher perceived this incident as an opportunity to crush opposition to her power, or at least she observed this as an opportunity to centralise her position. This was evident in the way she reacted employing drama and spectacle, in front of the entire class. If power was not constructed as the central concern, surely the incident could have been dealt with in a less public manner.

The incident provided an opportunity for the teacher to redress some self doubts, which were expressed in the opening sentences of the case. And, the way in which the incident was handled seemed to generate intended outcomes. We are told that subsequent class behaviour was exemplary. However, with power as the central and (practically) exclusive focus, there are a number of issues left unresolved in this case. We are not told what happened to the four boys punished. Did they ever return to the biology class? Aside from the reports of behaviour, we are not told the effect of this incident on the rest of the class. What was the impact of all this on their learning or interactions between themselves and the teacher? If these and other such issues had been examined, the teacher may learn that the importance given to contestation over relations of power may be an overstatement. Indeed, public displays of disciplinary behaviour, while they may cement the dominance of the classroom teacher, may also have some undesirable outcomes in teaching and learning.

★   ★   ★

Death of a cockroach

Nel Noddings, Stanford University

Two sorts of concerns arise on reading *More than murder*. One is concern for what the teacher did and a fervent wish that the current structures and policies of schooling supported more educative strategies for dealing with disobedient and disruptive students. A second set of concerns centres on what I hope was done after the incident recounted here.

First, I do understand and sympathise with a teacher trying to establish her reputation in a new school and especially with students reputed to be 'ratty' or just emerging from a ratty stage. I taught for more than twelve years at the secondary level and know how keen the pressures are to maintain discipline. Still, it seems a shame to get control of a class by dismissing four students who might have profited greatly from a carefully constructed biology class. Was there no other way?

One possibility might have been to abandon the planned group work, gather the class together, and talk about what is required to do such work effectively. In what ways must we depend on one another? How should a group organise its work? Should there be a division of labour or should everyone share in all tasks? A reader cannot tell from the description given here whether such preparation was provided earlier but, even if it was, a significant breach in procedures would justify reviewing and extending the preparation.

In addition to a full class conversation about interdependence and responsibility, the teacher might have invited an important discussion in the treatment of laboratory animals. Is it acceptable to kill a laboratory animal gratuitously? Does it matter that this one was a cockroach, a creature we regularly attempt to exterminate? What if it had been another creature? This kind of discussion could be very valuable and might add to a host of interesting and controversial questions about our moral obligations to non-human animals.

But it was just a cockroach. Again, a reader doesn't know how the teacher followed up the 'practical' lesson and this observation leads to a second set of concerns. How might she have followed up? One hopes that the students learned something about the evolutionary success of cockroaches. Despite human attempts to exterminate them, they have survived while many other creatures have disappeared. What did the students learn about these hardy creatures? For example, how long does an individual cockroach live? How many familiar types are there? How do they reproduce? Why are they so hard to eliminate? And why are we so bent on eliminating them? Do they bite? Are they dirty? People do associate cockroaches with dirt and, in fact, cockroaches are said to create an objectionable odour. But this may occur as a result of their cleaning themselves and leaving behind a smelly residue. Could students think of a way to test this conjecture?

Here both teachers and teacher educators might pause to ask about the practicality of five-minute observations. What was to be accomplished in that short time? Again, we can't tell from this brief anecdote what was intended. If the activity was meant as a prelude to in-depth study and observation, it might well have been pedagogically justified. However, would a scientist expect to learn much in a five-minute observation?

Having mentioned scientific activity, another possibility arises. Were the students introduced to the work of some great naturalists? Were they told some true stories about naturalists or invited to read biographies? Will the names Darwin, Tinbergen, Wilson, Andrews, Muir or Audubon mean anything to them?

The class might also get into some geography. Where in the world do cockroaches flourish? Are any parts of the world cockroach-free? Do they have natural enemies? For that matter, what do they eat? Are there people who hesitate or refuse to kill them? Why? In addition to conducting discussions of contemporary peoples who reject killing insects for religious reason, the teacher might mention Albert Schweitzer and his 'reverence for life'. Who was Schweitzer and where did he do his great work?

Some history might be fun too. Paul Theobald tells the story of medieval ecclesiastical courts that actually tried insects and other animals on various charges. He writes:

> One didn't wantonly destroy, say, beetles, despite the fact that they may have been jeopardising a harvest. In such a case, the matter was brought before ecclesiastical courts, learned counsel was appointed to defend the beetles, and more often than not, the rights of the pests were upheld. They were a part of the natural order – God's natural order – and as such, they had a right to exist.
>
> (1997, p. 17)

Theobald points out that such affairs now seem silly. But he also notes that earlier notions about intradependence and the organic embeddedness of human life in nature were not silly. Somehow, we need to find ways to combine an earlier wisdom with the power of current technology. When we are threatened by 'pests', what is the wisest move? Can some be held in check by natural methods? When we decide that we must use pesticides (and surely there are times when we must), how can we be sure that they are safe for humans and other living things? Here is another enormously important topic for study and thoughtful discussion.

The more deeply we explore what might be done to redeem the 'murder' of some small cockroach, the more we regret the dismissal of four students who clearly had much to learn. Even more, as teacher educators, we might regret our failure to act more forcefully to relieve teachers of the intolerable and highly artificial pressures of contemporary schooling: rigidly prescribed curricula and demands to 'cover' the material; demands for control that dominate all else; formal chains of commands that enforce narrow behavioural rules; and the isolation of teachers in subject-matter departments. And we might think more deeply about how to prepare teachers so that they can comfortably go beyond the specific demands of their own discipline. A story like this one should arouse our sympathy for both teacher and students. More than that, it should arouse us to think more clearly and imaginatively about the enterprise of teaching.

★   ★   ★

Truth and murder? Alternative readings

Peter C. Taylor, Curtin University of Technology

> Multiple perspectives make our engagement with the phenomena more complex. Ironically, good research often complicates our lives.
>
> (Eisner, 1997, p. 8)

> Dialogically constructed texts allow us to recognise our lives in the mimicry of stories and conversational anecdotes.
>
> (Van Manen, 1990, p. 144)

First, a critical reading

My first reaction (while not halfway through reading Karen's story) was one of growing dread that a happy ending might not be in store. And I was right. Karen's militant tone towards the 'criminal' students transformed into an air of supreme indignation which, for her, justified sacrificing the students on the altar of her narrow sense of self-righteousness.

No final sense of irony breaks through to cushion the sensibilities of the liberal humanist reader for whom care and compassion are principles that should not be compromised. No final confession of guilt or regret to assuage the concern of the critical theorist interested in empowering the disempowered and the dispirited. The story ends on a tragic note: a sardonic one-liner that cements in place the privileged status of the cockroach and (by implication) the teacher as the victim of adolescent perfidy.

The essence of this tragedy is that the possibility of rapprochement between teacher and students is all but ruled out by the school-wide perception of the legitimacy of Karen's totalitarianism.

Then, a critical self-reading

Haven't we all felt like Karen at some stage of our teaching careers? Well, at least those of us who have taught in schools where trial by fire is a standard practice of recalcitrant students!

I think back to my early twenties, fresh out of university where I had enjoyed a bizarre mix of (conscription-avoidance) military training, several years of self-indulgent socialisation laced with left-wing political activism, and many of the (worst!) didactic science lecturers ever invented. And there I was, encountering adolescents for the first time; inflated with implicit expectations about my 'natural' classroom role as a presenter of specialist subject-matter knowledge and my 'natural' right as a teacher to be granted unlimited respect. And without the (much later earned) practical wisdom of parenthood to warn me about the need for children to test the limits of adult authority or to prepare me with educative strategies for managing their behaviour. I shudder to recall that quixotic young man licensed to shape children's educational opportunities.

So, how did I react to the real world of classroom teaching? What were my early teaching priorities? Control with a capital 'C'! No, that's not altogether true; that came a little later, after the drawn-out agony. For the first year, I struggled with the disillusionment of shattered ideals. I wanted learning to be fun and games to have a serious role in my classroom. I wanted self-directed and self-paced learning and, of course, self-motivated learners. I wanted to innovate, to revolutionise teaching and learning, just like the radical educators I had read about in those captivating 1970s texts by A.S. Neill, John Holt, Ivan Illich and Paulo Freire. Like most of my colleagues in that alternative government high school, I eschewed exams and competition as educationally unsound practices. We even vetoed participation in inter-school sports carnivals.

And how did the students react to my reform-minded zeal? Well, many flourished but some gave me hell, provoking me into angry outbursts of self-righteous indignation. My drill sergeant's voice must have frightened the hell out of the (majority of) placid students. During my second year, I quickly developed a reputation as a teacher who did not tolerate misbehaviour. I was even called on by other novice teachers to quell riots in their classes. And from the third year on, my reputation preceded me. Only the occasional adolescent playground bully managed to intimidate me.

So, back to Karen's story. It seems to have suddenly lost its demonic aura, the one that I constructed from the rich store of educational theory that I now have access to and which I use (ever the idealist) to indulge my social reform fantasies about a better world. My first reading now seems like an account of a moralist, one who perhaps occupies the high plateau of an ivory tower populated by exceptionally well-behaved adult learners (if only that were true!).

And yet, despite my embrace of a pragmatic approach to teaching, I have learned not to dispense with a vision of a better world and a better way to teach, one that engages all students in enriched learning experiences. For without a vision I am trapped hopelessly within the narrow horizons of my daily life and am buffeted mercilessly by the exigencies of circumstance (mostly of economic rationalist origin in the current era!). But my vision is no longer one of static idealism. Its dynamism and fluidity result from it being informed by my (equally dynamic and fluid) teaching practice. As a teacher (of teachers) I continue, therefore, to both re-invent and re-vision my teaching self, judging my efficacy against ever-changing standards.

So, I do not condemn Karen for her heavy-handed approach to managing students' (mis)behaviour. To condemn is to close down the possibility of learning (from the skeletons in one's own closet). Although I believe that there are better ways of resolving problems of inappropriate student behaviour, I feel that it is important to understand and appreciate the complexity of teaching and the enormous difficulties facing inexperienced teachers as they struggle to deal professionally with conflicting priorities over which they have little control.

And more possibilities

Now, that seems a much more balanced account. And a carefully crafted one at that! Yet, it is a highly selective reading, shutting out some interpretive possibilities in favour of others while constructing characterful images on perhaps questionable foundations. Other readings compete for my attention.

How, I wonder, might my second reading have changed if I had decided that the character of Karen was not a novice teacher but one of twenty-five years' experience starting up at her tenth school; a control freak who was well practised in resorting to ultimate sanctions for the merest infringement of her rigidly set code of behaviour? An unreflective teacher impervious to the challenge of learning from experience? Perhaps my first (demonising) reading makes this assumption.

Or, how might my second reading have differed if I had focused on the issue of the meaningfulness for students of the seemingly mundane practical cookbook activity of recording observations of living 'things'? I could have constructed Karen as an unwitting captive (a victim, an agent) of the mythos of modernist science, through whose agency is perpetuated the sanctity of a positivist scientific ethos. Such a teacher would assume scientific observation to be a theory-free activity that, with appropriate rigour, yields identical understandings for all (scientists and students, alike). Science controls nature, teachers control students, students control …?

But, then again, what if I had constructed the storied character of Karen as a radical reformer (a hero) with a constructivist view of the contingent nature of scientific knowledge, one who is struggling to contest the traditional positivist image of science, an image that is entrenched by both the senior school curriculum, the culture of the science department and, significantly, the lived experiences of her students? Such a teacher would experience severe conflict with students unwilling to reconstruct themselves as self-determined and socially responsible learners.

The value of reading, and reading

What value is there in reading Karen's story if there are many possible readings? For me, the value lies in the power of the story to provoke what Max van Manen (1990) calls *pedagogical thoughtfulness* about an important and contentious issue facing many teachers. At first glance, the story presents a poignant tale about a teacher battling to control inappropriate (perhaps monstrous) student behaviour, a story that would speak graphically to most teachers at some time in their careers. But what I have tried to demonstrate is that there is added value in continuing to read critically the story while at the same time reading critically ourselves. By persisting, I began to delve into my autobiography from which I retrieved vivid memories of my own lived experience as a teacher, empathic memories that ameliorated my initial hard-nosed (perhaps ideological) stand on the issue of teacher control. From a perspective born of practical wisdom, I felt compelled to make a fairer judgement about Karen's actions. On further reading, I felt compelled to consider how Karen's actions may have been shaped by widely divergent contextual factors such as the (possibly distorted) nature of the long-established science curriculum, over which she had little control, or a curriculum reformist role in which she struggled gamefully to overcome student resistance. By this stage, I was conceiving of Karen as a professional educator situated socially and politically as an agent of either cultural reproduction or cultural transformation.

For a critical educator, the experience of reading a text about teaching and learning can never be a simple exercise of germinating a single privileged truth planted by the author. Reading elicits one's own lived experience and opens up a provocative inner dialogue. In this case, the issue of student discipline, for me, metamorphosed into a number of related issues, each of which added potential value to my growing understanding of the socio-political nature of a teacher's actions.

★   ★   ★

Editors' synthesis

'Don't smile before Christmas' is the advice often given to young North American teachers to prepare them for the classroom fray. The storyline is a familiar one – frisky students misbehaving in class and a teacher firmly establishing standards of acceptable classroom conduct in the early weeks of the semester. This scenario is so commonplace in schools that it has become part of the folklore of teaching – as if it were some necessary opening ritual dance between students and teachers. One of the purposes of this chapter is to raise some questions about this ritual, focusing particularly on issues of power in classrooms and the dilemmas faced by teachers as they walk the difficult line between power with and power over.

A central issue concerns the conception of power used in the story and the various commentaries. All four contributors employ the notion of power as a property, owned principally by the teacher. McNamee refers to the importance of establishing (her) standards of behaviour and the need for the students to follow (her) instructions. In sending the recalcitrant students to the deputy principal, in the words of her colleague, Atwood, she 'identifies clearly to the class that she occupies the dominant, central power position'. While Noddings does not directly mention power in her commentary, she too refers to the incident in terms of the teacher gaining control over the class. Many of Taylor's 'multiple readings' are also about analysing the use (and abuse) of the teacher's power in various contexts.

An alternative and sometimes parallel reading looks at the teacher's actions in terms of the wider social milieu – in other words, a relational notion of power. The teacher, for example, hints at the role of the administration in this incident – in tolerating crowded and unsafe laboratory conditions while, at the same time, expecting her to maintain discipline. Noddings lists several of these contextual pressures within which teachers are required to operate –

rigid curricula, demands for control, formal chains of command and teacher isolation. In a similar vein, Taylor suggests that the teacher could be constructed as an 'unwitting captive of the mythos of modernist science'. He also acknowledges the role of students in creating the conditions of power in classrooms.

These two ways of looking at power are used side by side in the various descriptions and analyses of this story. Under the first conception, the teacher is a 'perpetrator', freely and willingly exercising control over herself and her students. Under the second conception, she is a 'victim' of a set of circumstances and constraints beyond her control. The teacher, it would seem, is both powerful and powerless or, in Taylor's terms, an agent and a victim at the same time. A consequence of this both/and view of the exercise of power is that it invites both criticism of and sympathy for the teacher in this story. Noddings, for example, 'regrets' the dismissal of the students and is sympathetic to the plight of both teacher and students. Criticism and sympathy are most evident in Taylor's commentary as he interprets and reinterprets the story through various theoretical and autobiographical lenses.

All four contributors offer their views about consequences and alternative courses of action. McNamee, for example, sees her actions as motivated by the need to 'prevent future [behaviour] problems' and to influence the administration to change her teaching circumstances. Atwood would have preferred that the cockroach incident be dealt with in what he calls a 'less public manner'. Noddings offers several alternatives to the teacher's punitive actions, focusing on promoting 'interdependence and responsibility'. Further, she proposes some practical ideas about capitalising on the cockroach incident as a teachable moment rather than as a trigger for a power struggle. Taylor takes a different view, encouraging the teacher to engage in the role of curriculum reformist – a form of social action in which contestation of the prevailing images of science, curriculum, school organisation and student roles may be inevitable.

McNamee's story – and the different levels of advice offered by our commentators – illustrates the difficulty faced by teachers in the exercise of power. One set of suggested strategies would have teachers work *within* the system and *with* their students to co-construct a positive and rewarding teaching and learning environment. However, the system is not always supportive and some students are not easy to work with. Under these circumstances, teachers must exercise power *over* others in order to achieve their pedagogical goals. It would seem that these two forms of action – power with the power over – are held in constant dialectic tension. Freedom, according to Shor and Freire (1987), cannot be found in the absence of authority. Hence the promotion of freedom for self and for others often requires the exercise of power, and the act of teaching means knowing how, why, when, where and for how long to exercise that power.

References

Boler, M. (1999). *Feeling power: Emotions and education*. New York: Routledge.

Burbules, N. (1986). A theory of power in education. *Educational Theory*, 5, 95–114.

Davies, B. and Hunt, R. (1994). Classroom competencies and marginal positions. *British Journal of Sociology of Education*, 15 (2), 389–408.

Dewey, J. (1966/1916). *Democracy and education*. New York: Free Press.

Eisner, E. (1997). The promise and perils of alternative forms of data representation. *Educational Researcher*, 26 (6), 4–10.

Ellsworth, E. (1992). Why doesn't this feel empowering? Working through the repressive myths of critical pedagogy. In C. Luke and J. Gore (eds), *Feminisms and critical pedagogy* (pp. 90–119). New York: Routledge.

Foucault, M. (1978). *The history of sexuality: Volume 1: An introduction*. New York: Vintage Books.

Giroux, H. (1988). *Schooling and the struggle for public life: Critical pedagogy in the modern age*. Minneapolis, MN: University of Minnesota Press.

Gore, J. (1993). *The struggle for pedagogies: Critical and feminist discourses as regimes of truth*. New York: Routledge.

Habermas, J. (1972). *Knowledge and human interests* (2nd edn). (J. J. Shapiro, Trans.) London: Heinemann.

Kreisberg, S. (1992). *Transforming power: Domination, empowerment and education*. Albany, NY: State University of New York Press.

Lather, P. (1986). Research as praxis. *Harvard Educational Review*, 56, 257–277.

McLaren, P. (1989). *Life in schools: An introduction to critical pedagogy in the foundations of education*. New York: Longman.

Noddings, N. (1984). *Caring: A feminine approach to ethics and moral education*. Berkeley, CA: University of California Press.

—— (1998). Care and moral education. In H. S. Shapiro and D. E. Purpel (eds), *Critical issues in American education: Transformation in a postmodern world*. Mahwah, NJ: Lawrence Erlbaum Associates.

Ropers-Huilman, B. (1998). *Feminist teaching in theory and practice: Situating power and knowledge in poststructural classrooms*. New York: Teachers College Press.

Shor, I. and Freire, P. (1987). *A pedagogy for liberation: Dialogues on transforming education*. South Hadley, MA: Bergen & Garvey.

Theobald, P. (1997). *Teaching the commons*. Boulder, CO: Westview Press.

Van Manen, M. (1990). *Researching lived experience: Human science for an action sensitive pedagogy*. Albany, NY: State University of New York Press, 144.

Waller, W. (1932). *The sociology of teaching*. New York: Wiley.

Part III

Dilemmas about representation

Chapter 8

Textbooks

Contributions by Catherine Milne, Noel Gough and Cathleen C. Loving

Editors' introduction

Students in science practical classes in high schools are confronted with a range of sources of authority. Perhaps most obviously, there is always the personal authority of the teacher. Students set to work on practical activities in a spirit of inquiry but know that at any time the teacher may arrive, hover over the bench, ask a pointed question or explain what they are really supposed to see or do in the activity. Students also work in the shadow of the authority of the textbook and the test. Whatever they might see, draw, measure or conclude from a practical activity they know that what they are supposed to learn about a topic has been established and recorded in the textbook and will be measured by tests that reflect the knowledge of the textbook. At its most extreme, the authority of the textbook leads some students to play by 'Fatima's rules' (Jegede and Aikenhead, 1999; Larson, 1995), attending only to the boxed, emboldened words and phrases that they predict will turn up in the test. Alongside these powerful sources of authority, there is a much weaker pull towards the 'authority of experience' (Munby and Russell, 1994), to trusting their own capacity to observe and interpret the physical world through the lens of the science practical.

One of the epistemological commitments science teachers share is a belief in the importance of practical experience in school science. Just as the laboratory sets science apart from other school subjects, so does science teachers' commitment to laboratory activities. Whether they do so because of a Baconian preference for observation, or because of a constructivist commitment to beginning with students' practical experience, science teachers spend substantial time and resources on laboratory practical activities. In the story that follows, Catherine Milne describes a practical class in Grade 8 science. She asks students to dissect a flower and then draw and label a representation of the flower. As her students undertake this activity, Milne is disappointed to find that some students look to the authority of the textbook rather than the authority of experience. Milne's story is followed by commentaries from Noel Gough and Cathleen Loving.

The flower dissection

Catherine Milne

I was busy. In fact I felt like the White Rabbit, 'I'm late, I'm late for a very important date!' I was running out of time to cover all the objectives for Plants and Animals with my average ability Grade 8 Science class. This was only the second unit of science that this class had done since starting high school and it is always a struggle to get all the work done in the time available – especially with our objective-based approach to teaching science. Our department also has an emphasis on practical activities which I am personally in favour of but this approach requires more time to teach the relevant material than does 'chalk and talk'.

The class had been examining various plant phyla and classes. Already we had studied fungi, mosses, liverworts and ferns and today we were to study flowering plants. I had asked the students to bring some flowers from home so that we could do an activity on dissecting flowers. As usual, some students had remembered and some had not. I spent the first half of the lesson discussing with students the characteristics of ferns and their benefits to humans in order to finish the section on ferns and then we moved on to flowering plants.

I instructed the students to open up their workbooks to Activity 10 and showed them the equipment that was available for the dissection – hand lenses, blades, forceps and probes so that they would recognise them in the activity. I introduced the instructions by saying to them, 'Activity number 10 class, "To investigate the structure and functions and parts of a flower"', and I went on to say, 'Well, we're proceeding one step further past ferns and we're going to have a look at some flowers today.'

As I said this, the students opened up their workbooks to Activity 10 and I read some of the activity to them. I didn't think it was necessary to go through the full activity because it was described clearly in the workbook. So I read through some of the instructions expecting that they would follow in their workbooks: 'Carry out the instructions set out below. Answer the questions in your book as you work through your flower dissection. Part B – now look at the coloured petals. Part C – the stamens. Now look at the male reproductive structures called the stamens. Blah. Blah. Blah.'

I realised that not all the students might be familiar with the terminology that was being used in the activity so I continued, 'Right let's see if there's some help in your own textbook. Have you got your own textbook ready? The reddish one.'

There was general movement in the lab as students got out their textbooks. I asked them to look at the book to see if perhaps a diagram of the parts of a flower was drawn in their textbook so that they would have something to refer to when they were doing their dissection. As the students were sitting quietly waiting to start the activity I looked for a reference to flowers in the index of the text but couldn't find one. As I looked, I spoke out loud to the class, 'It doesn't seem to have a diagram of a flower. I would have thought it would have. What are we up to? About page 86? Green plants. Ferns. Yeah, it does. It's just not listed in the index. On page 92 class. There it is. The sepals. The petals. If you have trouble with the male parts, they are here. Female pistil part. That is there. So, page number 92 will be a big help to you if you are having some difficulty when you are doing Activity number 10.'

I described what they should be doing for the activity: 'Right, so proceed, put your headings, do your parts, answer your questions and then we'll finish with about ten minutes to spare because we've got two other things to do in today's lesson. Now you can start writing like mad. I know you're really keen to.'

The students immediately started working on the activity although some needed a little bit more encouragement than others. I gave permission for some groups to collect flowers from the school gardens and started to walk round to each of the groups which ranged in size from two to five students. Although one group of girls was more interested in discussing what they were going to wear to the next school dance, most groups were involved in dissecting the flowers. One group of boys proceeded to massacre their plants and I had to hurry some groups along who were not exactly on task by saying to them with some emphasis, 'Do your work. See what it says and do it. Life is simple, you make it hard.'

As I was walking around the class towards the end of the lesson, I noticed two of the girls deeply engrossed in the activity. Jane and Fiona were each drawing diagrams of their observations of the eucalyptus flower that they had dissected. Although neither Jane nor Fiona are going to be Curies, they both work well in class. Their diagrams were excellent. They had drawn cross-sectional diagrams which were very accurate and clear showing stamen, style and ovaries of the flower. However, as I watched, Fiona erased the stamen that she had drawn and proceeded to copy the diagram of the flower from her textbook into her science notebook.

Jane leant over and said to Fiona, 'Why did you rub that answer out?'

To which Fiona replied, 'What? That one?' as she pointed to the eucalyptus diagram.

'Yeah', said Jane. 'Why did you rub that one out?'

'Oh, 'cause it had too many of those things', responded Fiona as she pointed to the stamen on the diagram in the textbook.

'Why?' said Jane. 'How many should it have?'

'Five', replied Fiona.

'Why should it have five?' asked Jane.

To which Fiona responded triumphantly, 'Because it has five petals', as she pointed to the diagram in the textbook.

Both girls then quite happily proceeded to finish copying the generalised diagram of a flower from the textbook into their notebooks.

I consider this story to be the tip of the iceberg. To me it indicates a limitation of my classroom. Clearly Jane and Fiona did not value their voice in science. Instead, they bowed to the voice of the textbook. I had not encouraged them to be independent constructers of knowledge but rather they have become reflectors of 'significant' facts that are presented in the textbook. Jane and Fiona have learnt that all the activities that they do in class and the sense that they make of these activities have no value. The only knowledge to be valued is the 'knowledge' that comes from the textbook. The discourse of power is the discourse of the textbook.

★   ★   ★

A postmortem on dissection
Noel Gough, Deakin University

Catherine Milne introduces her vignette, *The flower dissection*, by referring to the White Rabbit – and rabbits invariably remind me of Spike Milligan's (1979, p. 46) poem, 'Open heart university'. Dedicated to BBC-TV's Open University programmes, the poem begins as follows:

> We've come a long way
> said the Cigarette Scientist
> as he destroyed a live rabbit
> to show students how it worked.

I realise that Milne's story is not centrally concerned with the ethical dilemmas posed by dissection as such – although there may be a hint of disquiet in her reference to the group of boys who 'proceeded to massacre their plants' – but such is the power of narrative allusion that I was immediately drawn to revisit questions of the moral defensibility of dissection in schools. Is dissection necessary? Can we justify destroying a living organism 'to show students how it worked'? Should we tolerate students 'massacring' anything – be it a pithed toad or a flower? A related issue concerns the gender-related differences in students' enthusiasm for dissection to which Milne alludes. In my years as a biology teacher I found that girls were often reluctant to dissect animals whereas boys tended to be much more enthusiastic, wielding their scalpels like samurai swords and overtly or covertly ridiculing the girls for their squeamishness. Later, as a teacher educator visiting student teachers in schools, I found that many teachers (both male and female) would also try to persuade girls to suppress their abhorrence of dissection by modelling or encouraging a dispassionate and clinical approach – for example, it seemed to me that lab coats were more often donned for dissections than for other laboratory activities. I frequently found myself pondering the appropriateness of such tactics. Doubt, suspicion and even revulsion are perfectly reasonable – and indeed healthy – responses to destroying living things in the name of education. Why would anyone deliberately seek to suppress such feelings in others?

In principle, I am no more opposed to dissection for educative purposes than I am to eating meat to satisfy our nutritional needs or epicurean desires. But I also abhor waste, and believe that the decision to kill (or to condone the killing of) another organism should not be taken lightly. I used to keep a colony of hooded rats in my biology classroom – clean and friendly animals that students enjoyed caring for – so that those who chose to participate in dissection activities (and I always made it clear that it was *their* choice) were not distanced from the experience of killing an animal to satisfy their curiosity about 'how it worked'. The slightly melancholy mood that usually prevailed during the ensuing dissection classes suggested that students took their complicity in (and personal responsibility for) the rats' deaths seriously. There were no 'massacres' or casual mutilations of the kind I have observed in classes where students were given preserved specimens from biological supply companies. Such specimens are, I believe, indefensible wastes of animals' lives. Students are not only distanced from the opportunities for moral development that may accompany a more personal encounter with the ethical questions surrounding dissection, but they are also robbed of the sensuous experiences and tacit knowledge that comes with seeing, touching and smelling the insides of an animal that has only just died. Students are likely to learn less from dissecting the cold, hard, bloodless and shrivelled organs of a preserved rat that stinks of formaldehyde than they are from disassembling a scale model or manipulating a computer simulation. But I would much rather give students the opportunity to feel the warmth and wetness of bodily fluids and soft tissues before rigor mortis sets in, to see the glistening translucence of membranes and mesentery, to unpack the slippery mass of abdominal organs and intestines, and perhaps to reflect a little on whatever they find wondrous or disquieting or ineffable as they expose – and are exposed to – the fleshly embodiments of life's complexity and transience.

All of the above may seem a long way from Catherine Milne's story of a flower dissection, but you can blame her invocation of the White Rabbit for that. And you haven't heard the end of the Rabbit yet, because I'm enough of a trivialist to note that Milne quotes the Walt Disney movie version of the White Rabbit's entrance line rather than Lewis Carroll's (1939 [1865], pp. 13–14) original text in which we are told what Alice was actually contemplating when she was interrupted:

> She was considering in her own mind (as well as she could, for the hot day made her feel very sleepy and stupid) whether the pleasure of making a daisy-chain would be worth the trouble of getting up and picking the daisies, when suddenly a White Rabbit with pink eyes ran close by her.
>
> There was nothing so *very* remarkable in that; nor did Alice think it so *very* much out of the way to hear the Rabbit say to itself, 'Oh dear! Oh dear! I shall be too late!' (when she thought it over afterwards, it occurred to her that she ought to have wondered at this, but at the time it all seemed quite natural) ...

This passage resonates with aspects of Milne's tale in interesting ways, for Alice is consciously pondering a very similar question to one which teachers and students should be encouraged to attend: is the 'pleasure' of dissecting flowers worth the 'trouble' of picking them? I trust that it will be clear from my discussion of rat dissection that this is not a rhetorical question: the troubling moral dilemmas of dissection can – and perhaps should – mute the pleasurable aspects of the experience but need not extinguish them. Picking flowers is not lethal to the plants from which they are excised, but I would still prefer living material not to be wasted. Milne writes, 'I had asked the students to bring some flowers from home so that we could do an activity on dissecting flowers'. If I were in Milne's position, I would be less disappointed by the observation that, 'as usual, some students had remembered and some had not', than by the absence of any response from students that might resemble Alice's: 'when she thought it over afterwards, it occurred to her that she ought to have wondered at this, but at the time it all seemed quite natural'.

We ought to wonder – and encourage our students to wonder – at much that seems 'quite natural' in science classrooms. For example, Milne's story illustrates the extent to which we have 'naturalised' a privileging of *science-as-representation* over *science-as-performance* in science education. Milne's comment on practical activities in her first paragraph is familiar: teachers are usually 'in favour' of them but note that they require 'more time to teach the relevant material' than 'chalk and talk'. In other words, the valued outcomes of practical activities are not performance skills but those which can also be represented through 'chalk and talk'. Milne's student, Fiona, has similarly naturalised the expectation that the valued outcomes of her flower dissection are not the skilled performances of using specific instruments to assist close observation of a real flower but, rather, the reproduction of a representation of a flower that matches another representation (in this case, the textbook diagram). I would prefer the activity of dissection to be seen as an end in itself, completed when the appropriate parts and structures of the plant or animal are displayed. As Fiona's second drawing demonstrates, a student's ability to produce a cross-sectional diagram of a flower does not necessarily provide us with evidence that s/he has actually observed it. Milne's story reminds me that I was not in the habit of asking students to draw diagrams of what they had dissected – though not (at least consciously) for the reasons I would now offer, but because I modelled my approach on that of my own high school biology teacher. For example, he would ask us to use a blunt probe to carefully lift a rat's ureter from the back wall of the abdomen so that we could trace its path from kidney to bladder and, when he was satisfied with our display, we could move on to the next stage of the dissection.

Activities such as dissection may be most worthwhile if they are emphatically empirical – object-oriented 'experiments' in the pre-Baconian sense (as in the Latin *experimentalis*, based on experience not authority or conjecture). The language in which we frame such activities should initially focus students' attention on their own performances relative to the objects with which they are interacting, and encourage a sense of achievement by reference to *demonstration* rather than more abstract forms of representation. Of course, as I have argued elsewhere (Gough, 1998), practical work in school science education is always a 'theatre of representation', but teachers exert a good deal of control over which representations are privileged through the students' performances. The mere presence of textbooks as 'props' for such performances encourages students to defer to languages of abstraction and authority and discourages them from focusing on their own experience by using their own colloquial languages.

One of Jay Lemke's (1990, p. 172) recommendations for 'teaching against the mystique of science' is pertinent here, namely, bridging the gap between colloquial and scientific language by encouraging students to 'translate back and forth between scientific and colloquial statements or questions'. This sort of translation cannot occur if students are presented too soon with the language of textbooks as the privileged mode of representing their own experiences. Thus, for example, in the conversation between students that Milne reports, Jane and Fiona seem to be moving too hastily from observing and counting 'those things' in a eucalyptus flower to representing them as the 'stamens' that are labelled in their textbook. The missing step here is a performance – displaying and counting 'those things' to each other and/or the teacher – a performance that needs no textbook or labelled cross-sectional diagram to authorise it.

★   ★   ★

Flower power

Cathleen C. Loving, Texas A&M University

This Saturday I will serve as a rules judge for a regional science bowl here at our university. High schools from all over the area will compete for the right to go to the National Science Bowl, sponsored by the US Department of Energy. While I enjoy the whole process and love to interact with the students, I was struck today in one of our volunteers' practice sessions by the extent to which a student could correctly answer all the questions about the right diameter of an average comet, the role of plasmids in recombinant DNA technology, or the meaning of the mathematical term 'amicable' and still have little understanding of how science is actually done or how it should be done – the nature of science. The questions are, of course, all dealing with what Duschl (1990) calls 'final form science' (p. 69). Here the dynamics, both human and scientific, leading to current best explanations never seem to find their way into classroom discussions, or in this case into bowl questions. What it took to get to the point of being able to measure a comet and identify the role of plasmids is what I am more interested in – and what I think students find fascinating. Unfortunately, most of our school science has little time for such exploration.

Just as there is much explanation behind those science bowl answers, a generalised diagram of a flower in a textbook represents the result of many years of research on flowering plants. For example, recognising that there are both male and female flowers or being able to classify flowering plants as either monocots or dicots took botanists years of work. What appears to have happened in *The flower dissection* is that a generalised textbook diagram of the parts of a flower got confused with generalisations one can make about all flowers. They are not the same thing. This highlights the challenge of how best to use texts in class. While the intent in the flower lab was for the text to be used for clarification of terms and to assist students in making their drawings, the generalised diagram served to shut the lid on student exploration, conjecture and the kind of free thinking that needs to go on in order for some authentic science (albeit school science) to be experienced. While the lab activities did encourage students to work with flowers first hand, the emphasis on dissection, drawing and answering questions immediately reduced the intent to one of a comparative anatomy lesson at best – presumably comparing all those other plant phyla with this one.

While we would like to think an objectives-based approach to teaching science is a good one, we should look at the objectives and ask ourselves, 'How do these daily objectives connect to our larger learning goals for students?' 'Are our learning goals ones that are important enough that everything we do in their name is worth the time and effort?' The danger in focusing on objectives too much and not looking beyond them is that individual objectives may be fine when viewed separately. But, when they are viewed collectively, do they result in worthwhile learning goals being achieved?

In the case of our *Flower dissection* classroom, the phylogenetic approach to learning about plants was clearly emphasised. Students were moved from phyla to phyla – presumably learning about increasing complexity and, perhaps, success (although Stephen J. Gould would question that notion). Frankly, I find that approach to teaching biology (and I taught it for many years) rather boring to teach and boring to learn. It encourages a kind of linear learning, where organisms are presented out of any deep context other than their classification scheme and where we often try to cover so much so quickly. This is illustrated by our *Flower dissection* teacher who felt compelled to finish ferns, conduct the entire flowering plants lab activity, and have ten minutes left to do 'two other things' – all in one class session. What meaningful connections related to important concepts about ferns and flowering plants can we expect to develop in the schema of our students? And what do we know about student prior conceptions and how they might have been altered as a result of today's session? There seemed to be no time to find out.

I am reminded of a series of units produced under the auspices of the US National Academy of Sciences and its National Science Resources Center. One involves second graders studying butterflies for eight weeks (NSRC, 1990). Students begin by talking about butterflies and drawing them according to their current conceptions. Those drawings hang on the classroom wall for the entire unit. Next children are given a cage for each table in which there is a Painted Lady Butterfly caterpillar. They watch over the time of the unit as the caterpillar turns into a chrysalis and then to a beautiful butterfly. Before it is over, they have learned a lot about the butterfly, fed it and set it free outside. They revisit their drawings and make new drawings of their newly formed conceptions of a butterfly. The Plant Growth and Development unit for third or fourth graders (NSRC, 1991) also has a diagram of a flower. But this is a particular flower, one from the crucifer family known as *Brassica*. These students plant Wisconsin Fast Plant seeds, watch the *Brassica* grow, pollinate using dried bees, and then watch as the flowers wither and seed pods emerge. What could these students do in Grade 8 (the level of our *Flower dissection* class) that might involve more meaningful, better connected learning goals than comparing plant phyla anatomically and physiologically?

One suggestion for eighth graders is a unit on plants in *Science Directions 8* (Winter *et al.*, 1991). What one notices about the work students do with plants in this series is that the learning goals are either related to the nature of science and its processes, to the relation of science to technology or the relation of science and technology to society. The unit entitled 'Managing Plant Growth' involves activities on various ways one can grow plants, what is going on in different plant organs during growth, how modern technology assists these natural processes, how plants have been and are currently used medically and for food, and how we are constantly challenged by plant pests and disease. There are two diagrams of a flower in this text also. One is a generalised cross section in the unit review which asks students about the function of each labelled part (p. 271). The other diagram is earlier in the section on sexual reproduction. It is a beautiful, stylised drawing of a tiger lily, with its reproduction-related organs labelled (p. 255).

It seems evident from this description of our *Flower dissection* classroom that our teacher has a good relationship with her class. There seems to be a climate of honesty, comfort and rapport with students. She appears to hold them fairly responsible for seeking additional information if they need it, and yet is helpful. The stage is set – if she has the desire and the freedom to do so – for her to involve her students in more engaging, more meaningful activities without having to drastically alter her current programme. A personal experience is followed by a few suggestions.

During my nearly twenty years of teaching biology, I profoundly changed the way my Grade 9 or Grade 10 students learned about a lot of things. One was how I introduced the frog. I moved away from a phylogenetic approach and the traditional lab involving the dissection of a preserved frog (after a series of 'lower creature' dissections) and substituted the BSCS 'Green Version' lab (Biological Sciences Curriculum Study, 1963). Here students spent one or two class periods answering questions about and examining big, live frogs – watching them jump on their lab tables, swim in aquaria, catch insects, move their eyes and breathe. Only after thoroughly investigating frogs as living creatures did students examine them freshly pithed. (I did sacrifice and pith myself, with help from a trained lab assistant before school, enough frogs to supply teams of two students in three classes.) It was the only animal dissection we did in the ecologically based course. For the next three days we watched as the reflexes of the freshly pithed frogs (they *were* dead) slowed down and finally stopped reacting to our probes and chemicals. In the meantime, all sorts of questions addressed the fresh-looking external and internal organs and some of the adaptive features we had been noticing over the last few days.

In some ways, dissecting a flower is like dissecting a preserved frog. Neither is looking very alive or connected to the rest of the world. We literally take them apart to their components and in the process lose sense of their symmetry, know little or nothing about their niche, and rarely have time to compare different flowering plants in their environment to discuss the relationship between their size, structure, colour, organ arrangement and their success.

What if there had been time for students to compare each other's flowers and diagrams? Would not they have discovered some differences between eucalyptus, poinsettia and a rose? Would they then have been able to make generalisations based on the many different kinds of flowers represented in the room? This could serve as an exercise in observation, hypothesis-building and seeking some kind of generalisation. Instead students studied isolated examples and let the text diagram shut down their imagination and their decision-making.

Time was against them. Time was against their teacher. There was just too much to cover. There was no time to talk of the evolutionary mechanisms that might have been at work encouraging the success of one species instead of another – some of the behind-the-scenes questions getting at millions of years of change. There was no time to talk of the adaptive capacity of flowering plants or why they have been successful in so many environments, taking many unusual and varied forms. And what of relationships, connections to the rest of the living world?

I am struck by one statement made in the Project 2061 *Benchmarks for science literacy* (American Association for the Advancement of Science, 1993) which gets at the need for middle school students to have opportunities to enrich their knowledge about diversity of life on the planet. It says, 'By the end of 8th grade, students should know that … animals and plants have a great variety of body plans and internal structures that contribute to their being able to make or find food and reproduce' (p. 104). What an important learning goal! It says on the same page that students should 'begin to connect that knowledge to what they are learning in geography'. Suddenly the flowers in the dissection lab take on a whole new dimension as they become connected to the real world.

The 'flower power' youth of the Haight-Ashbury neighbourhood in San Francisco used flowers to symbolise love and peace during the tumultuous 1960s. Science teachers can design and promote a kind of biological 'flower power', inquiry opportunities which result in more powerful, connected learnings. This may be the most important lesson we can learn from this case study. Thanks for the opportunity to comment. Good luck with *your* 'flower power' labs!

★   ★   ★

Editors' synthesis

In her coda to *The flower dissection* Catherine Milne identified the dilemma in the story as the conflict between knowledge from textbooks and knowledge from observation. Jane and Fiona, she says, have learned that 'all the activities that they do in class and the sense that they make of these activities have no value'. Although both Gough and Loving comment on the text/activity dilemma, they both also take up the challenge of dissection.

For Gough the canonical school science activity of dissection provides an ethical as well as a pedagogical dilemma. The ethical dilemma is not whether in principle dissection can be justified, but whether classroom dissection can be managed in a way that is respectful of living organisms. His resolution to the ethical dilemma involves managing students' contact with the animals, alive and dead. He argues that students should not be distanced from the act of killing by white coats, formaldehyde smells or computer simulation, but confronted with 'the glistening translucence of membranes and mesentery' and 'the fleshly embodiments of life's complexity and transience'. Similarly, Loving's response to *The flower dissection* involves a commentary on the moral and pedagogical possibilities in classroom dissection of frogs. Like Gough, she objects to dissection of preserved frogs, disconnected from the rest of the living world and from their ecological niche. Her preferred classroom strategy is to help students understand frogs as living, breathing, jumping organisms before they encounter them prepared for dissection. Whether a lab activity concerns rabbits or flowers, neither commentator is comfortable with reducing a living thing to an object in a lesson 'to show students how it worked'.

Beyond these shared concerns about the practice of dissection, Gough and Loving take up different opportunities offered by *The flower dissection*. Gough focuses on the way in which the language and structure of textbooks can short-circuit students' opportunity to develop performance skills in the laboratory. For him, the outcome of a dissection is not representation, either by the student or in a textbook, but skills in a practical performance such as physically tracing a ureter's path from the kidney to the bladder. Unfortunately teachers – and students such as Fiona – have naturalised the expectation that the outcome of a lab is to produce a representation that matches the textbook. One of the reasons for this displacement from performance to representation is time. As Loving points out, it is hard for students to make meaningful connections when teachers are rushing to cover the content. It may be that there is just too much to cover in the course Milne describes, or that the course is wrong-headed in propelling students and teachers through a phylogenetic sequence from fungi to ferns to flowering plants. Working at a slower pace, the teacher may have been able to build Fiona's and Jane's capacity to make adequate generalisations about many kinds of flowers that were available in the room, rather than reproducing a generalised textbook diagram.

Despite Milne's personal preference for making sense of science through practical experience, the tyranny of the objectives, tests and textbooks presses down on teachers. Rushing through the syllabus, like the White Rabbit, the issue of time remains at the heart of the displacement from science as experience to science as representation.

References

American Association for the Advancement of Science (1993). *Benchmarks for science literacy*. New York: Oxford University Press

Biological Sciences Curriculum Study (1963). *High school biology* (BSCS Green Version). Chicago: Rand McNally.

Carroll, Lewis [Charles Lutwidge Dodgson] (1939 [1865]). *Alice's Adventures in Wonderland*. London and Glasgow: Collins.

Duschl, R. A. (1990). *Restructuring science education*. New York: Teachers College Press.

Gough, Noel (1998). 'If this were played upon a stage': school laboratory work as a theatre of representation. In Jerry Wellington (ed.), *Practical work in school science: Which way now?* (pp. 69–89). London: Routledge.

Jegede, O. J. and Aikenhead, G. S. (1999). Transcending cultural borders: Implications for science teaching. *Research in Science and Technological Education*, 17 (1), 45–67.

Larson, J. O. (1995, April). Fatima's rules and other elements of an unintended chemistry curriculum. Paper presented at the American Educational Research Association annual meeting, San Francisco.

Lemke, Jay L. (1990). *Talking science: Language, learning, and values*. Norwood, NJ: Ablex Publishing Corporation.

Milligan, Spike (1979). *Open Heart University*. London: M. and J. Hobbs in association with Michael Joseph.

Munby, H. and Russell, T. (1994). The authority of experience in learning to teach. Messages from a physics methods class. *Journal of Teacher Education*, 45, 86–95.

National Science Resources Center (1990). *The life cycle of butterflies* (Teacher's guide, Field-test edition). Washington, DC: National Academy of Sciences.

—— (1991). *Plant growth and development* (Teacher's guide). Washington, DC: National Academy of Sciences.

Winter, M. K., Gore, G. R., Grace, E. S., Lang, H. M. and MacLean, W. (1991). *Science directions 8*. Toronto: John Wiley.

Chapter 9

Student reports

Contributions by Catherine Milne,
Clive R. Sutton and J. R. Martin

Editors' introduction

Among the distinguishing rituals of school science, there is nothing quite so familiar as the lab 'experiment' and the lab book formula of Aim, Apparatus, Method, Results and Conclusion. As much as students are expected to learn from the practical activity, they also are expected to learn to reproduce the structure of the lab report, to mirror its passive voice and third person, and adopt its tone of studied certainty. Learning these language conventions has long been an essential part of school science, but in recent years teachers and researchers have taken issue with this tradition. For some, the objective language of lab reports obscures the radically interpretive nature of knowledge in science. As Sutton (1992) has argued, figurative language is central to scientific theorising. Scientific language is always already theory laden, so it is epistemologically inauthentic to stress the objectivity of the language of lab reports. For this reason, it is argued that school science should make more use of personal language and contingent text forms.

Linguists with an interest in the language of science have, however, proposed an alternative view. From this perspective, science has its own discourse, its own distinctive forms of organisation and vocabulary. Many of these language features go to the heart of science as a system of thought, with particular standards of evidence, argument and proof. To study science without learning to master the discourse would not be studying science as we know it (Lemke, 1990). Students who cannot master the structures and language of science textbooks are cut off from a significant source of understanding; students who cannot reproduce these textual forms run the risk of being misunderstood as not really understanding science. Even in elementary schools, some people argue that it is essential for students to learn to master the forms of scientific discourse (Martin, 1990). Without the discourse, it might be said, where is the discipline of science?

The fingerprinting report, the story that begins this chapter, provides an opportunity to weigh up these competing views about the value for students of mastering genre structures such as the lab report. Catherine Milne's story about a Grade 9 and 10 unit on forensic science explores her dissatisfaction with the language conventions of school lab reports. She feels obliged to teach the approved science department report format, but is concerned that this highly structured approach might take the fun out of an otherwise interesting unit of work. In the commentaries that follow, Clive Sutton argues for the authenticity of more personal forms of writing, and Jim Martin argues that making the genre structures of science the object of inquiry opens opportunities for understanding the nature of science and the ways in which it is changing.

The fingerprinting report

Catherine Milne

In this story I describe with some embarrassment one of my lessons on the conventions of scientific report writing. Even as I presented this lesson I had started to have reservations about the formal methods that we (the science department) presented to students as requirements for the writing of experimental reports in school science. My concerns, which have crystallised since I presented this lesson, were that an algorithmic approach to report writing reinforced for students the notion that science was a very structured discipline with a specific way of doing something in which nothing exciting happened.

The science department, in which I taught at the time, had an agreed policy on the structure of experimental reports and the language that was appropriate for students to use in these reports. The report was to be presented with the following structure using these headings: (1) Aim, (2) Apparatus, (3) Method, (4) Results and (5) Conclusion. The reports were to be written using both third person (students were not to use 'I' or 'We' in their sentences), and using the passive voice (in these sentences they were to emphasise the outcomes of the activity rather than their involvement in the conduct of the activity). The structure of the report and the use of third person and passive voice was consistent with the requirements of our school system.

It was early in fourth term and I had just started teaching a new unit called Crime Detection to a class of Grade 9 and 10 students. We had negotiated the content and assessment of the unit and the students had elected to begin the unit with fingerprinting as the first area of forensic science for us to investigate. As a result we were embroiled in looking at different techniques for collecting fingerprints from different surfaces.

Over a period of a few lessons the students had been experimenting with the effectiveness of various powders on various surfaces and they had been asked to submit an experimental report of this practical activity for assessment. I had marked their reports and began this lesson by revising the features of experimental reports with the class because after reading their reports I had some concerns about the structure and language of their reports. I decided to use the student reports to emphasise to students the type of language that they were expected to use.

At the beginning of the lesson I said to the class, 'Let's look at the experimental report that you completed on collecting fingerprints using powders. I want you to check and make sure that your method is a series of instructions. Is there anyone here who can tell me what is required for a good instruction?' I paused and waited for a response from someone in the class because I wanted to be sure that students had fully understood the characteristics of a good instruction.

Carole volunteered, 'A verb.'

I responded with delight, 'A verb. Right, Carole.' I then turned to the rest of the class and continued, 'So we start with a verb. All method is a series of instructions. In school science you'll notice that the method written by other people has the same characteristics as your method has. So an instruction must contain a verb. What else must an instruction contain?'

Karl answered, 'A verb refers to an object.'

'That's very good, Karl', I replied.

I then elaborated the features of an instruction by telling the class that a clause might also be needed for a good instruction. I wrote on the whiteboard the features of a good instruction and then said, 'So when you're writing the method it should be written as an instruction. It should not be a recount or a story about what you did. For example, some people wrote, "I went and collected the powders from the front bench. I placed my fingerprints on the glass". Well, we don't consider that a good instruction and in science we expect people to write their method up as a series of instructions because their method must look like a series of steps to follow, a procedure.'

A classroom discussion ensued over appropriate instructions. Students proposed a series of instructions for the collecting of fingerprints using various powders and I whiteboarded them as we proceeded. These were examined in critical detail by the rest of the class and each student compared the model with their own work. Notes were made by students on the areas of their own method section that could be improved.

I drew together this section of the lesson by saying that I would like everybody to get into the habit of writing instructions for their method because they were giving everybody their procedure, a procedure that another person could follow to do the same experiment. I explained to them that 'Somebody should be able to pick up your book, read your set of instructions, and do the experiment correctly.'

Next I started describing to the class what I expected to read in the results section of their experimental report. This was different from the methods section because here students were expected to compare the effectiveness of various powders. I told the class that I liked Michael's results because he not only presented a detailed description but he also included samples of the fingerprints that he had collected from surfaces and he compared the powders used on various surfaces with the quality of the collected prints. Thus he analysed as well as described his results. Also Michael made the most of his opportunity in this section to present samples of his work from this experiment. I indicated to the class that I would like to see them all doing something similar to Michael's efforts in their results section because Michael's presentation was an excellent example of analysing his data thoroughly.

I completed the lesson by commenting on the type of language that they were expected to use in writing their conclusion section for the report. I said to the class, 'When you write a conclusion, it should be written as a summary or an explanation of the results. In your conclusion you should relate the results and the aim together. Everybody in this class has had lots of experience writing up science experiments in their school science classes. You know that when you are writing the conclusion you are writing an explanation and you don't need to describe, "I think this", "We think that". Your explanation should be written as a series of sentences which relate the results to the aim without referring to your involvement in the experiment.'

As an example I read out to the class Daniel's conclusion which followed the conventions as I had described them. One of these conventions was that he made sure that the language that he used to write his conclusion emphasised the object of study, i.e. the fingerprints and not his involvement in the practical activity.

This part of the lesson was completed here. I tried to ensure that I had presented the algorithm clearly to the students to prepare them to write other reports in this unit in the appropriate way. Regardless of my reservations about any slavish adherence to a particular approach to report writing I had tried to ensure that my students would not be disadvantaged when they were compared against other schools in the moderation process. They knew how to write up their reports!

★　　　★　　　★

Doing, thinking and writing

Clive R. Sutton, University of Leicester

How glad I am that no-one is expecting me to check whether Catherine Milne has got the right section headings and the proper forms of expression. Free of some of the pressures she experienced in class, I can just try to listen to what I think she is saying, but in school that job of listening sometimes seems to be over-ridden by a different one altogether – getting the pupils to do things in the 'proper' way. Other people's expectations about what is proper then come into play and there is even the long shadow of examiners to cope with – and our ideas about their ideas of what is expected. That's what Catherine found as she tried to use her professional judgement and give the pupils good reasons for what she asked them to do, and so she writes in the language of personal dilemma.

We can hear her voice as she lets us in on her thinking – her hopes and doubts and her reasons for a particular action as she saw it at the time. She shows us not just what she did but why, and that's what keeps the story interesting. Isn't it exactly that kind of mixture of action with reasoning which can keep both a reader and a writer involved, whatever the topic? I would like school learners to write that way for at least some of their time, to express their uncertainties, try out their understanding, gain confidence in their ownership of scientific ideas, and gradually become skilled at explaining them. I could say the same for ideas in history or geography as well as in science, but our dilemma is that to encourage such involvement is wrongly thought to conflict with something special about the subject. Why do some of us feel uneasy about encouraging 'I thought ...' 'We tried ...' or 'What I expected was ...'?

The short answer is that this unease comes from erroneous beliefs about science that developed in schools a century and a half ago and have become fossilised by tradition. This dilemma is not just about writing; it concerns the actual conceptions of science that underpin our reasons for setting the writing. These include the idea that practical experience is the main source of knowledge (and so the teacher's prime task is to train pupils to 'write it up'), and the idea that scientists write 'impersonally'. To be charitable to our predecessors who introduced science into schools we might say that beliefs of this kind were suited to the purposes of their time, but since then they have come to be treated as an account of how scientists work and in that they are extremely misleading.

The inflated centrality of practical work and reporting 'what happened'

In school we constantly imply that what matters most is the practical work. Scientists, we appear to be saying, learn by doing experiments, 'seeing what happens' and telling the world about it. Children can try to learn that way too, we say. Scientists however do not learn mainly by doing experiments. They learn by having an intense desire to understand, by wondering, by thinking, by talking and planning in ways that are linked with observations and experiments. The fallacy perpetuated in school is that one just gets on with observing and experimenting and this leads directly to new reliable knowledge. Writing in school is set with words like 'describe' and 'report' much more often than 'argue' or 'explain' or 'set out a mental picture of what might be going on'. Case studies of scientists-in-action on the other hand show the crucial importance of theory both for designing investigations and for interpreting 'what might be going on'. Scientists spend a good deal of their time on this mental orientation and re-orientation; school science focuses too much on the experiment itself and has, in effect, elevated doing above thinking, especially thinking away from the bench.

Writing is thus cast as 'reporting'. What else could it be for? For formulating ideas? For checking out with your teacher whether you have understood? For wondering and speculating? For arguing a case? For explaining an idea to some public audience? Those uses have been almost eclipsed by the traditional belief that writing should be for describing 'what happened in the experiment'. Did the school policy to which Catherine Milne refers have anything to say on how to get pupils to write about the big picture of relevant scientific ideas, not just about the bench work?

Do scientists write 'impersonally'?

No, they do not, but in schools we have been confused about this for several reasons. The confusion arises partly through a misreading of what scientists are doing when they try to separate opinion from evidence and mainly because of too little exposure to scientists' original writing and over-exposure to 'finished' science which is no longer controversial and from which the personal voice has faded. When ideas are new and fluid, there is no mistaking the human voice of the author. Try showing pupils some writing by Robert Boyle or Charles Darwin or Michael Faraday (for example, see Sutton, 1997), or show them the recent writings of Harry Kroto about his struggles to visualise a structure for the fullerenes.

The personal voice is stronger in some kinds of writing than in others and there are actually many different kinds for active scientists – laboratory notebooks, conference presentations, e-mail letters, articles for first journals, reviews of recent research, bids for research funds and so on. For a better understanding of how science 'works' we should be showing more of these different kinds of texts in school. Our emphasis on the doing rather than the debating has drawn attention mainly to the laboratory notebook and then to a fantasy stereotypical version of the experimental report for a journal. These two, or a confused mixture of them, have been held to encompass what schoolchildren should be taught. They began in the 1860s when science was gaining its place in the elite private schools as a form of pre-professional study. To be a laboratory scientist you must learn to set out your record of what you did – 'to determine the specific gravity of paraffin oil', or whatever. You must make a disciplined notebook with easily retrievable figures. In chemistry you were trained how to record your qualitative analysis in columns headed Test, Observation and Inference. These technical routines did form a *part* of science as it was then, but they certainly never formed the whole of the 'process of science'. The second one for example omits a crucial piece of thinking, i.e. reasons for choosing a particular test in the first place. Nevertheless in school they were gradually taken to represent the scientific way of doing things and were ritualised in various other systems of headings which I have surveyed elsewhere (Sutton, 1989). One of them was the Aim – Apparatus – Method – Results – Conclusion system which Catherine Milne mentions. It developed a life of its own for pupils as 'what you have to do in science lessons' and helped to eliminate from school science any genuine personal attempt to communicate.

For the active scientist, on the other hand, even the most clinical of research articles is a strongly personal communication, composed with great care. Researchers publishing such a paper do not 'report' a 'fact', much as they might like to do so. Rather, they make a claim which they hope will be accepted by others, and eventually be taken into the body of accepted scientific facts, and they support this claim with evidence. They make strenuous efforts to suggest that what they present is 'not just our opinion ... look at what the equipment says ... try it for yourself', but their readers are in no doubt who is making the claim or that it is still only in the realm of 'potential fact' at this stage. Myers and others (Myers, 1990) have shown that the personal voice stands out strongly in today's journal articles regardless of how many times 'I' and 'We' are used or not used. The writers may replace 'We counted how many caterpillars were eaten each day' by 'Caterpillars were counted' or even by 'Table 3 shows the measured predation rates', but this does not remove the personal authorship, nor the need for the authors to argue a case and be heard.

That kind of initial scientific paper forms a distinctive genre of writing, developed for specific purposes. Anything we teach teenagers about such papers should help them to understand the context and purpose, not just to mimic the structure. The context and purposes of their own writing in school are not the same, and what they write must be functional in their own situation. But it could share with the scientist's papers the need for a writer to argue and persuade with evidence, making personal choices about how to present it.

The personal voice diminishes later. Successful research articles get quoted by other people in a ladder of re-reporting and citation which is a very important part of 'process' of science (see Sutton, 1996) and it is then that a more substantial de-personalisation occurs, as ideas become surer and more widely accepted. What began as a debate about ideas gradually becomes instead a set of accepted facts to be transmitted. 'So-and-so has suggested that the continents move about' gets transformed into a set of apparently unproblematic factual statements about 'tectonic plates' which move and 'subduction zones' at their points of collision. The creative human and personal contribution is forgotten. Pupils can easily misunderstand this mature language of established science and see it as 'plain description' if teachers do not unpack some of it for them and show the human involvement in formulating the concepts. The two genres – research report and review textbook – all have a part to play in establishing the factuality of scientific 'findings'.

The form and functions of various genres of writing in science

Scholars in the history of science and in linguistics can teach us a lot about scientists' writing, especially where the two types of study come together. This happens, for example, in Charles Bazerman's history of how the experimental article developed over many decades and in Steven Shapin's analysis of how Robert Boyle and others developed a new 'technology' of writing in certain ways in the early days of the Royal Society (see Bazerman, 1988; Shapin and Schaffer, 1985). Scientific communities have refined their ways of working substantially by developing new written genres and it is important therefore for teachers to understand the genre concept. Perhaps it is all the more important because some experts in linguistics in parts of Australia have recently urged, perhaps over-urged, an emphasis on genres in school. They see this as a means of 'empowering' pupils for life in the modern world, providing youngsters with access to the kinds of discourse that characterise different subjects and professions (see, for example, Cope and Kalantzis, 1993; Halliday and Martin, 1993).

Let me repeat that there isn't just one way of writing in science, but a whole range of scientific genres. A section of a data book for example is very different from the preface to a research review and it does a very different job. All the various forms can be understood in terms of their functions – we write in a certain way in a certain context in order to get certain things done. If we want a set of instructions for how to use a thermometer it will be a sequence of commands, but if we are composing a letter of apology to a technician for breaking the thermometer a different style will be needed. That will be different again from the letter which the technician might write to a supplier to order a replacement. 'Directions for building a wormery' will be very different from 'a general account of the biology of earthworms', because here again a different job is being done in the two situations. The features of these various ways of writing should be discussed in class by means of examples to raise the pupils' awareness of how form is related to function.

Generally, appreciation of the form will follow an understanding of the function, whereas simply to demand a particular set of headings is indeed likely to be dull, mechanical and alienating and it will fail to engage the pupils in making an effort to communicate.

Several of the examples I have mentioned could be justified in school both as a means of coaching pupils in functional literacy and as a way of developing their understanding of the science. Two of them involve composing instructions and it is interesting that Catherine Milne casts 'method' in that form. Pupils need an image of what they are trying to do and they value the security of a structure within which to write, once they have understood the overall intention. Composing instructions, sometimes as a numbered list, provides a fairly simple structure and helps them to think about the logic of the task and the logic of communication. It is also something they can check for themselves. What comes next? Is that clear? Have I missed out anything? Composing instructions is not however the one and only way to communicate in that situation; it is just one of several possible ways – another could be to make a flow chart of what to do in what order.

Had the work on fingerprinting been a technology project, the most logical outcome would have been a numbered set of instructions *to tell* your assistant, Dr Watson, what he must do to reveal and record the prints; everything would focus just on the best method. It was however a science project and the function of a section about methods in science is a little different – essentially *to persuade* the reader that the tests of more than one powder were fairly conducted. A numbered list is still a legitimate approach and a sub-heading for 'results' is of course a good idea to follow it. The purpose of the results section is also to persuade the reader – this time that the fair tests yield useful and trustworthy information. Tables of comparison and samples of the prints are just two of the ways this purpose might be fulfilled.

Before the pupils compose a section at the end called 'Conclusion' or 'What use is this?' or 'So what?' there should be a bit more discussion of the audience to be addressed. Are they writing for the local police department to get them to give the school funds for further investigations? ... or to cast doubt on long-used practices? ... or what? Are they to write for local 'victims of crime', to let them know that people in the local school studied fingerprints? ... Or who else? For some of these audiences a guarded approach would be appropriate: 'Fingerprints are not easily revealed by using technique x, but technique y has advantages.' Others cry out for a more overtly personal voice of the writer: 'What we think now is ....' or 'Based on our results we recommend that ... '

For all the more complicated written genres, to get children to appreciate them we need examples and questions such as the following: 'How does this kind of writing usually start off? Why does the writer start that way? ... What comes next? ... Has she rounded it off well and why?' Catherine Milne was surely working in that direction with her questions to the class, and once they understand that form is for a function, then genuine composition becomes possible.

★   ★   ★

To teach or not to teach: why the question?

J. R. Martin, University of Sydney

I was intrigued by the tensions in this recount – the teacher taught the genre (experimental report) and its features, so her students would know them when they needed them; but she wasn't happy about doing it because it makes science look like a place where nothing exciting happens. For me, of course, there is no tension. The teacher has negotiated the curriculum with the students; working on fingerprinting does sound exciting (but then I love crime fiction). The class has come to a point in their work where writing happens; the teacher has let the students have a go and is trying to fix the writing up (but then I don't mind intervention). Good models are presented and discussed, both with respect to their generic structure and language features (but then I don't mind using knowledge about language to teach with). The teacher attempts to motivate the structure and features in terms of its functionality (what it achieves) and appropriateness (its status) – but then I do think the structure and features of experimental reports really are functionally motivated; it's not just a matter of taste, for markers, in public examinations. The teacher's anxious; I'm becalmed. How to bridge between?

I'll try and approach this is two ways – first by talking about linking language to science, and second by thinking about making science exciting for students. In both cases I'm trying to argue that the language matters because it is motivated; if we can recover this motivation, this functionality, maybe some anxiety can be resolved.

Let's start with language features. The teacher refers to the third-person and to the passive voice and clauses beginning with a verb. Here the teacher draws on some terminology from traditional school grammar, which she seems to know more about than her students (who stumble, saying 'a verb refers to an object', which isn't really how grammarians speak). To her credit the teacher does try to justify these features, which she refers to as conventions: 'Somebody should be able to pick up your book, read your set of instructions, and do the experiment correctly.' And later, 'he made sure that the language he used to write his conclusion emphasised the object of study, i.e. the fingerprints and not his involvement in the practical activity'. I'm not sure, however, how convincing or transparent these justifications were. The teacher's actual position seems to be that these features are a matter of form … part of an algorithm agreed on by the science department, reflecting conventions attracting evaluation in the moderation process. So the real reason she teaches them is because scientific etiquette insists on them (at least in school examinations) and she doesn't want her students to be disadvantaged for not knowing them.

The problem here seems to be that the way in which the features are described is so formal that a link to why science behaves this way cannot be made. And here we confront the general problem that most science teachers and students share next to no language for talking about language, and what they do share are relics of school grammar that are next to useless. As an alternative, we might look at the kind of grammar which functional linguists who study the evolution of science discourse deploy – and especially at what these linguists call Theme (Halliday, 1994; Martin *et al.*, 1997). The basic argument here is that a clause can be interpreted as a wave of information, and that in English the beginning of the clause is used as a kind of orientation to what the clause is on about. So the reason clauses begin with verbs in the Methods section of an experimental report is that in this section the clauses are on about activity; their perspective is action. In the Conclusion section, on the other hand, the clauses are on about fingerprinting techniques, not what the students did; the recurrent clause perspective is that of results in relation to aims.

This understanding of the clause as a wave of information orienting us to what we're on about is useful for explaining grammar in relation to science. Grammatically, it explains why clauses begin with verbs in the Methods section and are written in the third person (and in the passive where necessary) in the Conclusion. Scientifically, it allows us to go back into the history of science to see when and why scientists started writing in this way. Halliday (see Halliday and Martin, 1993) and Bazerman (1988) provide fascinating accounts of Newton's discourse and the problems he had getting his ideas accepted. Newton was among the first major scientists to write up their work in English; and interestingly enough he wrote up his methods as recounts, in the first person. From Bazerman, however, we learn of the terrible problems Newton faced when people replicated his experiments, coming up with different results; Newton realised that his work was not being replicated precisely, and subsequently took great pains to document his experiments more carefully. Judging from Halliday's analysis of the evolution of scientific writing, it is clear that social pressures of this kind were instrumental in shaping the language of science as we inherit it today. And the way in which information unfolds, from one task to another in scientific writing, has been critical to this process of evolution.

Taking this back to school, I'm arguing that if the language for talking about grammar were a little richer, and more sensitive to meaning and considerations of discourse, then the motivations for using language in scientific ways would be easier to explain – not just in terms of what students are doing in school, but also in terms of what scientists have been doing redesigning and expanding English for the past 400 years. With some functional grammar, we can begin to explain why science is the way it is, and how it differs from other subject areas, which have their own histories, equally exhilarating and equally fraught. Australian linguists and educators have been at the cutting edge of these understandings for more than twenty years (see Christie, 1998; Halliday, 1994, 1998; Rose, 1998; Unsworth, 1998; Veel, 1998).

So I'm suggesting that if we draw on functional linguistics, rather than school grammar, we can make some links. What about excitement? Will deploying ideas about functional grammar and genre make science too dry? Even drier than students expect, as our science teacher fears?

One way around this might be to use grammar and genre to explore changes in science, and the language of science, even as they occur. An obvious place to begin might be with what Veel calls the 'greening' of science in secondary school, as ecology and environmentalism impact on textbooks and curriculum. Veel (1998) points out that as science changes, its genres and grammar change with it. So we find new 'multimodal' texts, incorporating news arrays of language in relation to images (including figures, diagrams, drawings and photos); we find new genres that argue issues and urge change; we find renovated genres – descriptions of animals for example that involve consideration of endangerment of the species and what might be done about it; and so on. And all these changes involve new uses of grammar (for example persuasive language and evaluative language) and new graphology (formatting, layout, colour). It is easy to study these developments as they happen – as traditional textbooks are replaced with green ones, as traditional topics are supplanted by environmental ones, as traditional exam questions are replaced by more expository ones, and so on. I find it hard to see how changes of this kind wouldn't be exciting … since the future of the planet depends on them; and I find it hard to see how studying the repercussions for genre and language features wouldn't be exciting too (but then I love analysing texts; it brings them ever more to life for me – it never dulls them down).

There is an opportunity here for what is termed critical literacy (Walton, 1996; Morgan, 1997). Martin (in press) worries that green geography means having the right attitudes about the environment without necessarily incorporating the ecological understandings required to salvage a biosphere, or anything in it. Is green science speeding down this unfortunate route? If so, is this because what we are looking at is simply a partial takeover of the science curriculum by the humanities – English genres and language features in the science classroom? If so, to what degree are we selling our environment short? To answer these questions we need to look hard at science discourse as it greens – in textbooks, in classroom lessons, in moderation processes. We need to look at science and its genres and language features (but then, I think that science is made up of genres and language features – that its own distinctive genres and language features are what science is).

There's a bridge to walk across. Make the grammar richer, so it can show why science discourse is the way it is. Then use genre and grammar to analyse change … for example the greening of school science. Or whatever teachers might negotiate with students that seems exciting.

The teacher's anxious; I'm becalmed. Frankly, I was rather impressed by the lesson (but then I don't think teachers should feel bad about teaching, especially when they're doing a damn good job).

★   ★   ★

Editors' synthesis

Catherine Milne introduced *The fingerprinting report* by confessing to some embarrassment at the recollection of teaching the writing conventions of lab reports. Does such an algorithmic approach reinforce students' perception that science is an unexciting and over-structured discipline, she wondered. Clive Sutton shares her concern. In his response he emphasises the historical contingency of the now conventional genre structure of lab reports. The structures taught in school science, he says, are built on 'erroneous beliefs' about the practices of science, 'fossilised by tradition'. Real science, he argues, does not elevate doing above thinking, and involves a much broader and more personal range of writing than the conventional lab report suggests to students.

Although Sutton and Martin draw on some of the same intellectual resources – Bazerman's historical accounts of the emergence of the report genre and the functional linguistics of Halliday – they draw different conclusions about the merit of students learning to use scientific genre frameworks. For Martin the linguistic features of conventional science text forms carry forward the intellectual history of the discipline. Rather than characterising the lab report as a genre that must be mastered for the sake of exams and etiquette, he argues that the grammatical structure carries the part of the genre's meaning. Clauses begin with verbs in the Methods section, for example, because 'the clauses are on about activity'. Similarly, changes in school science as a result of the greening of the curriculum may be traced through grammatical and graphological changes in textbooks.

Good lessons like the one described in *The fingerprinting report* provide more pedagogical opportunities than any one class or teacher can take up. In the story, Milne's limited objective is to ensure that students understand and use the correct genre framework. Given more time and the benefit of hindsight, she might unpack Martin's suggestion that the features of the genre are not arbitrary, and that understanding of the genre structure builds understanding of the nature of science. Alternatively, and equally worth pursuing, is Sutton's desire to disturb the taken-for-granted use of science's historical text forms and provide students with opportunities to try more personal and persuasive ways of writing up their lab reports.

References

Bazerman, C. (1988). *Shaping written knowledge: The genre and activity of the experimental article in science*. Madison, WI: University of Wisconsin Press.

Christie, F. (ed.) (1998). *Pedagogy and the shaping of consciousness: Linguistic and social processes*. London: Cassell.

Cope, W. and Kalantzis, M. (eds) (1993). *The powers of literacy: A genre approach to teaching literacy*. London: Falmer and Pittsburgh: University of Pittsburgh Press.

Halliday, M. A. K. (1994). *An introduction to functional grammar*. London: Edward Arnold.

—— (1998) Things and relations: Regrammaticising experience as scientific knowledge. In J. R. Martin and R. Veel (eds), *Reading science: Critical and functional perspectives on discourses of science* (pp. 185–235). London: Routledge.

Halliday, M. A. K. and Martin, J. R. (1993). *Writing science: Literacy and discursive power*. Lewes: Falmer Press and Pittsburgh: University of Pittsburgh Press.

Lemke, J. (1990). *Talking science: Language, learning and values*. Norwood, NY: Ablex.

Martin, J. R. (1990). Literacy in science: Learning to handle text as technology. In F. Christie (ed.), *Literacy for a changing world*. Melbourne: Australian Council for Educational Research.

—— (in press). From little things big things grow: Ecogenesis in school geography. In R. L. Coe, R. L. Lingard and T. Teslenko (eds), *The rhetoric and ideology of genre: Strategies for stability and change*. Cresskill, NJ: Hampton Press.

Martin, J. R. and Veel, R. (eds) (1998). *Reading science: Critical and functional perspectives on discourses of science*. London: Routledge.

Martin, J. R., Matthiessen, C. M. I. M. and Painter, C. (1997). *Working with functional grammar*. London: Edward Arnold.

Morgan, W. (1997). *Critical literacy in the classroom: The art of the possible*. London: Routledge.

Myers, G. (1990). *Writing biology*. Madison, WI: University of Wisconsin Press.

Rose, D. (1998). Science discourse and industrial hierarchy. In J. R. Martin and R. Veel (eds), *Reading science: Critical and functional perspectives on discourses of science* (pp. 236–265). London: Routledge.

Shapin, S. and Schaffer, S. (1985). *Leviathan and the air pump: Hobbes, Boyle and the experimental life*. Princeton, NJ: Princeton University Press.

Sutton, C. R. (1989). Writing and reading in science: The hidden messages. In R. Millar (ed.), *Doing science: Images of science in science education* (pp. 137–159). Lewes: Falmer Press.

—— (1992). *Words, science and learning*. Buckingham, UK: Open University Press.

—— (1996). Beliefs about science and beliefs about language. *International Journal of Science Education*, 18 (1), 1–18.

—— (1997). New perspectives on language in science. In B. J. Fraser and K. G. Tobin (eds), *International handbook of science education* (pp. 27–38). Dordrecht, The Netherlands: Kluwer Academic Publishers.

Unsworth, L. (1998). 'Sound' explanations in school science: a functional linguistics perspective on effective apprenticing texts. *Linguistics and Education*, 9 (2), 199–226.

Veel, R. (1998). The greening of school science: Ecogenesis in secondary classrooms. In J. R. Martin and R. Veel (eds), *Reading science: Critical and functional perspectives on discourses of science* (pp. 114–151). London: Routledge.

Walton, C. (1996). *Critical social literacies.* Darwin: Northern Territory University Press.

Chapter 10

Questioning

Contributions by Joan Gribble, Sue Briggs,
Paul Black and Sandra K. Abell

Editors' introduction

Questioning has long been a conspicuous feature of primary classrooms, comprising about one-fifth of teachers' utterances (Galton *et al.,* 1980). Teachers ask questions for many purposes – to control behaviour, as well as to seek, test, prompt, and reveal children's ideas. At best, questioning is a powerful strategy for accessing students' science knowledge and promoting learning. Yet there are aspects of the questioning strategy that often work against teaching and learning for understanding. When teachers lapse into what Elstgeest (1985) calls the 'testing reflex', students play the game of figuring out and responding to what they think is in the teacher's head. In passing judgement on the student's response, the teacher reinforces her role as the knowledge authority. This kind of interaction forms part of a three-part pattern of teacher–student dialogue, often referred to as Elicitation, Response and Feedback or ERF (Cazden, 1986; Mehan, 1979). Teachers and students learn this pattern as one of the unwritten and ingrained rules of the game of teaching and learning (Lemke, 1990).

Shapiro (1998) raises several concerns about the ERF pattern of questioning. For example, students who do not possess the necessary language or social skills of answering in group settings may be disadvantaged. The triadic pattern invariably encourages single-word responses from children, limiting opportunities to scaffold knowledge and experiment with scientific language. In this exchange, students' talk is with the teacher rather than with peers. Shapiro (1998) suggests that under the ERF regime, only the boldest students find the courage to ask questions of the teacher or risk putting forward an uninformed thought. This situation fosters a kind of intellectual dependency, with students lacking confidence to promote their ideas or judge the worth of knowledge claims (Munby, 1982).

Altering the asker–answerer relationship (Sarason, 1996) so that students become more responsible for their own learning is an important issue for many educators. Elstgeest (1985), for example, emphasises the advantages of asking challenging questions, where students are encouraged to figure out for themselves how to meet the challenge. Harlen (1992) argues that the most effective form of questions are those which are both open (rather than closed) and person (rather than subject) centred. Person-centred questions are phrased to ask for the student's ideas rather than the 'right' answer. Using the image of 'child as theory builder', Chaille and Britain (1991) argue that children, like scientists, need opportunities to raise and generate answers to questions about the physical and natural world. Harlen (1992) says that predictive questions are useful because they require students to use their own ideas as possible explanations. The aim, according to Baird (1998), is for students to ask evaluative questions of themselves (such as, What am I doing? and Why am I doing it?).

For teachers, schooled in the ERF triadic pattern, it is difficult to break the long-established mechanisms of control (over content and behaviour) which this form of interaction promotes. Changing the patterns of questioning is not only difficult to do (because it takes practice) but risky (because it means letting go). Thus teachers' use of questions is related to the dilemma of holding on to, or letting go of, the classroom controls – with the risks and rewards associated with each course of action. In this chapter, we illustrate this dilemma with a case study written by a researcher Joan Gribble about a teacher, Sue Briggs, and Briggs' experience with a preschool class. The case is called *Attracting learners: is it in the question?* and is followed by comments from Sue Briggs, Paul Black and Sandra Abell.

Attracting learners: is it in the question?
Joan Gribble

The tranquillity of morning spread over the kindergarten centre that I was visiting. Peacefulness was broken only by the working noise of busy preparation as the teacher and her assistant quickly and methodically organised the day's activities in readiness for the arrival of their throng of twenty-seven 5-year-olds. In addition to the cornerstone indoor activities for the day such as block play in the block corner, dramatic play in the home corner and art and craft work at a work bench, with new or additional props, a special science topic centre had been planned for the purpose of introducing the children to magnets and their properties. Part of the planning for the session had been to set up a small designated area with a table displaying bar, horseshoe, round and fridge magnets, paper clips and iron filings. String was attached to the horseshoe magnets so that they could be suspended. Also, a retort stand, with a bar magnet clamped at the top, and a paper clip tied with cotton fixed at the base, was placed with the equipment. The secured paper clip could be raised close to the magnet, but not touching, and held up 'in the air'. The science centre had been neatly and conveniently arranged near the reading area where new books on magnetism were displayed.

Soon the peace of the morning's preparation was disturbed as children, accompanied by their parents, gradually began to drift in to start their learning for the day. The effervescence of excitement floated into the air as children and adults exchanged greetings with one another and as children unpacked their tote bags proclaiming the hidden treasures they had brought with them to school for the News telling session. In due course, the teacher gathered the children together to sit on a mat area for formal greetings and introductions to the day. The events in News telling came and went with some children's treasures being put on display for later inspection. Relative calm descended on the group of eager, shining faces while the teacher explained the options in activities from which they could choose for investigation and exploration. Beside the ongoing activities of block play, dramatic play and art and craft work, the children could decide to participate in some special activities involving cooking biscuits in the kitchen, discovering all about the new computer activity in the math corner or experimenting at the science centre.

Five boys made a bee line to the science centre and delightedly grabbed for the equipment. The play with the equipment was investigatory with the boys' chatter mostly about what they had observed as they turned different pieces of equipment this way and that. When the teacher approached the science centre and began to question the boys about what they were doing they were particularly eager to demonstrate what they had discovered about some of the equipment. The boys' responses reported discoveries such as: 'My magnet can pick up lots of paper clips.' 'My magnet's got more clips on than yours.' 'These round magnets stick together.'

As the teacher acknowledged each boy's report and congratulated them on what they had found, she decided to probe them for further conceptions about magnets and magnetism.

'Why do you think the paper clips stick to the magnets?' she asked.

'Because they are magnets', replied Mark in a wondrous tone expressing his surprise that the teacher couldn't work that one out.

The teacher persisted. 'What do you think makes the magnets attract the paper clips?'

'I think there is glue in the magnet', volunteered Anthony, knowing that another question meant there must be more his teacher was trying to find out. He liked to be helpful.

'What makes you believe that, Anthony?'

Like Mark, Anthony now thought his teacher really needed some help.

'Because they stick', he explained patiently.

'Do you think the magnet is made of glue or another substance, Anthony?'

'Ummm ... That question brought a ponderous look to Anthony's face. Perhaps his teacher did know a thing or two after all.

'It's another substance but I don't know what it is', he conceded.

'I do! I do!' Matthew excitedly cried out as he danced up and down. 'Let me say it. It's metal.'

'Yes, Matthew, that is a good name for the substance in the magnet. What do you think, Anthony?'

'I knew that,' Anthony responded defensively, 'but I couldn't think of the word.'

'Why don't these things stick to the magnet then?' asked the teacher, trying to confirm with the boys what they might know.

'Because they're plastic, of course', replied Matthew with disdain, and the other boys nodded their confirmation.

The teacher then directed the boys' attention to the retort stand and asked, 'What can this magnet do?'

The boys puzzled and talked about what might happen but it was Matthew who lifted the paper clip up towards the magnet. There were gasps of wonder as the boys watched Matthew in awe.

'Look everyone. Look what's happening. The paper clip is spinning around. It's magnetised. It's up in the air', shouted Matthew in a series of commands to the watching boys. He had captured their full attention and they were hanging on his every move and word. His performance equalled that of a magician. There was instant jubilation from Matthew's small audience.

The teacher glanced around the classroom reassuring herself the other children's play was in order and that her assistant was coping with the challenges presented by a group of young chefs cooking biscuits in the kitchen. The parent helper for the day also was coping admirably with the children's art and craft activities. She turned back to the boys working at the science table comforted that everyone was safe for the time being at least.

'Boys, why do you think the paper clip is staying up in the air?' asked the teacher. There was confounded silence from the boys. Matthew, however, was obviously grappling with the phenomenon.

'I don't know ...' Matthew's words wafted into nowhere as he became preoccupied with his own thoughts for a few moments. Suddenly his eyes gleamed with recognition. 'Yes I do ... because the magnet is pulling it up and it's going all around', replied Matthew with satisfaction.

'What is going all around the paper clip, Matthew?' queried the teacher.

'There is magnetic stuff all around the paper clip. It comes from the magnet', responded Matthew.

'Do you mean magnetic force?' probed the teacher.

'Yes the magnet field is all around the paper clip like this', replied Matthew waving his arms in the air in a circular motion. 'The magnet force must be very strong to hold the paper clip up in the air.'

'How do you know about the magnet force of a magnet?' asked the teacher curiously.

'Because I saw a show on the TV', Matthew offered in a matter-of-fact way.

Meanwhile the other boys had become quietly fascinated by the conversation between the teacher and Matthew and showed their willingness to stay with the activity by continuing to suspend the paper clip under the magnet. The teacher realised that the boys needed to be drawn back into the talk and asked:

'Do you think the paper clip will act like a magnet?'

'I don't know', was the consensus.

'Perhaps you can test it with this pin', suggested the teacher.

'That is absolutely amazing,' exclaimed Matthew, 'the pin sticks to the paper clip.'

Once again Matthew was in control of the activity. As the teacher pursued the questioning of Matthew to capture the teachable moment for his learning, the other boys, obviously now lost in the discussion, wandered away to play with different activities.

Other children, this time, three girls, came to play with the magnets while the teacher and Matthew were talking. The teacher suddenly dashed off to rescue a child hammered with a wooden block in the block play area. But, Matthew stayed at the table and began to explain to the girls what he was doing.

'See this paper clip. If you hold it up here, look what happens. Do you know what is going on? Well, I can tell you ... '

The forty-five minutes of free choice activity was drawing to a close and the teacher began to check on who had made a biscuit. Except for Matthew, everyone had their very own made biscuit for morning tea. Thank goodness her assistant had made some extra! The morning coffee break would pass happily.

Teacher commentary

Sue Briggs

One of my beliefs about teaching young children is to listen to them carefully and not make assumptions about what they are trying to tell me. I try not to assume what they do or do not know. Rather, I work on the premise that if I listen carefully and interpret their body language sensitively, I will identify their level of conceptual development much more pointedly. In the reality of classroom practice, this belief is a constant challenge. Some days, when all the best laid plans go astray, or some child needs total attention because some sadness has befallen his or her world, it is so easy to put words into a child's mouth. Sometimes, the lack of time, energy placed into planning or expectations that children in my care will achieve, create a compelling inner desire to achieve my teaching intentions regardless of unexpected events and the feelings and achievements of my children.

A complicating layer in planning and evaluating young children's science learning, especially when children are involved in experiences with non-observable phenomena in physical science, is their grasp of language. My dilemma is finding the level of any developing conceptions and whether their language development impedes or facilitates their thinking. It is often difficult for young children to define the attributes of a concept that is not directly perceptible, such as magnetic force. Even more difficult is my task to first become aware of the level at which the child is operating and then formulate questions, often spontaneously, to capture the learning moment for that child. How to capitalise on the moment when a child 'cottons on' to an idea is critical to the building of his or her new knowledge. Questions, as much as interesting props and materials, are the irresistible lures into learning. I am always thinking of ways to attract children into a learning activity and, once 'hooked', how to find out what they know. Not only do my questions need to probe understanding, but they need to initiate the children's sensory observations and investigations. More, the idea of the occasional bizarre question to bring a touch of the whimsical to these interactions, and observing the children's reactions to such questions, heightens my capacity to define what children are learning and how they are making interpretations of their observations.

Before I began my conversation with the five boys at the science table I had observed their type and level of experimentation, or 'play' as I usually call it, to see what they were doing. All the boys were involved at the tactile level trying to determine what the magnets would do and what types of material they would attract. None of the boys initiated any play with the retort stand. After a few minutes of observation I thought it appropriate to question the boys about what they were doing. Predictably, I had the chorus of responses which recounted their work. Next, my idea was to question them further to define what thoughts each of them had about their investigations. With my initial questioning I tried to give the boys a sense of empowerment in their knowledge. Children always feel confident when they are in the teacher role.

Of course, it soon became evident to me that terminology for some boys, like Anthony, became a stumbling block, although I believe he had the developing notion of the properties of magnetism. It is at these moments that I frantically search for the appropriate, yet non-threatening question, to introduce new language to children. It seemed to me that Anthony would not have heard the word substance before but would understand my question because of the context. It was interesting, of course, to see Matthew respond with the information. I am always overjoyed when a child's peer can adopt the teacher role.

In directing the boys' attention to the retort stand, it enabled Matthew to assume considerable control of the learning situation. This was another of my dilemmas. Matthew is a wonder child, who, for his age, has a store of knowledge about the world that belies his years. I could see that Matthew's friends were happy to observe his experimentation for a considerable time, but, as I commenced questioning him more closely about the depth of his understanding, I could feel the growing lack of interest of the other four boys. Should I sacrifice the teaching moment of one child to the detriment of others?

Questioning techniques can impinge on the emotional status of young children. Even at a young age, many children are well socialised into the approval of giving the correct answer; guessing what is in the adult's head. Taking a risk and guessing wildly or in a considered way about what might be happening during their investigations and experiments, without fear of recrimination from peers or adults, is not always a predominant problem-solving behaviour for many children in my classroom. Risk taking and responding to questions often have to be gently fostered. Questioning of young children needs to encourage their independence in thinking and enable them to risk being wrong with their language and their ideas. As I pressed Matthew further about his understanding of the paper clip on the retort stand I believe the other boys in the group became aware that they did not know the facts and felt coy about their lack of knowledge. More of a tragedy was that they felt inadequate to guess at what might be happening to the paper clip. Thus, they moved away to safer ground.

My work with young children encourages me to be reflective. I am continually reflecting on what children do and say. I ponder about my planning and evaluation and recall my observations about children and the questions I ask them. Teaching to me is a conscious process although I know I carry out much of my practice intuitively.

★   ★   ★

The dilemmas of dialogue

Paul Black, King's College, London

To begin at the end – what did they learn? There are three possible aspects to discuss.

First: That science was interesting, fun

Matthew certainly learnt this – but what about the other boys who were fascinated but then drifted away as Matthew's dialogue with the teacher went beyond them? *It's fun at first, but they soon make it boring* might have been the lesson for them. And did the girls just learn that this is boys' stuff? Attractiveness on its own can be a hostage to fortune. It's the way you build on this – the transition from fascination to thinking – that hits the pot-holes.

Second: Skills in observation and experiment

Things to observe, things to try, opportunities to express, were certainly there, although inevitably cued and curtailed by the pre-prepared materials. However, in this episode, several features – the possibility of suspending the horseshoe magnets, the provision of several different types of magnet, the iron filings, the use of the books – were not taken up.

The teacher channelled work in specific directions – 'What can this magnet do?' 'Perhaps you can test it with this pin?' – these were significant moves by the teacher to direct the thinking. Yet several reported observations, e.g. 'My magnet's got more clips than yours', 'These round magnets stick together', were acknowledged but not taken further: these were not on the teacher's agenda. Later, for the girls, their play with the magnets was overlaid by Matthew's eagerness to pursue his agenda. What does all this teach the children about the purpose of observation?

Third: Concepts of magnetism?

It could be silly to expect 5-year-olds to develop abstract scientific ideas. But modest first aims ought to be attainable, for example:

1   Magnetic influences act across empty space, even with some, not all, materials in the way.
2   Magnets can pull or push things.
3   There are magnets, things are affected by magnets, things which are not affected by them. Things affected by magnets are always attracted, and can become magnets themselves, but usually only while the original magnet is around. Some children might generalise from 'some things' to 'all things made of certain materials'.
4   Magnets can attract or repel one another – depending on which way round they are when brought close together.

The teacher's questions reflect different aims – 'Why … ?' Anthony bravely tries to invent a reason, but the teacher's response is not to ask him or the others to think it through (e.g. 'How could we test this idea?'), rather it conveys to Anthony, through a *reductio ad absurdum* ('Do you think the magnet is made of glue … ?'), that his idea is wrong. The response also gives a clue to the answer the teacher wants ('… or another substance?'). So the response 'metal' is evoked, which Anthony could not think of. What would Anthony feel like at this point? And what lesson would he learn about proposing his own ideas in the future?

There follows a further 'Why' question about non-magnetic materials. It is hard to know what answers could possibly be given, either to this or to the previous 'Why' question, for such answers such as 'Because it is (metal) or (plastic)' are not genuine reasons, they are simply first attempts at empirical generalisation. No reason is possible at this level. A 'Why' question can have value if the children's responses can be followed up and tested by them – but Anthony learnt that this was not the game being played here.

The game here could have been as set out in (1) to (4) above, i.e. to generalise from limited empirical data in order to synthesise and simplify so that empirical predictions can be made. If questions had been framed to lead discussion in this direction, children could have been expected to give reasoned answers, which might have led them to extend their observations.

The next question changed the agenda. 'What can this magnet do?' is a pseudo-question – there are thousands of things that it can do (serve as a doorstop, break a window, and so on). But Matthew is sharp – he guesses what the teacher wants. The dialogue with Matthew then takes off fruitfully – 'magnetic stuff all around' is a remarkable and imaginative attempt to express the idea of a field. The response 'Do you mean magnetic force?' is weak. A field is not a force: the deep conceptual puzzle of the idea of field is that there is a 'something' everywhere around, but there is no force until you put a real thing at a particular point. Matthew's response, both in his use of 'field' before 'force', and his waving his arms around, indicates that he is onto this idea. But the discussion does not develop his insight – it is moved on to a further idea – that the paper clip itself becomes magnetic. Further pursuit of this loses the others, and the discussion becomes Matthew's alone. He is now canonised, and goes on to cut short exploration by the three girls and to introduce them to the transmission mode of teaching.

Reflections

The comments above, and what follows here, must all be qualified. The evidence in a brief description must be incomplete. We do not know the history of this teacher's relationships with these children – if Matthew had been a difficult child and this was the first occasion on which he had opened up, or if Anthony had a history of arrogant presumption which stifled the responses of his peers, then what is presented might be judged differently. Also, we do not know what had preceded this episode, or what the teacher might use from it on the next occasion. What might be seen as missed opportunities could well be the agenda next time.

Reflecting at a distance, with time to read, re-read and think, is all too easy, but the teacher had only a few seconds to respond on the spot. Therefore, it is absolutely essential to think through the rationale for anything that is put before children. In particular, any teacher should anticipate the purposes and possibilities inherent in her particular collection of materials and equipment. What can the children do with it? What questions can it raise? What process or content/concept aims might it help me to pursue with them?

Here we come to the nub of the matter. Between the farce of transmission teaching and the potential desert of so-called discovery learning, this teacher is committed to the only sensible course – guided heurism. The ground is well laid – interesting materials, attractive to the children, freedom for them to choose, teacher intervention to refine, challenge, guide thinking. What appears to be missing are two vital elements. The first element is a clarity of purpose which can reconcile a conceptual analysis (teasing out the potential concepts and skills accessible as the first useful steps in exploring magnetic phenomena) with a theory of learning (which would point to the potential of young children to engage with the ideas and find value in their own capacity to think about the phenomena). In the present case – what can they get out of thinking with magnets in their hands?

The second element is a general strategy about the conduct of the question–answer dialogue. The familiar trap is the 'guess what I am thinking about now?' question; a trap which opens up when the desired response is unrealistic, so that the target can only be reasonably achieved by telling the children the answer. Here one has a simple choice – either abandon the purpose, or just tell them (there's no sin in that – they just won't learn much if you do too much of it). The thing to avoid is the pseudo-question wherein the teacher tries to avoid this choice. The pupils are then baffled, the teacher gives heavy clues, and the bright ones make guesses. This can be deeply corrosive. It teaches children that in science learning you don't have your own thoughts about it, you try to read the teacher's mind and pick up clues; if you can't do this, keep quiet, the answer will come along anyway.

The trap takes another form when a child gives an unanticipated response, one which might seem at first sight to be silly or unproductive, and leading off the path which the teacher had pre-determined for the dialogue. The temptation is to suppress, for there is no time to think out whether the idea will lead anywhere, the fear that the limitations of one's own understanding will become too evident is ever present, and the pre-determined target will not be reached. I suggest two guiding principles – assume that the question is thoughtful and so has to be taken seriously, and be brave to the point of accepting that you might have to admit that you do not know. These are tough principles to live with – but the alternative is to teach children that thoughtful science is a sham, and that the aim of observation and experiment in science is to get the right answer. Sadly, the evidence is that the majority of children do learn these negative lessons, and seem to carry them through their school careers and beyond.

★   ★   ★

Placing the 'What if?' before the 'Why?'

Sandra K. Abell, University of Missouri-Columbia

Young children are naturally inquisitive. They love to mess around with stuff. Cooking, hammering, writing, shovelling, making music, drawing and building are intrinsically motivating activities for them. They love to hear new words. How often have you heard a multisyllabic dinosaur name glide out of the mouth of a preschooler? They are attracted to interesting facts. 'Did you know that the sun jellyfish is the world's longest animal?' a 5-year-old excitedly asks. They notice patterns in their world. My 4-year-old son states confidently, 'That moon is getting bigger every day.' They even make predictions and invent explanations to account for their observations. 'That toy is gonna sink because it's too heavy.' It appears that the preschooler is every teacher's ideal science learner – interested, enthusiastic, curious, thoughtful. Why do these traits seem to diminish each year a child is in school, until by secondary school we see so many students uninterested and bored with science?

The other day we had a dinner party at our house. Seven children, ages 4–15, as well as their parents, were in attendance. For most of the evening the children interacted by age groups, finding things to do that interested them apart from the adults. But towards the end of the evening, something quite surprising occurred. Someone noticed an old physics demonstration apparatus high on a shelf and inquired, 'What's that?' The apparatus consists of a row of four open glass tubes of different volumes and shapes (straight, zigzag, hour glass, and curvy) connected at the base to each other through a horizontal tube hidden behind a metal bar. The apparatus is used to demonstrate that water level is dependent on air pressure, not on the shape or volume of the tube. Since the air pressure on each tube is the same, when one of the tubes is filled with water, the water flows into the bottom connecting tube and up into the other tubes to the same level simultaneously.

Recognising the teachable moment, I pulled the apparatus off the shelf and explained that the tubes were all connected at the bottom, and that water could be poured into one of the tubes. Before I had a chance to ask my first question, all seven children, not to mention all of the adults, had gathered around, curious about the apparatus. At this point I had a decision to make. Would I demonstrate the apparatus by adding water and then ask the inevitable 'why' question? Or would I ask for predictions and see where we went from there? I opted to take the second path. 'What do you think will happen when I add water to this tube?' I asked, pointing to the straight test-tube-like glass on one end. Each child, from age 4 to 15, had a prediction. Some predictions came complete with reasoning. 'The water will go up faster in the skinnier tube because it will take less water', said one. 'They'll go up one at a time, and the one closest to the straight tube will fill up first since it's

closest to the water', predicted another. 'I don't think there will be any difference', commented a third. I added the water and watched the children's faces.
Eyebrows raised, mouths opened, hands raised in the air. Before I had a chance
to ask another question, one of the adult observers stepped in. 'What would
happen if I sealed off one of the tubes?' he asked. More predictions followed.
We tested the apparatus by placing a finger on the end of one tube before
pouring into another. Other 'what if' questions and tests readily followed.
'What if we start pouring into a different tube?' 'What if we keep pouring
until it overflows?' Finally one of the children asked her own 'why' question.
'What's going on?' she queried, to no one in particular. We did not solve the
problem of the tubes and water that night, although when the children went
back to their play, the adults proffered their own theories to explain what they
had seen. My guess is that the children also were inventing explanations for
what they had seen, although at that point they did not articulate them.

I was left wondering how the activity would have changed had I chosen
my first path and started with the 'why' question. I realised that choosing the
prediction path had opened the floor to each observer, not only to the older
or the more sophisticated of the boys. Furthermore, the prediction path had
opened the floor to new 'what if' questions from the children themselves. Yet
even with all of the questioning, predicting and testing, we still came back to
the 'why' question in the form of one girl's 'What's going on?' I was
convinced I had chosen the most productive questioning path.

This brings me back to my earlier question about why students don't retain
their natural curiosity and motivation for learning science. Could part of the
answer relate to a teacher's questioning paths? How do those questioning paths
come about? How do teachers make decisions about which path to take?

Over the past thirty years many science educators have asserted that a
teacher's questions do make a difference. I am in good company when I assert,
then, that the questioning *path* a teacher chooses leads to specific student
outcomes. This questioning path is not only about the types of questions that
are asked, but also about the sequence of asking and about who does the
asking. For example, in the tubes and water example, 'what if' questions came
first, followed much later by the 'why' question. Moreover the children themselves were engaged in raising questions as well as answering them.

If we re-examine the preschool classroom that Joan Gribble has written
about, we find that the teacher's first question to her students was the 'why'
question, 'Why do you think the paper clips stick to the magnets?' Why did
she feel compelled to begin with the 'why' question? Her question seems
incompatible with the exploratory nature of the magnet centre she had
designed. And why did she persist in following this 'why' questioning path to
the exclusion of asking 'what if' or other types of questions that would have
helped students focus their actions on the objects and help them generate
new questions of their own? First of all, let us not be too hard on the teacher.
She designed an exploratory centre for the children that was rich with possi-

bilities for age-appropriate activity. The children had opportunities to observe the effects of their actions on objects, and to produce various results with various actions. The reactions of the objects were immediate and observable. And the children had opportunities for social interaction as they interacted with the objects. All of these are important criteria for preschool science (Harlen, 1985). However, the teacher's interaction with the children seemed to momentarily block their actions and their thinking.

If this teacher is like many teachers of young children, it is reasonable to expect that her own science background is limited. Furthermore, it is reasonable to expect that the formal science education that she experienced, like most, focused narrowly on the products of science (facts and information), rather than on broader notions of science as inquiry. I have found in my own research into teacher beliefs about science teaching and learning that teachers of young children often face a dilemma in their beliefs (Abell et al., 1998). They envision themselves making science accessible to all children via experiences with science phenomena and science talk. They design activities that begin much like the magnet exploration in this classroom. However, their school science experiences have led them to also believe that it is a teacher's responsibility to make sure all children take away the products of science from the lesson. Thus they often reach closure on science activity by expecting or presenting the scientific explanation. I think it is this products-of-science perspective that influences the proliferation of questioning paths which start with and emphasise 'why' questions in our science classrooms. That and the fact that the 'what if' path is much riskier because a teacher can't easily predict where the path will lead.

What can we do about this situation? The topic of teacher questions is addressed in most textbooks that are used to teach future teachers of science. Are question types too simplistic? Maybe we need to develop instead a variety of questioning *paths* that might work in different science teaching and learning situations. Not that we would teach teachers the paths and which situations to use them, in a sort of a rule-applying approach to science teaching. Not at all. Much like we want our science students to be in control of their own science learning, as Matthew was at the end of the magnets story, we should also desire that teachers be in control of their own learning about science teaching. Perhaps if teachers analyse the questioning paths they take and the resultant classroom outcomes, they can begin to develop teaching strategies that are most compatible with their instructional goals. Concomitantly, through their analysis teachers may uncover discrepancies in their own thinking about science teaching and learning that lead to changes in their practice.

★   ★   ★

Editors' synthesis

Abell's reading of this story is that teachers of young children often face a dilemma in choosing between activities that open up or those that close down scientific explanations. While teachers design activities to open up exploration of scientific phenomena and encourage science talk, they often feel the pressure to seek closure on a science activity by expecting a scientific explanation. Briggs, the teacher in the story, says that she often experiences this pressure as 'a compelling inner desire to achieve [her] teaching intentions'. In Abell's words, it is the 'products-of-science perspective that influences the proliferation of questioning paths which start with and emphasise "why" questions in our science classrooms'. Abell's reading provides an interesting way of examining the questioning dilemma and of understanding the reason for Briggs' actions.

This dilemma is well illustrated in the interaction between the teacher in the story and her student, Matthew. Black's analysis is that the teacher's questions consisted of a combination of why questions (where Matthew was invited to guess an answer), absurd questions (where the teacher's proposal was clearly wrong) and pseudo-questions (where the meaning of the question was ambiguous). All three commentators suggest that the interaction was unsatisfactory from several perspectives. First, it reinforced the authority of the teacher as the source of knowledge about magnetism. Secondly, it canonised Matthew among his peers as a person who was able to converse with the teacher on scientific matters. But, importantly, it failed to advance Matthew's understanding of the phenomenon or his responsibility for his own learning.

Briggs describes questions as part of 'the irresistible lures into learning'. All three commentators suggest that effective questioning requires a clear understanding about the purpose of the activity and the line of questioning. According to Abell, the questioning path a teacher chooses leads to specific kinds of student outcomes. 'What if' questions, for example, help students focus their actions on the objects and help them generate new questions of their own. 'Why' questions can be useful but they often lead the teacher into what Black calls a trap – deciding what to do when the student comes up with an unrealistic or unanticipated response. Black's advice for the teacher is simple – either tell the student the answer or admit that you do not know. Either way, the teacher needs to assume that the student's response is thoughtful and to be taken seriously. In Briggs' words, students' responses need to be 'gently fostered'.

Reflecting on the wisdom of a particular course of action after the event is relatively easy. Making snap decisions about what to say in the moment of an interaction is far more difficult. As Briggs points out in her commentary, decisions about what to say are enormously complicated. Levels of language, conceptual development and readiness for learning vary considerably from one student to another. Balancing the needs of one student against another provides an additional layer of difficulty. In picking her way through the strategy of what Black calls 'guided heurism', the teacher is faced with the ever-present dilemma of when to allow students to discover things for themselves and when to provide guidance. Deciding what to do, and when, is a matter of careful planning and astute professional judgement.

References

Abell, S. K., Bryan, L. A. and Anderson, M. A. (1998). Investigating preservice elementary science teacher reflective thinking using integrated media case-based instruction in elementary science teacher preparation. *Science Education*, 82 (4), 491–510.

Baird, J. R. (1998). A view of quality in teaching. In B. J. Fraser and K. G. Tobin (eds), *International handbook of science education* (pp. 153–167). Dordrecht, The Netherlands: Kluwer.

Cazden, C. (1986). Classroom discourse. In M. Whittrock (ed.), *Handbook of research on teaching* (pp. 432–463). New York: Macmillan.

Chaille, C. and Britain, L. (1991). The child as theory builder. In C. Chaille and L. Britain (eds), *The young child as scientist: A constructivist approach to early childhood science education* (pp. 3–17). New York: HarperCollins.

Elstgeest, J. (1985). The right question at the right time. In W. Harlen (ed.), *Primary science: Taking the plunge*. London: Heinemann.

Galton, M. J., Simon, B. and Croll, P. (1980). *Inside the primary classroom*. London: Routledge & Kegan Paul.

Harlen, W. (1985). *Teaching and learning primary science*. New York: Teachers College Press.

—— (1992). *The teaching of science*. London: David Fulton Publishers.

Lemke, J. (1990). *Talking science: Language, learning and values*. Norwood, NJ: Ablex Publishing.

Mehan, H. (1979). *Learning lessons: Social organisation in the classroom*. Cambridge, MA: Harvard University Press.

Munby, H. (1982). *What is scientific thinking?* Ottawa: Science Council of Canada.

Sarason, S. B. (1996). *Revisiting the culture of the school and the problem of change*. New York: Teachers College Press.

Shapiro, B. (1998). Reading the furniture: The semiotic interpretation of science learning environments. In B. J. Fraser and K. G. Tobin (eds), *International handbook of science education* (pp. 609–621). Dordrecht, The Netherlands: Kluwer.

Chapter 11

Analogies

*Contributions by Grady Venville, Lyn Bryer,
Brent Kilbourn and John K. Gilbert*

Editors' introduction

Analogies form part of a family of creative devices — including similes,
metaphors and models — used by scientists and teachers to convey explanations, arguments and questions about science. The basis of the analogy is that
it enables unfamiliar concepts to be understood by comparing them with
familiar objects. It is this feature which makes analogy central to the understanding of science and understanding in science. As Robert Oppenheimer
(1956) observed:

> Analogy is indeed an indispensable and inevitable tool for scientific
> progress. ... We come to new things in science with what equipment we
> have, which is how we have learned to think, and above all, how we have
> learned to think about the relatedness of things. We cannot, coming into
> something new, deal with it except on the basis of the familiar and the
> old fashioned.
>
> (Oppenheimer, 1956, p. 129)

In recent years, there has been a considerable effort in the science education
community to understand how analogies are used in the science classroom to
convey meaning. Much of this effort has focused on better ways of matching the
analogy with the scientific reality or the target. This approach suggests that it is
incumbent on the teacher to select an analogy with the closest fit to the target
(Gentner and Gentner, 1983). Where the analogy does fit the target, the teacher
should take care to map out the similarities and differences between the analog
and target (Glynn, 1991; Treagust, 1995). Others (Gentner, 1983, 1988; Thagard,
1992; Zook, 1991) point out the advantages of students developing their own
analogies to describe and explain scientific phenomena, although this process is
expensive in terms of time. Gentner (1983) argues that only deep systematic
analog mapping enhances understanding.

While this work has done much to highlight the importance of analogy in
science teaching, there is still a poor understanding of the relationship
between analogy and science. According to Gilbert and his colleagues

(Association for Science Education, 1994), science is the development of theories explained by models which have analogical origins. The analogy therefore serves the purpose of conveying a particular meaning and simplifying the theory to the point of being understood by the proponent of the analogy. Over time, this simplification enters into the language as fact (Sutton, 1993) and the historical origins of the analogy get lost in history. The result is that both teachers and students often believe that analogies are simple copies of reality (Grosslight *et al.*, 1991).

So there appears to be a paradox in the use of analogies to understand science. On the one hand, we need to understand that analogies are not reality, that they are only representations and inventions and are, by definition, flawed. On the other hand, analogies are the *only* way we have of representing science; they provide a common basis of language and understanding so that learning can progress. As Sutton (1993, p. 1,223) puts it, 'As a learner, one has to know the right labels.' Von Glasersfeld (1983) uses a similar line of argument: 'So the paradox is that in order to find out if our understanding is "true" we would have to know what we were trying to understand before understanding it' (von Glasersfeld, 1983, in Solomon, 1994, p. 14).

In this chapter we illustrate this paradox with a case study written collaboratively by a researcher, Grady Venville, and a teacher, Lyn Bryer, about Bryer's attempts to use the analogy of the city to teach the concept of cell structure. Venville worked with Bryer to capture the events in Bryer's voice. The case is called *A sanitary problem* and it is followed by comments from Grady Venville and Lyn Bryer, Brent Kilbourn and John Gilbert.

A sanitary problem

Grady Venville and Lyn Bryer

I find teaching Grade 8 students about the organelles of a cell really difficult. You can have a bit of fun with microscopes but when it comes down to the functions of the organelles it's all so abstract. What I wanted to do was to make it more concrete for the class. I didn't have enough time to devote to the construction of models this year, so one of my colleagues suggested I try an activity where the students make up an analogy between a city and a cell. The way a cell functions as an integrated unit with different subunits performing different functions can be compared with the way a city functions. Comparisons can be made between the nucleus of a cell that controls the activities occurring in the cell and the city council. Ribosomes, the structures in a cell that construct proteins, can be compared with building sites, and mitochondria are like power stations because that is where the energy for the cell is produced. Many other similarities exist and the analogy can be extended as far as the students' ability and creative energy permits. It sounded like an interesting activity and being the kind of person who likes to try new things I decided to give it a go.

It was an early morning lesson, so the students were fresh and cooperative. We had completed a microscope laboratory lesson the previous day and the students had been asked to read their textbook for homework and make a list of the organelles in a cell and their functions. I started the lesson with a discussion about the city of Fremantle, where our school is situated, so the students would start to think about the various functions parts of the city perform. We talked about the transport system including roads and railways, the city council and how it has control over the buildings in the city, the local power station, and various other parts of the city. I tried to emphasise the idea that the city functions as an integrated unit with each part of the city having an individual job to do. The students were animated and lively and participated with enthusiasm.

After the discussion I asked the students to work in groups and discuss among themselves the similarities between the functions of various parts of a city and the functions of different parts of a cell. Each group was given a large piece of paper and they were to make up a table with the organelles of a cell down the left-hand side, the parts of a city which they thought were similar on the right-hand side and the reason why they were similar written in the middle. I circulated around the class and the group activity seemed to go really well with the students working on the task, discussing, sometimes disagreeing, making all sorts of suggestions, laughing and then coming to a consensus and making up the table. At the conclusion of the activity one member of each group stood up and displayed their table and explained to the rest of the class the reasoning behind the comparisons they had made. Some were pretty creative, but from my point of view, most were plausible.

I had a home period next lesson and as I have a Grade 8 home room I was able to talk to a few of the students from my Grade 8 science class about the activity they had just completed. The first student I talked to, Pia, seemed to have a pretty good understanding of the functions of the organelles. For example, she knew the mitochondria are like power stations because they supply energy to the cell for its activities and she knew the nucleus is like a city council because of its control function. I asked her, 'Do you think this activity helped you to learn about the cell?'

'Yeah, I think it made it a little better because I sort of remembered more of the things compared to a city. But it confused me a bit because I forget what the cell's parts really do when I compare them together. I just like to talk about the real science. I think it would be easier for me just to remember what the cell's parts do than compare them with the city', Pia replied. Initially she thought the analogy helped her to remember the parts of a cell and their functions, then on second thoughts, she felt the analogy was confusing and made her forget the 'real science'.

I wasn't quite sure what she meant by her answer so I asked her, 'What's the difference between what the parts of a city do and what the parts of a cell do?'

'Well, the power station makes power for the city, which is electricity, and the mitochondria make power for the cell, but it isn't electricity. I'd rather just think about what the mitochondria do than think about the power station first and then the mitochondria, it's too confusing', Pia argued.

'But once you can remember what mitochondria do you're not supposed to think about the power station anymore. It's just an activity to help you picture the situation in the first place', I defended.

'Yes, I see, that's why I said I think it helped me in the first place, but I wasn't sure whether we were supposed to think about the city all the time', Pia said.

Joe, another student I talked to, really seemed to find the activity helpful. He was still having problems with the terminology of the cell's organelles, but that's not surprising at Grade 8 level. I asked him to tell me about some of the parts of a cell that he had learnt about that day.

'Well, there's this part in the cell which supplies energy to do all the things it does, we compared that to the power station. I can't remember what it's called though, the matrodania or something. And there is a part of the cell which helps build up structure just like building sites in a city, and the nucleus controls all the activities in the cell', Joe explained.

'Did you find doing the activity about the city useful in helping you understand the cell?' I asked Joe.

'Well, it's a lot easier. We learn about the city council where we live and I know about the things that happen in a city, but you don't hear "nucleus" or any of those other words. I didn't know about what's in a cell, but I understand about the things in a city and that helped me understand how a cell works', Joe said.

Lara was the third student I talked to and I just didn't know what to make of what she said. She seemed to have a preoccupation with sanitation! She said the analogy was really helpful to her because 'I've lived in a city for a while now, and I didn't know about the cell'. When I asked her about the functions of the organelles Lara astonished me by confidently saying that the nucleus cleans out the wastes from the other parts of the cell, that the mitochondria form the garbage and the endoplasmic reticulum is the sewage. I really couldn't understand why she thought everything in the cell had to do with sanitation so I asked her what they had compared the nucleus to in her group. She said it was like the city council, so I asked her what she thought the city council does in the city of Fremantle.

'It takes the rubbish from the houses', she replied.

'Ok, can you explain that to me?' I probed a little further.

'Well it just sort of cleans up the place, different areas need cleaning like the roads and parks and stuff', Lara explained.

'What other things do you think the city council does, Lara?' I asked as a last resort.

'Oh, they have a big rubbish day once a month.'

So I guess even though I had discussed the city council and the controlling function it has at the beginning of the lesson, in Lara's experience all the city council does is take away the rubbish.

So the analogy was reasonably helpful to two students, but downright misleading to the third student I had talked to. I was left with the decision of whether to use the activity again next year or whether to abandon it all together. The experience also left me with a deeper concern about the many other analogies and group activities I use in my science lessons.

Commentary

Grady Venville and Lyn Bryer

Two things really disturbed me after this experience. One was the use of the analogy and the contrasting effect it had on the students' learning and the other was the group work and how the efforts of the group may conceal an individual's progress.

Joe clearly benefited from the use of the analogy. He had no idea of the way a cell functioned previously and at the end of the lesson it seems he had a clear notion of the cell as an integrated unit with individual parts performing different functions. Even though Joe was unsure of the terminology, he was successfully able to transfer appropriate process ideas he had about the concept of a city to the concept of a cell. This is what I had assumed the lesson would do for students. Pia too found the analogy useful, but was confused about the object of the lesson. She was unsure about whether she had to remember the analogy as well as the science content and this clearly shows she is inexperienced and unfamiliar with the use of analogy as a teaching/learning strategy. Of course she didn't have to remember the analogy once she had good understanding of the cell concept. It is simply a way of creating a picture, or giving an advanced organiser to the students from where they can further develop their concept of a cell. Perhaps I should have been more explicit about my use of the analogy in the teaching process and made it clearer that using an analogy is just one way of understanding something difficult to comprehend. Perhaps it is too much to assume that students can use analogies appropriately and know why teachers use them.

For Lara the analogy was an absolute disaster. Lara's limited prior experience of a city council, that it simply takes away the rubbish, was all pervading and clearly dominated her subsequent ideas about the organelles of a cell. Even though I had carefully discussed the different roles that different parts of a city have early in the lesson, the rubbish-collecting image had dominated Lara's thinking to the point where her ideas had been inappropriately transferred to the cell through the use of the analogy. Through my teaching I had probably created a misconception in Lara's mind.

This analogy has certainly shown to be a double-edged sword. A clear thrust forward for one student and a nasty stab in the back for another. Would such a situation have happened no matter what teaching strategy I had used? No matter what you do, you would expect some students would learn less than others, but Lara wasn't a particularly weak student, so the fact the analogy really misled her is of great concern to me. On the other hand, for Joe the analogy was very useful. I still haven't decided whether to use the analogy again next year. Maybe I should and then interview all the students at the end of the lesson. If only I had the time!

The other thing that concerned me was that previously I had assumed the lesson had gone really well. The groups had worked well together and the group leaders had made presentations with plausible similarities between the city parts and the cell organelles. This indicated the students seemed to have clearly understood the functions of the organelles. It wasn't until I sat down on a one-to-one basis with Lara that I realised the problems it had caused for her. The group work had masked her misconceptions which persisted even though the group as a whole had come to different conclusions. The group work had done nothing to enrich her experience and develop her ideas of a cell.

★   ★   ★

Focusing on matrodania

Brent Kilbourn, Ontario Institute for Studies in Education/University of Toronto

This is an interesting and thought-provoking story. It avoids tedious detail that would render it lightly skimmed or unread. Brevity and craft carry a reader effortlessly to the end which has a delightful touch of sanitary levity. But brevity has a price, a point implicit in my comments and one to which I'll return at the end. My initial thoughts are about analogies.

Pedagogical analogies are, in a sense, half-truths. They illuminate some parts and shade others. The pedagogical power of an analogy comes from its familiarity and its degree of correspondence to the phenomenon to be understood. Normally an analogy is better understood than the phenomenon it illuminates. The usefulness of an analogy comes from its simplicity – helpful analogies tend to be less complex than the phenomena they are meant to depict. Careful painting and quick sketching represent two pedagogical approaches to using analogies. Sometimes the usefulness of an analogy lies in carefully painting the detailed parallels between it and a phenomenon to show texture and highlight subtleties – learning comes from methodically painted comparison. Other times the usefulness of an analogy lies in quick sketching to move towards understanding a phenomenon in its own terms – quick sketches, quickly discarded if unhelpful. The degree to which an analogy sheds light depends, then, on the demands of the learning situation and whether the analogy is quickly sketched or carefully painted. It also depends on who the analogy is for; in a typical classroom the same analogy will likely be helpful for some students but confusing for others.

Maybe cities are as complex as cells, or vice-versa. Perhaps painting detailed parallels between cities and cells will not always work well with some students to help them learn about the functions of cell organelles. Although most Grade 8 students are more familiar with cities than with cells, they may understand how a city functions no better than how a cell functions, unless they have studied the structure and function of city parts, as has Joe. Alternatively, it is possible that for some students the analogy is less central in shedding light than is the duration and challenge of the activity itself. Some students might understand more about organelles simply because they spent more time attending to them. The analogy itself may play an incidental role. The extent to which these kinds of observations are true likely varies from student to student and is open to empirical inquiry, a process the teacher has already begun.

Pia found the analogy initially helpful, but then a bit confusing, and she was not clear as to whether she should have been working as hard to understand a city as she was to understand a cell. Perhaps for Pia the nature and duration of the activity was out of proportion to the pedagogical function the analogy was meant to serve. It is not entirely clear how much Joe knows about the cell, but whatever he does know seems to have come through his studied understanding of cities. Joe thought the analogy helped, but on balance I wonder if his understanding of the city was illuminated while cell organelles remained safely out of direct light. Lara is an interesting case. From one view, the analogy was not useful since she came away misinformed about the functions of specific parts of the cell. From another view, Lara herself thought the analogy was helpful, and it could be argued that her imperfect, sanitary understanding of the city did move her incrementally forward. She now understands that the nucleus is important to a cell, just as the council is important to a city. When Lara said 'I've lived in the city for a while now', I fantasised that she had moved from the country to a new, unfinished subdivision and that her parents had made persistent phone calls about sewage problems and garbage pick-up, an interpretation that reinforces the idea that students will construct meaning with whatever materials are at hand. But as suggested, the truth of these interpretations are matters for empirical inquiry.

The teacher's pursuit of Pia, Joe, and Lara about the analogy is significant. It struck me how seldom as teachers we simply ask students about the usefulness of the pedagogical moves that we make and, when we do, how powerful that experience can be. It also reminded me of how the press of classroom life can divert attention from monitoring students' understanding and how, over time, the issue can almost fade from view. It has not faded from view for Lara's teacher. The observations (it worked for some, not for others) and the questions (Is this analogy pedagogically useful? Should students be using it in a group setting?) the teacher raises are important. These questions initiate a form of personal, professional inquiry that over time will add to pedagogical understanding; further insight will be gained as to in what circumstances the analogy has merit, what kind of context to provide, what kind of discussion to foster, what kind of follow-up to pursue, and what kind of self-monitoring to engage in. Such inquiry can be more or less formal, and its significance derives from the self-monitoring attitude towards teaching and learning that it fosters.

What form of classroom data would be relevant to inquiry of this nature, how could they be collected, how might they be framed, and what questions might be asked of them? With respect to overall form, details are important because the elements of understanding and misunderstanding in learning lie in the details and patterns of what is said and done, just as with other forms of human interaction. In the present case, three areas seem critical: First, there are details that relate to whatever talk the teacher has with the class as a whole before they begin the group activity. Pia 'wasn't sure whether we were supposed to think about the city all the time'. Her puzzlement suggests why it would be important to know exactly what was said and done in setting up the exercise. How, precisely, was the analogy of the city introduced? Not generally, but precisely. What exactly was said? What terms were used? Was the city analogy talked about as a way of learning? Were there opportunities for questions? Second, as the teacher suggests, it would be important to know what went on in each of the groups. What exactly was said and by whom? Who participated and who did not. Who dominated? What patterns seemed to be established? Did Joe lead his group and harp on the power station? Did his group come away from the activity mainly understanding how cities function? Third, it would be important to have data on how the exercise was brought to a close. What kinds of connections were made at the end, in what way, and who made them? The tentative answers to all of these kinds of questions, while not carved in stone, will suggest various moves that a teacher may make to increase the likelihood that an analogy will be helpful for learning. As to framing, it would be important to look for patterns among the details, especially those concerning the meaning and conceptual continuity of what is said and done by teacher and students against the backdrop of the task at hand; what patterns seemed to contribute to learning about cell organelles and what ones did not?

Answers to questions of whether and how to use the city analogy, or any pedagogical analogy, are seldom crystal clear. The picture drawn by the patterns and details of teaching and learning will not by themselves answer the questions because the process of inquiry ultimately involves a teacher's professional judgement about where to draw the pedagogical line. Inevitably the decision of what to do will involve the aesthetics of teaching, questions of balance and proportion. For instance, from numerous possibilities in the present story, the patterns and details revealed by inquiry might indicate that the analogy is useful so long as the teacher is clear about its function and promotes discussion among students about the nature of analogies as tools for learning. But it is a matter of professional judgement as to how much of that discussion is useful if the primary intent is for students to learn about the functions of cell organelles rather than the functions of analogies. Well-intended discussion could grow out of proportion to its value, as one interpretation of Pia's remarks intimates. The important questions concern on what occasions the analogy seems to be useful, whether it should be painted or sketched, and what sort of conversation between teacher and students should accompany it.

Let me return to initial observations. There is a degree of irony in a story like this, at least as it relates to how the questions the teacher poses at the end are to be addressed. Telling a story to provoke inquiry and telling a story to inquire are different things. Inquiry needs an exploratory phase in which too many details may prematurely channel thinking about a case, and a brief story serves well to open up possible courses to pursue. Brevity serves less well in the pursuit itself. The very detail called for in an actual inquiry usually must be omitted if a story is to capture our attention and provoke inquiry.

★   ★   ★

Consensus models and teaching models

John K. Gilbert, University of Reading

The problem with trying to help students understand a consensus model (one that is accepted by the scientific community) by providing them with a teaching model (one specially designed to do so) is how to do so appropriately, i.e. so that their future understanding of the subject is not inhibited (Gilbert *et al.*, 1998). The criteria for a good teaching model are well established. It must: address a real need, in that the consensus model is difficult to understand; be based on a source which is familiar to the students; contain major features which approximately match in numbers those of the consensus model; have a high degree of similarity to the consensus model (Treagust *et al.*, 1992). Applying those criteria in a particular case is more difficult! The components of a chosen source may be divided into the objects (or elements which may be treated as if they were objects) of which it is composed and the structural relations (temporal, spatial, causal) between those objects. A teaching model of high access to students (one which they can readily use) will place an emphasis on the analogy between objects, whilst one of high inferential power (one which can provide causal explanations) will place an emphasis on the analogy of structural relations (Gentner, 1988). The balance will be decided upon by considering the purpose(s) for which the teaching model is to be used and the achievements and expectations of the students (Holyoak and Thagard, 1995).

Developing a teaching model for the eukaryotic cell poses a great challenge. First, it must relate to a consensus model of an hypothetical general cell, so that the future consideration of specialist cells is not hindered. Second, the level of detail given about the objects of which the cell is composed and the relations between them will have to be carefully gauged in order to be appropriate to the needs of the students. For example, the phases of mitosis and the factors which control the interphase period are clearly not needed at Grade 8 level. 'The cell' crops up at every turn of the biology syllabus up to graduate

Table 11.1   The teaching model 'The cell is like a city'

Cell component	Functions of cell components	Analogy with city
cell wall and membrane	protective boundary, exchange with environment	city limits
nucleus	envelope of sub-structures containing chromosomes (overall control), ribosomes (protein synthesis), nucleoplasm (organisation)	city council, building sites, city administration
endoplasmic reticulum	synthesis of proteins, liquids, steroids	manufacturing industries
mitochondria	production of convenient form of energy (ATP)	power station
chloroplasts	storage of light energy in carbohydrates	?
golgi apparatus	protein modification and distribution	service industry
lysosomes	digestion, waste discharge	sewage pipes
vacuoles	storage of waste, water, salts, sugars	sewage plant, reservoir, food depots
vesiles	transport of materials	roads, railways

level: a prematurely sophisticated treatment has to be avoided. A teaching model based on the 'positive aspects of the analogy' (those aspects which map across, to any extent) (Hesse, 1966) of 'the cell is like a city' is given in Table 11.1.

The analogies for lysosomes, vacuoles, vesiles, ribosomes and mitochondria might be readily understood by Grade 8 students. They might reasonably be expected to know what the source objects are, what their functions are, and how they relate to each other in the life of the city. Those for the endoplasmic reticulum and the golgi complex will be appreciated if some economic geography has been studied. However, those for the chromosomes and the nucleoplasm are inherently rather abstract: students may have little appreciation of the objects themselves, let alone their functional interdependence and structural relations. Almost nobody, in any community, knows where the city limits are! The notion of a chloroplast (assuming that it is to be included in the general consensus model) cannot, I think, be addressed within the city-based teaching model. Does this mean that the city is like an animal rather than a plant?

There are, of course, some aspects of the source which do not map onto the target (e.g. the different groupings of people within the city, the public parks). These are examples of what Hesse (1966) called 'the negative aspects of the analogy'. Hesse (1966) also referred to 'neutral aspects of the analogy': those aspects of the source whose significance for the target were not clear. For example, how significant is the weather that the city experiences, or the nature of the environment outside the city limits?

The key issue is: what purposes was the teacher addressing in introducing this model? Students were certainly expected to get to know the names of the organelles. This learning had been begun by the use of the textbook, where sketches and photographs of a cell would have been included, and was continued when those names were matched to objects experienced in the microscope work. This latter seems to have been largely what Hodson (1993) called 'learning science' (acquiring theoretical knowledge), with only a little 'learning about science' (understanding the nature and methods of science) or 'doing science' (developing expertise in scientific enquiry). The emphases were on providing an *intentional* explanation, where the phenomenon of 'cell' is isolated from the continuum of nature and named for a specific purpose, and on providing an *interpretative* explanation, where the objects of which a cell is composed were identified and their spatial distribution explored (Gilbert *et al.*, 1998).

The use of group work, built around an exploration of 'the cell is like a city' analogy, offered opportunities for students to develop *causal* explanations. Criteria for good practice in the conduct of group work are known, both in general (Jacques, 1984) and in science education (Bentley and Watts, 1989). The structural and functional relations of the component objects within a cell were identified by discussing individuals' understandings of the source of the model. At the end of the group session, an activity to pool and evaluate the collective understandings achieved is usually included. The overall success of group work does depend on the clarity of the instructions given by the teacher at the start, the nature of the prior experiences of the source found among the students, their skills of working together in the group(s), and the teacher's skills of debriefing the class at the end of the activity.

The interviews conducted after the group session show the value that teacher research can add to the educational process. In this case, the full spectrum of problems in understanding the nature of the objects within the source of the model (the city) and their structural relations, in understanding the nature of the objects within the target of the model (the cell) and their structural relations, and in understanding the scope and limitations of the possible analogies between the two sets, are all evident. Pia demonstrated a good understanding of the objects and their relations within the source (the city). She was able to analogically transfer some of the objects within the city to the cell. However, she was unable to develop the structural relations within the cell. It seems likely that she could have, with help, taken that last, crucial, step. Joe also demonstrated a good understanding of the objects and their structural relations within the city. However, he made an incomplete transfer of the objects within the city to the objects within the cell, and hence was further away than Pia from being able to understand the structural relations within the cell. Lara had a very incomplete understanding of the objects and structural relations within the city. She gave a highly incomplete transfer of objects from the city to the cell. She also had no real appreciation of the relations within the cell. In short, she made little progress. These three cases demonstrate the two criteria that must be met if extended analogies are to be drawn. First, the students must be fully conversant with the nature of the objects and the structural relations within the source. It does seem worthwhile spending time on this set of issues alone. Second, students need to be explicitly taught the rules for drawing an analogy.

However, one must never forget that teaching models are only used to aid understanding of a consensus model. Indeed, there is virtue in using several such, so as to be able to address specific aspects of the target. The nightmare scenario is that students remember the teaching models and never use the consensus model *per se*.

★   ★   ★

Editors' synthesis

The use of the analogy of the city and the cell, which Venville and Bryer refer to as a double-edged sword and Kilbourn describes as a half-truth, leads to a dilemma for the teacher. Should she persist with an analogy which is unhelpful or insufficient for some of her students, or should she seek some other explanation that is more closely aligned to the students' experience? As Kilbourn points out, the disadvantage of developing the analogy (what he calls 'careful painting') is that the details of the analogy are less likely to match the details of the cell. On the other hand it is difficult if not impossible to find an analogy that matches the experience of all students. As this case illustrates, students have quite different understandings of the nature of a city (as they would have if the teacher had chosen an alternative analogy such as a factory or a shopping centre).

Gilbert's account adds to the complexity of this dilemma by pointing out that the phenomenon itself (in this case the cell) comes in different shapes and sizes. So the teacher's task of trying to match a variable phenomenon with a class of students with a variety of experiences, by using a single (static) analogy is an additional challenge. As Gilbert suggests, this challenge may be made more achievable by two strategies. One strategy is to probe more deeply into students' experience and increase their understanding of the analog. The second is to help students understand the status of the analogy as a consensus model of a variable and complex phenomenon, agreed by communities of like-minded scientists. This latter approach has the effect of presenting the enterprise of science as a tentative, sense-making experience rather than as a unitary and final truth. Analogies, therefore, can serve the larger purpose of bridging or scaffolding students' understanding of the phenomenon to bring their understandings closer to the consensus held by the scientific community.

Decisions about the selection of analogies and about how to make the links to students' experience require teachers to make judgements, and to continue making judgements as they meet each new class of students. Although the search for a better analogy is alluring, context, as well as the quality of the analogy, will determine the usefulness of any of the analogies teachers may choose to use.

References

Association for Science Education (1994). *Models and modelling in science education*. Hatfield, UK: ASE.

Bentley, D. and Watts, D. M. (1989). *Learning and teaching in school science: Practical alternatives*. Milton Keynes: Open University Press.

Gentner, D. (1983). Structure mapping: A theoretical framework. *Cognitive Science*, 7, 155–170.

—— (1988). Analogical interference and analogical access. In A. Prienditis (ed.), *Analogia* (pp. 63–88). Los Altos, CA: Morgan Kaufman.

Gentner, D. and Gentner, D. (1983). Flowing waters or teaming crowds: Mental models of electricity. In D. Gentner and A. Stevens, *Mental models* (pp. 99–130). Hillsdale, NJ: Erlbaum.

Gilbert, J., Boulter, C. and Rutherford, M. (1998). Models in explanations, Part 1: Horses for courses? *International Journal of Science Education*, 20 (1), 83–97.

Glynn, S. (1991). Explaining science concepts: A teaching-with-analysis model. In S. Glynn, R. Yeany and B. Britton (eds), *The psychology of learning science* (pp. 219–240). Hillsdale, NJ: Erlbaum.

Grosslight, L., Unger, C. and Jay, E. (1991). Understanding models and their use in science: Conceptions of middle and high school students and experts. *Journal of Research in Science Teaching*, 28 (9), 799–822.

Hesse, M. (1966). *Models and analogies in science.* London: Sheed & Ward.

Hodson, D. (1993). Towards a more critical approach to practical work in school science. *Studies in Science Education*, 22, 85–142.

Holyoak, K. and Thagard, P. (1995). *Mental leaps.* Cambridge, MA: MIT Press.

Jacques, D. (1984). *Learning in groups.* London: Kogan Page.

Oppenheimer, R. (1956). Analogy in science. *American Psychologist*, 11 (6), 127–135.

Solomon, J. (1994). The rise and fall of constructivism. *Studies in Science Education*, 23, 1–19.

Sutton, C. (1993). Figuring out a scientific understanding. *Journal of Research in Science Teaching*, 30 (10), 1,215–1,227.

Thagard, P. (1992). Analogy, explanation and education. *Journal of Research in Science Teaching*, 29 (6), 537–544.

Treagust, D. (1995). Enhancing students' understanding of science using analogies. In B. Hand and V. Prain (eds), *Teaching and learning science* (pp. 44–61). Sydney: Harcourt Brace.

Treagust, D., Duit, R., Joslin, P. and Lindauer, I. (1992). Science teachers' use of analogies: Observations from classroom practice. *International Journal of Science Education*, 14, 413–422.

Zook, K. B. (1991). Effect of analogical processes on learning and misrepresentation. *Educational Psychology Review*, 3 (1), 41–72.

Part IV

Dilemmas about teaching and learning

Chapter 12

Teaching ethics

Contributions by Vaille Dawson, Roger Lock, Nancy W. Brickhouse and Jan Crosthwaite

Editors' introduction

As Michael Matthews has observed, 'philosophy is not far below the surface in any science classroom' (1998, p. 995). Complex epistemological questions may emerge from even the most routine classroom treatments of the scientific method. What counts as evidence in a particular lesson? What is the epistemological status of the models and analogies students are expected to reproduce in tests? Similarly, metaphysical questions separate the truth claims of western science and indigenous knowledge, and evolutionary science from creationism. In addition, many students bring to class strong views about the medical and environmental issues that they cover in science. Whenever science and social policy intersect, such ethical questions arise. As the history of Bovine Spongiform Encephalopathy in the United Kingdom shows, ethical and scientific issues cannot be disentangled (United Kingdom, 2000). How soon did the scientific consensus emerge that the disease was a risk to humans? How much sooner did some suspect it? What social judgements would have been drawn if they overestimated the risk, announced it too soon, and needlessly slaughtered the British cattle herd? In a society dominated by risk (Giddens, 1999) scientists are forever caught between the possibility of panic and the fear of involvement in a cover up.

Some of the most pressing ethical dilemmas of our time are dilemmas that have arisen as a result of the technical successes of science. Among the most contentious of these may be counted access of non-traditional families to reproductive technology; fine distinctions between euthanasia and the withdrawal of futile treatment in end-stage cancer patients; and judgements about rationing of scarce organ transplant resources. In this chapter, Vaille Dawson describes a lesson in which she asks students to explore the ethical dilemmas inherent in organ transplantation. Although she sets out to provoke students' reactions to one of the dilemmas of medical science, she soon finds herself with a dilemma about her own moral authority in the classroom. Dawson's story is followed by commentaries by Roger Lock, Nancy Brickhouse and Jan Crosthwaite.

Playing God

Vaille Dawson

As I wait for my Grade 10 science class to arrive, I mentally preview the lesson plan in front of me. We are halfway through a unit called transplantation technology, an innovative unit that in addition to helping students understand a complex scientific topic also raises a number of ethical dilemmas for which there are no right or wrong answers. Most of the students relish the opportunity to engage in rich discussion about ethical issues although some have reacted angrily to the change from their regular science classes.

The students file in and sit down. I recap on the previous lesson. Students had completed a conflict map designed to help them identify the rights, needs and duties of those involved in transplantation (from Hildebrand, 1989). I remind them of some of the conflicts that they identified. Does the donor family have a duty to comply with the wishes of the donor? Also, does the donor family have a right to refuse to donate their kin's organs when a recipient will die without a transplant?

'So, girls, you are aware that one in three recipients die before they can obtain a transplant. Given a limited number of donors how can we decide who should receive an organ?'

I pause. Caitlin and Sophie raise their hands. 'Caitlin?'

'Well, I think it should be compulsory to donate your organs when you die.'

'Caitlin, we discussed that last week and I think that most of us agreed that the donor and their family have a right to decide what happens. Sophie?'

'Why don't they have a ballot and if your name is picked you get the transplant?'

'Why, Sophie,' I reply, 'that's an interesting idea and in fact, that is how some states in America select their recipients. Can anyone see any advantages or disadvantages with that system?'

'What if the person was really sick and died after the transplant? Then the organ would be wasted', says Caitlin.

'Or how about if the person was a criminal in jail?' says Emma.

'So what?' responds Sophie. 'He (*sic*) has just as much right as anyone else.'

'OK', I interrupt. 'If we have time we'll come back to this later. I would like you to make some choices about who receives a transplant. You will need to form groups of about three or four and select four patients from this list of ten patients. All of these patients will die unless they receive a liver transplant in the next twelve months. Large hospitals in Australia often budget to carry out a set number of transplants. This particular hospital will only carry out four transplants this year. You have about twenty minutes to select your patients. I suggest you read the list first and then as a group discuss your choices. There is some information available on the age, sex, race and family status of each patient. Any questions? Yes, Maree.'

'I don't think I can do this', says Maree.

'Why not?' I query.

'Well, it's a bit like playing God, deciding who will live or die … ', her voice trails off.

I walk over and sit down beside her. 'I know it's difficult to choose Maree, but it's only a role play. I can see that you appreciate how it feels. Just do your best. Read the list and discuss it with your friends.'

I return to Maree's group a few minutes later and listen as they discuss Patient A, a 4-year-old Vietnamese orphan who will be adopted by an Australian couple if he has a successful transplant.

Peer discussion

'I chose A because he's young and he's got his whole life ahead of him', says Maree.

'But maybe his life won't be that good', says Caitlin.

'Yes, but he's got a family that will adopt him', says Maree.

'He's too young to know any better', says Caitlin.

'But that's discriminating against him because of his age', says Maree.

'No, but you don't know that she's doing that, Maree', said Sophie. 'Patient A is quite a good one, actually, because, you know, he's young. And like he's coming to Australia so he can have a good life.'

'And – yes,' says Maree, 'you can just think of his family, who are waiting to adopt him. He can start a new life in Australia with all these opportunities.'

'We don't really know what his life's going to be like', says Caitlin.

'He's still got the opportunity to make it anything he wants', says Maree. 'He's only four years old. He hasn't even had a chance.'

Hearing laughter, I turn. Emma, Candy, Janine and Josie are discussing the contents of a Dolly magazine. 'How are you girls going?' I enquire.

'We've finished', Candy replied.

I inquire as to how they have arrived at a consensus so quickly and Candy says they have let Emma (a popular and forthright student) decide. I stay with this group and through questioning help them to consider each patient in turn.

Debrief discussion

At the end of the group discussion students write on the whiteboard the names of their groups' selected patients. I ask each group to outline why they chose or rejected certain patients. We begin with patient A who has been selected by half of the groups. Maree says he should have a transplant because 'he hasn't had much of a life' and 'deserves a chance'.

'No', states Emma emphatically. 'I don't agree. Who is going to miss him? He has no family. It's no great loss.'

'I agree', says Candy (Emma's best friend). 'We should not take them. We should look after our own kind first.'

I query, ' Do you think we have an obligation to look after those from other countries who are less fortunate?'

'No', says Candy.

'Definitely not', says Emma. 'It won't matter if he dies.'

Maree interjects. 'I actually think everyone has a right to life.'

'Oh yeh!' says Candy sarcastically.

'No they don't!' says Emma.

'It would be nice if every one could get a transplant, but he hasn't paid taxes in our country. What right does he have to our technology?' asks Candy.

In my mind I am weighing up my next move. I view my role in the classroom as one of helping students reflect on and critically evaluate their views through discussion with their peers. It is neither my role, nor my right, to impose my ethical values onto students. Rather, I want them to think critically about their own values rather than adopt mine. Yet, last year when students expressed similar views I remained silent and regretted afterwards that I had let the comments pass. Was my silence then interpreted as tacit approval? No, not this time.

'So Emma, do you think those types of views might be interpreted as racist?'

'I'm not a racist', retorts Emma.

'I didn't say that you were a racist, Emma, but I think that some people might think that the comments are. I would have to agree to some extent with Maree. All lives are important. What do the rest of the class think?'

As I think back now, I still question whether I should have spoken. Did my or Emma's comments cause other students to reflect on their values? What did the three Southeast Asian students in the class think? Are my ethical values any more valid than Emma's? I certainly have no right to impose my views. My ethical platform is fairly shaky and inconsistent. It comes down to a gut feeling most of the time. At least if I was teaching ethics from a religious perspective I could fall back on a theological view, 'We are all God's children.'

I asked a colleague who teaches Philosophy to Grade 10 students in Social Science how she coped with students' views who were totally opposed to hers. 'Ask them questions. Get them to defend their views and never give your own opinion', she advises. 'So what do you rest your own views on?' I ask. 'Honesty, truth and justice' is her quick reply. All very well I think, but whose truth is right and whose view is the honest one? In the end I must live with myself and admit that I will question views that I consider inappropriate.

Another colleague believes the students' views are just part of adolescent *naïveté* and that they will grow out of it. However, when I open the newspaper and read the Letters to the Editor and encounter letters urging the Government to reintroduce the death penalty and to halt Asian migration, I wonder.

★   ★   ★

Ethics and evidence

Roger Lock, University of Birmingham

Vaille Dawson concludes her first paragraph with the observation that some of her students have reacted angrily to the 'change from their regular science classes'. It is not just students who react in this way; many science teachers express similar feelings when it is suggested that there should be a space for considering bioethics in their lessons. What are the factors that lead students and teachers to think that teaching and learning of bioethical issues does not have a legitimate place in science schemes of work?

One key feature is, in my view, closely linked to the subject culture of science teachers. This is different from that of teachers of religious education, English and personal and social education who regularly include such topics in their teaching without difficulty even though their knowledge base about the specific issue may be less secure than that of their science colleagues. In the following paragraphs I will try to identify features of the science subject culture which lead to reluctance to engage with ethical issues.

Science is a subject which is seen as heavily cognitive; dominated by knowledge and involving an extensive curriculum content. Assessment of science is usually by written examinations which accentuate a culture of students regurgitating, often 'parrot fashion', a collection of ill-digested facts which are unconnected in any 'grand scheme' within their minds. It is all too rare for examinations to place an emphasis on understanding. Consequently, teachers get used to delivering lessons which develop recall skills and students become accustomed to associating class time in science with particular styles of teaching and learning that lend themselves to the transmission of significant quantities of information. Opportunities to interact with the information, to interpret and understand it, to interrogate it in order to develop a conceptual map of how it fits together are severely limited. The same is true of lessons dealing with ethics and this leads students to protest when their expectations are not met.

The major activity in science classes, other than the garnering of information, is practical work. This too contributes to a culture dominated by cognition and specifically the ability to recall. Practical work usually confirms the theory that has previously been taught. It is usually closed-ended in that there is a single outcome from the activity, one which reinforces the points previously covered in a theoretical manner. The practical activity may be presented as a problem-solving exercise, with a question to which the student has to find the answer, but there is usually a single experimental method by which the question might be approached and a unique answer to be obtained at the end of the lesson. Such a 'pseudo' open-ended approach does little to expand the students' views about either the nature of science or the way in which scientists work.

Practical work apart, many science lessons become teacher-centred and dominated by a limited range of teaching and learning styles. Science teachers are much less used to debates, role plays and simulations and are more confident with board copying, demonstrations and question–and–answer sessions. Student-centred strategies are more in the domain of teachers of English and religious education.

However, there is more to the science subject culture than content-dominated lessons, associated with closed-ended practical work and a limited range of teaching and learning strategies. Perhaps as a consequence of these, science teachers become accustomed to their students leaving lessons with a stock of new-found knowledge. They are much less used to students leaving with a dilemma to ponder or a new issue to chew over with friends in the dinner break. Science teachers feel less comfortable about teaching strategies which are designed to make students think. They are more familiar with telling students what to know and think and are less confident in giving students opportunities to deliberate and a range of different strategies through which this can be achieved such as the goals, rights and duties analysis referred to in the passage.

There is an explanation as to why science teachers behave in this way and part of it is linked to the nature of science curricula. These are usually much more tightly prescribed than curricula of other subjects. When syllabi themselves are content-laden, time and opportunity are reduced for science teachers to indulge their students in ethical issues related to the subject. Further than this, in England and Wales as recently as 1983 the Secretary of State for Education rejected out of hand a syllabus that suggested that science teachers should consider social and economic issues which arise from the application of scientific knowledge. In doing so, he suggested that students should not be engaged in the interesting questions of value and morality that many scientists face in their work. Later curriculum development has led to little improvement, for although the consideration of ethical issues was included in the statutory legislation of the 1991 National Curriculum, it was marginalised through a position in the programme of study which indicated that it was an appropriate issue only for the most able of students. Such marginalisation has, in my opinion, continued in the latest (1995) revision of the curriculum.

A further factor is that examination questions are not addressed to ethical issues. Consequently, teachers see them as a low priority in a system which is driven by examination success and the position of your school in the local league tables.

All is not bleak, however, as the number of teachers like Vaille Dawson is increasing, slowly. Often they recognise that science teachers have a key role to play and a unique contribution to make. In part, this is because of the knowledge and understanding that they have of the science involved in the topic. This, coupled with their familiarity with an objective, scientific approach to issues means that dispassionate, balanced lessons can result, lessons that help students to distinguish between fact and opinion, show respect for the evidence and keep an open mind on the issue.

With such an approach students don't just learn science and science practical skills, they also learn about science and the way in which scientists work. Through this latter perspective students may come to see scientists in a different light. No longer the cold, hard, uncaring, unsympathetic and eccentric, balding male but the warm, considerate, person concerned about the ethical dilemmas that her work produces. Scientists are not the cause of society's ills and problems but the agents who are trying to alleviate them. Such an approach is firmly tied in with current concerns about the wider accountability of scientists and ways in which they and their work are perceived by the general public. The moral high ground is not the exclusive preserve of non-scientists.

One critical dimension of the public is the students themselves, for it is they from whom the future scientists will be recruited. In England and Wales we face a situation where a smaller proportion of our 16–19-year-old population is choosing to study science beyond the period when it is compulsory. In Vaille Dawson's classroom it is significant that the students discussing the bioethical issue are female, for the evidence suggests that it is the humanistic side of science that appeals to women and hence is likely to encourage more of them to choose science.

The phenomenon of rejection of the novel is not new to science teachers. I well remember in the early 1970s when 'language across the curriculum' was the current buzzword and we were encouraging more students to write in a poetic style in science lessons. Naively I asked my students to produce a biological poem for homework. One such effort began well with

'Write a biological poem', he said with glee
Knowing none of us could do it
Including me!

but ended in rejection as described in the passage.

How do I go about writing a verse?
I don't wanna be a poet,
I wanna be a nurse.

The concluding section to the story highlights the dilemma for the teacher about the role that should be played in presenting a 'balanced' approach to teaching ethical issues. Is it possible to offer a range of views without indicating her personal thoughts? However balanced a teacher attempts to be, there will almost certainly be some influence on students' views. However, if there has been an even-handed lesson, conducted in a scientific manner, then students will have a model of how to approach controversial issues in other contexts. Having been exposed to a balanced range of viewpoints and encouraged to discuss their views with their peers, students should be allowed to make up their own minds about the issue. The significant elements here are coming to these views through a critical evaluation of the evidence which should be seen to support rather than contradict their opinion. The nature of the student opinion shouldn't be important, but the fact that it has been gained through critical reflection and respect for evidence should. However, if I found my students adopting racist or sexist positions then I, like Vaille Dawson, would be tempted to 'play God'.

★   ★   ★

Norms and authority in teaching science

Nancy W. Brickhouse, University of Delaware

When we ask students to talk or write about matters of substance, when we convince them that we want to know what *they* think rather than a regurgitation of the 'correct' point of view, then we have to be prepared that at least some of what drips from pens or comes out of mouths will be morally repugnant to us. There are lots of ways to think about these responses: as evidence that something is amiss with the teaching or that the students are particularly lacking in moral values. I think the best way of thinking about them is as artifacts of an oppressive culture (Lensmire, 1993). They serve as evidence of the oppressive social relations inherent in our society.

Schools, of course, teach values. The very fact of compulsory education is an imposition of the value that knowledge is good for everyone. Furthermore, the teacher has societal and institutional authority to enforce some values over others. Regardless of how much the teacher may want to relinquish this authority, she cannot. Some would argue she should not because she has a responsibility to educate students to be competent actors in changing an oppressive society (Counts, 1932). In the case described here, a laissez-faire approach will reinforce racist views both in the classroom and the society at large. The real question is how does the teacher respond to these views in ways that make explicit the moral and political referents for authority and develop in students concerns for social justice.

Lensmire (1993) faced similar problems in a third grade classroom writing workshop in which he had been working to support student efforts in developing personally relevant texts that are published and shared with other children in the classroom. When Maya writes 'The Zit Fit: The Lovers in the School', a text that demeans another child of lower social and economic status, he finds himself unable to support the child's writing efforts. The writing workshop literature, like the literature on values clarification, asserts that the role of the teacher is to simply support whatever values the child brings to his or her school work. The approach attempts to be value neutral. However, as Lensmire describes, it is both impossible and undesirable to be value-neutral. Clarification of values may result in simple clarification of racist values. In Lensmire's conference with Maya, he attempts unsuccessfully to convince her that it will be hurtful to share the text with the class. She claims that her text is 'just a story' – not to be taken so seriously. In the end, he uses his institutional authority and simply forbids her to share the text with the class since it would work against his goal of sustaining an engaged, pluralistic classroom community.

Similarly, the science teacher in this case could have the students interrogate the relationship between policy solutions and self-interest. She needs to think of ways to set norms for classroom discussion that make explicit the desire to derive solutions that account for the interests of the relatively powerless. This sort of norm ought to be explicitly discussed, but not necessarily debated. I simply would not leave open the possibility that the class could decide that a racist solution was acceptable. In the same way that we set norms such as scientific ideas being based on evidence, we can also set norms that policy solutions must be consistent with our commitments to care for one another, particularly those who may be unable to take care of themselves. This would mean that the teacher would insist that the student evaluate whether her solution is consistent with a commitment to care for everyone, especially the relatively powerless. While it may not be possible to prevent the student from voicing her opinion in the classroom and influencing peers, it is imperative that the teacher interrupt such activity, refuse to sanction it and redirect the classroom discussion in hopefully more fruitful directions. While we want to help our students develop voices of their own and to speak in ways that do not merely mimic the teacher, we can and should also refuse to aid in the development of morally objectionable voices. If that requires the teacher to act on the basis of her authority as a teacher and refuse to allow a class discussion to go in a morally objectionable direction, then so be it.

It seems to me that it would be preferable for the teacher to be able to get the student to critically evaluate her own beliefs rather than for the teacher to simply assert her authority and not allow morally objectionable views to be publicly engaged. I believe this is far more likely to happen if the relationship between the teacher and student is a challenging, yet caring one, and if the environment in the classroom is such that it is safe to change your mind and one is admired for giving reasons for decisions that go beyond self-interest.

I also think it is important that the teacher in this case is a woman. I doubt this to be a coincidence. I simply do not believe that many male teachers would have such difficulty coming to terms with issues of authority. Male teachers have less difficulty seeing themselves as authorities and serving as representatives from the worlds of science, moral philosophy, and so on (Pagano, 1988). For women, however, authority is more problematic. Women have been objects of scientific study (and often compared to a male model to show deficiencies), but rarely producers of scientific knowledge. To what extent are women speaking with their own voices when they are teaching science (or moral philosophy)? As Pagano (1988) repeatedly asks, 'Was there ever a life more riddled with self-doubt than that of a woman teacher?' Pagano (1988) writes:

> Authority in all of its meanings refers to some sort of power or right. When teaching is considered to be the enactment of narrative, authority refers to the power to represent reality, to signify, and to command compliance with one's acts of signification. ... Women exercise powers or rights to represent reality only as surrogates for men. Only by proxy have we the right to command, to enforce obedience to the father's law. Still it is doubtful we ever do it well. Part of the reason is that women are either not represented in the father's law or we are represented as a lack or deficiency.
> (p. 322)

At least partly because of this ambiguous relationship women have with the public worlds of knowledge, authority does not seem to be a natural right. However, it is necessary at times to act as though we do have the right and responsibility for the moral voices that are developed in our classrooms.

★   ★   ★

Moral authority

Jan Crosthwaite, The University of Auckland

This interesting teaching vignette raises a very important question for those of us who teach about ethics or ethical issues and the role of a teacher's own moral views in such teaching.

Any teacher is aware of the susceptibility of children (or students more generally) to acquiring their beliefs from (what they believe to be) those of their teachers. Most who teach about ethically important issues are concerned, like Ms Dawson, to encourage moral reflection and debate rather than to inculcate moral truths. But few who are sufficiently interested in ethics to teach in this area will not have given serious consideration to, and formed their own views about, the issues they are addressing. Hence the problem: should a teacher let students proceed in what appears to her as moral error, or intervene to correct their views?

In the scenario we are given, Ms Dawson faces the question of whether or not to tackle apparent racism in the views of some students. She frames her problem in the context of a particular conception of the role of the teacher of ethics, that of 'helping students to reflect on and critically evaluate their views through discussion with their peers'. While she construes this as incompatible with 'imposing the teacher's own ethical values on to students', her values do not permit her in this case to allow racism to go unchallenged.

It is clear that one's understanding of the professional role of a teacher, and of an ethics teacher in particular, is central to posing and resolving the question raised. Whether or not to correct wrong views is less of an issue in other areas of teaching, though it will arise if one accepts some versions of constructivist approaches to the teacher's role. The specific problem about whether it is appropriate to correct 'moral error' arises from a combination of views about ethics or morality and the teacher's role.

The prevalence of forms of relativism, both naive and sophisticated, in people's views about ethics, and the plurality of views which discussion of any significant ethical issue reveals, lead many to deny that there is any 'correct' ethical position. Reasonable, informed and conscientious persons can disagree about ethical issues. Though such disagreement is not sufficient grounds for denying the existence of moral truths, recognising its possibility makes ethicists and teachers of ethics reluctant to assume moral authority, or 'impose' their own views on others.

In the face of reluctance to accord moral authority to any individual and the difficulty of finding an agreed moral content which should be taught, many hold that what is to be taught in the area of ethics is not a set of moral truths, but a capacity for moral reflection, and 'sensitivity' to ethical issues or ethical dimensions of issues. But facilitating moral reflection cannot be easily separated from a conception of the nature of morality or from certain values associated with this. In the scenario Ms Dawson has described, she intervenes in the procedures of one discussion group (Emma, Candy, Janine and Josie) to ensure that they do deliberate on the issue of selecting transplant recipients. The four have worked out a way to make their selection, by delegating the task of choosing to one of their number. Ms Dawson indicates no qualms about rejecting this way of proceeding. Her intervention to alter their process of choice is compatible with the aims she has in teaching this material, and she does not seem to see it as imposing her own ethical values. I am not so sure. Delegation of responsibility for selection to a respected individual or group is, like choosing by lottery, a solution to the problem of distributing scarce resources which has been used and could be argued for.

Ms Dawson's intervention at this point could have arisen more from pedagogic than from moral concerns. As a teacher she needed to make sure that any decision procedure was a response to understanding the problem set, rather than a failure to engage with it at all (which seems more likely in this particular instance). But I think it is important to realise that the insistence on a kind of moral deliberation, and on the suitability of certain skills for dealing with ethical problems, may be as much an ethical stance as a pedagogical one.

Most who teach about ethics and ethical issues would accept the importance of teaching students processes of moral reflection. If we were to teach content without skills of deliberation, students would not be able to deal with new moral issues. They might also be easily swayed by alternative views, because they are unaware of and unable to articulate the grounds of their own. Some might also advocate teaching processes of reflection over content from a more proceduralist position, that the determinant (or more weakly, the mark) of correctness in moral judgement is the process by which it has been arrived at.

In teaching about ethics, we need to give students the basis from which to subject moral positions to critical appraisal, including not only their own views but also those held by authority figures or authorised by a community. Encouraging peer debate is an important part of this process, but it isn't all that is needed. I think that it is also important that the views of the teacher are not always absent or withheld from debate. This would make them protected from challenge in a way that the views of students are not. While the teacher's views must not dominate, they can be used to provide an example for students of how to be open to debate and the scrutiny of others. But I should say at this point that my own experience is in teaching university students, not Grade 10s.

I would argue also that there are certain fundamental values, generally accepted in some form or other, which can be advocated in teaching ethics, viz. respect and care for other persons. How these apply in particular situations is obviously problematic and disputable, but they would appear inimical to racism. Hence, I think the opportunity to raise and explore the issue of racism should not be allowed to pass. Nor do I think that raising this issue need be considered to be 'imposing' the teacher's own values on a class, though certain ways of addressing the issue would be closer to this than others. It would be wrong (and possibly inaccurate) to simply categorise Emma's or Candy's views as racist. It is also likely to be counter-productive; an accusation of racism, even one as gently worded as 'Do you think those views might be interpreted as racist?', is likely to be met with a flat denial and resistance to further reflection. The teacher might be able to elicit responses from other students which will bring up the issue of racism, without having to present it herself. But this could also produce a blunt accusation of racism, so it may be pedagogically preferable to lead the discussion through questions.

It is Candy who has raised the considerations Ms Dawson takes as inviting the charge of racism. The cluster of responses given by Candy suggests she (and Emma) may well be racist, but the grounds they articulate for not selecting the Vietnamese orphan are not necessarily so. Candy has said (with support from Emma) two different things in this context. First, that 'we should look after our own kind first', and that we do not have an obligation to look after those from countries who are less fortunate. Second she has suggested that a right to access technology is based on one's contribution in the form of taxes. Both these could be explored further in ways which would allow any racist element to become apparent, and also allow a range of non-racist criteria for access to scarce resources to be explored more deeply. Some would argue that care for one's own is a moral imperative; for example, parents who sacrificed their own children to give resources to others would be condemned by most people. Why should the responsibilities of health-care providers be more general? This immediately raises the question of who is 'our own kind', from which the possibilities of racism can very easily be high-lighted.

Candy's view that tax contributions are relevant to access to the resources of a country's medical or health-care system is also a position which many hold, without necessarily invoking race. It would be interesting here to ask whether children who have not paid taxes are entitled to health care. If an entitlement could be based on parents' contributions, should orphans in general be excluded? (And if not, then why candidate A?) Should level of access to resources be connected to the amount paid in taxes? Should people who have not paid taxes because they have not earned sufficient income be excluded? Does it make a difference that someone who receives a transplant may be able to pay more to the country in taxes in future as a result? The issue of migrants would obviously arise, and allow exploration of who counts as 'our own kind' as well. Pressure on these questions should start to expose whether it is status as a non-taxpayer, orphan, or 'foreigner', which is really being used to exclude patient A.

It is important to note that this idea of directing discussion to bring up consideration of racism does not avoid the fundamental problem about the role of the teacher's own values. The promotion of such a discussion presumably arises from the teacher's own moral views that racism needs to be challenged. But it is not an 'imposition' of the teacher's own values so long as the decision of whether or not to accept categorisation of a view as racist, or to accept or reject the view on this ground, remains with the student(s).

Directed discussion does however raise a further problem in the ethics of teaching, viz. the possibility of manipulating the teaching situation to present certain moral views or positions for consideration. Teaching fundamentally involves manipulating situations (or more politely, taking advantage of the possibilities in situations) to provide opportunities for learning. If one is dealing with ethically significant issues, then such manipulation will be directed by what one sees as ethically important and what one thinks might be learned. This cannot in the end be divorced from one's own moral views. This does not make the teaching of ethics unethical, but it does require that we engage in the sort of scrutiny of our aims and practices which Vaille Dawson has encouraged in providing this story.

*   *   *

Editors' synthesis

Much of school science, Lock argues, conspicuously ignores ethical questions. Teachers construct the subject as highly cognitive and lessons are packed with curriculum content. When teachers move away from the blackboard into activities, the practical lessons they organise focus chiefly on reproducing results that are already identified in their notes or in the science text book. The consequence, he argues, is that science teachers are uncomfortable with 'teaching strategies which are designed to make students think'. Lock welcomes bioethics lessons such as Vaille Dawson offered her students, not least because such lessons uncover some of the uncertainty in which scientists practise their science. Dealing in class with ethical dilemmas provides students with opportunities to weigh and balance evidence. Although he characterises the role of teachers in such instances as being 'even-handed', he acknowledges that he would be tempted to express his own opinions if he found students adopting racist or sexist positions.

For Brickhouse, such even-handedness in the face of racism is not an appropriate option. Relativist tolerance of expressions of racism such as those of Emma and Candy, she argues, reinforce racism in the classroom and in society more generally. Although Brickhouse shares with Lock the view that the teacher has an important role in encouraging students to critically evaluate evidence, she proposes that the evidence be evaluated against a set of ethical norms. One such norm, she suggests – a commitment to care for one another – is inconsistent with racist policy options. In the presence of racist expressions the role of the teacher is to 'interrupt such activity, refuse to sanction it and redirect the classroom discussion in hopefully more fruitful directions'. In refusing racism and redirecting the conversation, Brickhouse acknowledges that many women teachers will struggle with questions of authority. For women, she says, the exercise of authority is problematic but it is necessary that teachers such as Vaille Dawson take responsibility for the moral voices that are developed in their classrooms.

Crosthwaite takes up the issue of moral authority in a relativist world. 'Reasonable, informed and conscientious persons can disagree about ethical issues', she says, and this disagreement makes ethicists reluctant to impose their views on others. One solution in teaching ethics is to focus on the process of moral reflection. The process of moral reasoning, she argues, may be the mark of correctness in moral judgement. The skills of moral reasoning, however, cannot be taught without the content of moral problems. Teachers have several responsibilities in providing students access to a diversity of views, Crosthwaite argues. They should encourage peer debate; they should not allow their own views to dominate, but nor should they withhold their own views. Although Dawson was concerned not to impose her ethical values onto students, unless the teacher's views are shared they appear to enjoy a privileged status. And besides, the decision to deal with ethically significant issues such as liver transplantation is a reflection of the teacher's own ethical position. Teachers' own ethical positions cannot be separated from their peda-gogical decision-making, Crosthwaite concludes.

In this story Vaille Dawson sets out to provoke students to respond to the ethical dilemmas inherent in organ transplantation. In this she succeeds – students engage in a process of ethical deliberation about transplantation – but the discussion also provokes a pedagogical dilemma. How should she respond to a remark she regards as racist? Be even-handed and attend to issues of evidence, Lock suggests. Take responsibility for the moral voices developed in the classroom, suggests Brickhouse. Help students to engage in moral reasoning, says Crosthwaite, but don't expect to separate pedagogical action from your own moral views. All this leaves teachers such as Dawson not far from where she began: committed to classroom processes that uncover and explore ethical issues and uncomfortable about her ethical role in a relativist world.

References

Counts, G. S. (1932). *Dare the school build a new social order?* New York: John Day.

Giddens, A. (1999). *Runaway world: How globalisation is shaping our lives.* London: Profile Books.

Hildebrand, G. (1989). The liver transplant committee. *Australian Science Teachers Journal*, 35 (3), 70–73.

Lensmire, T. J. (1993). Following the child, socioanalysis, and threats to community: Teacher response to children's texts. *Curriculum Inquiry*, 23, 265–299.

Matthews, M. R. (1998). The nature of science and science teaching. In B. J. Fraser and K. G. Tobin (eds), *International handbook of science education* (pp. 981–999). Dordrecht, The Netherlands: Kluwer.

Pagano, J. A. (1988). Teaching women. *Educational Theory*, 39, 321–340.

United Kingdom (2000). *The BSE inquiry report*. London: Her Majesty's Stationery Office.

Chapter 13

Constructivism

Contributions by Barry Krueger, J. John Loughran and Reinders Duit

Editors' introduction

Over the last three decades there has been a major shift in the way that science educators have come to view the status of scientific knowledge. This shift was largely inspired by the theoretical work of philosophers of science such as Lakatos (1970), Popper (1972) and Feyerabend (1975). These scholars argued that knowledge is not discovered but rather constructed within communities of like-minded people. Consequently, scientific knowledge depends for its warrants and truth claims on the socially constructed knowledge of particular communities of scientists.

While philosophers questioned the scientific canon, cognitive scientists were observing that students' common-sense practical knowledge of physical phenomena is not necessarily contradicted by formal science knowledge. Studies in the 1980s focusing on the scientific understandings that children bring to the classroom (Champagne *et al.*, 1985; Osborne and Freyberg, 1985) led to various theories about student engagement, student misconceptions and conceptual change (Pines and West, 1985). Under the more familiar title of 'constructivism', these ideas have since been elaborated in considerable detail. They are based on the idea that learners are the constructors of their own knowledge. From the constructivist perspective, knowledge resides in individuals and cannot be transferred intact from 'the head of the teacher to the heads of students' (Lorsbach and Tobin, 1992, p. 9). At the heart of the theory is the negotiation of meaning, at a personal level and also at a social level (Tobin, 1990).

While cognitive scientists and philosophers of science share some common territory, there are important differences in their approach to science education. While the first group sees student knowledge as imperfect – and often in need of perfection – the second group views science itself as imperfect and imperfectible. These different perspectives on science knowledge have raised important issues about the nature of science, about the status of student knowledge and about how to teach for understanding. Solomon (1994), for example, highlights the difficulty faced by students as they struggle to comprehend the formal language of science used in textbooks. 'No amount of recollection of their own remembered territory with shut eyes', says Solomon (1994, p.16), will help them with the foreign task of understanding the canons of science.

For the classroom teacher, these issues create particular problems and tensions. For example, what value should be placed on students' practical knowledge? What is the status of canonical science as represented in textbooks? What does scientific understanding really mean when teachers are asked to 'teach for understanding'? and finally, How much should a teacher tell students (and what should be told)? In this chapter, several of these tensions are played out in a story by Barry Krueger, appropriately titled, *To tell or not to tell?* Krueger's story and commentary are followed by comments from John Loughran and Reinders Duit.

To tell or not to tell?

Barry Krueger

'The positive and negative currents flow from the power pack and they meet in the light bulb and they react together to produce light.' Janet looked towards Nicki and Cheryl for their approval. I cringed inwardly. I had been watching their exchange from the next bench. Nicki started to record Janet's explanation. However, Cheryl was less sure. She was struggling to remember what she had learned in Grade 9.

'But ... uhm ... isn't electricity ... uhm ... a flow of electrons?' Cheryl asked tentatively. 'Isn't that what Mr Daniels told us last year?'

Nicki stopped writing and I breathed a sigh of relief. Surely Janet would remember learning about electron flow. After all, she was one of the better students in the class, and she had scored an 'A' last year. Without even stopping to gather her thoughts Janet pointed towards the power pack.

'This is the positive electrode and the black one is the negative electrode', she replied matter of factly as she pointed to the wires. 'Electricity comes out of both of them. They are both connected to the light bulb. If you take away one of these leads the circuit doesn't work. Light can only be produced when the positive electricity and the negative electricity react together in the light bulb.'

Cheryl wasn't convinced, but she was at a loss how she could argue against Janet's logic. I was nonplussed. I don't think Nicki had any idea at all. It seemed that all my plans were awry. I had divided the class into small groups and set them the task of constructing a theory to explain why a light bulb glows when it is connected to an electric current. I was determined to avoid telling students the answer. It should have been a straightforward exercise, or so I thought. After all, the students were revisiting concepts they had learned in the previous year. However, it didn't seem to be working. I was bothered that Janet could hold such unusual views, and moreover, that she was so persuasive.

I moved over to Ian's group. A surfing magazine lay open on their desk. Ian and Nick were off-task. Nick pre-empted my question.

'The battery pushes electrons around the wire until it reaches the globe', Nick read. 'The globe has a thinner wire in the middle which acts as a resistor. This resistance causes heat and light energy to be given off.'

They sounded like Ian's words. What a contrast with Janet's group! Yet, I felt uneasy with their explanation. I wondered whether they really understood what they had written. The test of their understanding would come soon.

Moving to the front of the classroom, I called the class to order. Each of the groups reassembled into the centre of the laboratory. One by one they presented their theory about glowing light bulbs to the class – to their critical colleagues.

Janet's group was the fourth group to present their theory. Nicki wrote their theory onto the whiteboard while Janet explained it to the class. The class listened attentively. Janet's arguments made a good case for her theory. The trouble was its plausibility. Would the class subscribe to her theory? What would I do if they did? Would I have to end up telling the students the answer?

Stafford raised his hand and addressed his question to Janet. Cheryl breathed a sigh of relief at having escaped the question.

'Can you tell me what positive electricity is?' he asked.

The class was silent.

Without any hesitation Janet replied, 'It's the electricity that comes out of the positive terminal on the power pack.'

'Yes, but', Stafford frowned, 'can you tell me what it is? It can't be protons because they are in the nucleus and they can't move.'

Cheryl looked towards Janet to hear her answer. This was the question that she was unable to articulate. Janet blushed and she was silent for a moment.

'I don't know what it is', she replied. 'It's just positive electricity. It comes out of the power pack.'

Stafford won the day. The consensus of the class was that there couldn't be such a thing as positive electricity and that negative electricity was made up of electrons. The positive and negative aspects of Janet's theory were summarised and written onto the board while the next group came forward. Janet quietly returned to her desk. She was embarrassed, it would appear, not for her lack of knowledge, but for her inability to answer the question.

'Just where do they think the heat comes from?' she commented to Cheryl.

There were just a few minutes remaining when the final group finished presenting their theory. I thanked the students for their cooperation and directed their attention to the board. I asked that they work individually, take into account the content of the discussions and spend the remaining time writing their final theory. Most of the students picked up their pens and started writing. A few gave the appearance of being busy. Janet raised her hand.

'Aren't you going to tell us?' she asked. 'If you don't tell us the answer we won't know if we are right or not.'

Janet's question underscored the tension I experienced during the lesson. How would I know that the students were writing out the correct answer? Would they still hold misconceptions about electricity? I wondered, for a moment, if I should stop the class and tell them the answer. Or, perhaps, I could stop the class and highlight the essential aspects of the earlier discussion so they could string together an acceptable answer.

I smiled at Janet's question. I knew where she was coming from. Strengthened in my resolve, I replied.

'Just write out what you now understand. Look at all those ideas on the board. Pick out the ones that are right, that is, the ones which don't contradict each other and what we know about science.'

Janet stared back at her page and I moved to the front of the room. The bell rang several minutes later. I wondered what she had written. Did Janet still hold to her beliefs about positive and negative currents? Should I have told the class the answer, or at least highlighted particular aspects of their theories? I turned to check Janet's work but she had already packed her books and was leaving. She caught my glance and read my thoughts.

'Oh, it's all right, Mr Krueger, I'll look it up tonight when I get home. See you tomorrow.'

Teacher commentary

Barry Krueger

'To tell or not to tell', to teach or not to teach, to continue the allusion to Prince Hamlet's soliloquy, 'that is the question.' Does telling bring about understanding? I cannot help but recall Lawson and Renner's (1975) criticism that traditional approaches to teaching are based on the 'notions that (i) teaching is telling, (ii) memorization is learning, and (iii) being able to repeat something on an examination is evidence of understanding' (p. 343). These criticisms have had a profound influence on the way I have come to conceptualise my teaching. I assert that none of the practices that Lawson and Renner criticise promote the development of understanding. The story that I describe portrays the tension between 'telling' and 'teaching for understanding'.

Each year I have students in my classes who are somewhat like Janet. They are interested in science and they work hard at their learning. What they lack in ability is more than compensated for by their persistence. However, their successes diminish as they progress further into the senior school. The problem, as I see it, is that these students become too reliant on a steady diet of facts and information. Textbooks, television programmes, encyclopaedias and particular teaching practices deliver information that is all too easily swallowed, ready to be regurgitated with success on poorly constructed tests.

In this story we read of Janet's preoccupation with getting the correct diet of facts. She needed to know the right answer and she was unwilling to play at the game of constructing her theory any longer. Janet's tardiness seemed out of character. She was usually such an eager participant in class activities. The story ends with Janet ready to consult her encyclopaedias, her source of facts and information. Janet had more than enough ability to complete the exercise. I can only guess at the reasons why she didn't. Perhaps Janet realised that she would be assessed according to the textbook view and that her theorising would be of little consequence. Perhaps, she was perturbed by the smorgasbord of ideas that were presented during the lesson. Stafford's counter-arguments may have been troubling her, and she needed to consult an authoritative source to settle her uncertainties. Or, perhaps, there was a mismatch between our ideologies. Could it be the case that Janet didn't want to play the learning game according to my rules? She may have decided to wait, to see if I would eventually provide the right answer. I don't know. I can only guess.

I think I can understand some of Janet's reluctance. I too, as a student, subsisted on a regular diet of facts and learned theories. More recently, I have 'taught' my students in these ways, spoonfeeding them with a meal of carefully prepared knowledge. Like a chef preparing food, I would prepare my lessons and present knowledge in ways so that it would be palatable and easily digested. Looking back now, I see that I gave little for my students to chew. Vestiges of this ideology are present in the story that I described. I, too, was preoccupied with the students getting the right answer. I was disturbed that Janet spoke so persuasively to the class and that her ideas had a certain credibility. I cringed at the thought of her misleading the class. I am not sure what I would have done if Stafford hadn't have saved the day. Even so, I still contemplated whether I should tell the class the 'right' answer. However, I knew from my experience that if I did, students like Janet would memorise my words and repeat them back to me in tests, sometimes as answers to the wrong questions! I considered, as a compromise, picking out the important ideas and highlighting them, so that students could string together an answer that was substantially correct. Yet, I chose not to. Telling does not produce understanding. I hold that the development of understanding requires students to link ideas together for themselves. That is why I didn't intervene. Just as in a smorgasbord meal one would select apple sauce rather than mayonnaise for roast pork, so I held the hope that my students would make the right associations and meld them into a coherent theory. This is what I would call the development of understanding.

★   ★   ★

Teaching about electricity

J. John Loughran, Monash University

How does electricity actually work? Physicists know about electricity, we all experience electricity in everyday life, there is so much information available about it, surely it can't be that difficult to explain. A science teacher should 'know' the information and be able to explain it in a way that makes sense and is obvious and understandable to their students. I certainly remember being in science classes which handled concepts as complex as electricity in such a simple manner. So why did I struggle to understand? Teaching science concepts like electricity should be easy. The teacher just needs to make it clear, present the irrefutable evidence, show the students what they should know and *voilà*, they will all certainly understand.

It is little wonder that science teaching is often thought of as the delivery of information. Science is seen as a body of knowledge about how things work. Get the knowledge from the textbooks and transfer it to the students' heads. That is how it often appears; to parents, students and (sadly) many teachers. Yet Barry Krueger's narrative demonstrates a dilemma in science teaching, something that is not able to be easily resolved, something that science teachers are confronted by in many of their lessons. However, being confronted by a dilemma is one thing, recognising it and attempting to address it is another.

Barry illustrates how, as an experienced science teacher, the delivery of information alone is not sufficient to ensure that his students will genuinely learn about the concepts being explored. A problem for him though is that in trying to encourage his students to construct their own understanding, his uncertainty about their learning still remains. What is certain is that from Barry's experience, he clearly recognises that just because the students have the right words written down in their books there is no guarantee that the meaning of those words will be translated into understanding the concept. He recognises, and attempts to respond to, two concurrent issues/concerns. Simplifying science does not make science simple, and learning for understanding involves much more than knowing by recall.

A thoughtful teacher attempts to encourage learners to construct their understanding. But this is not such an easy task in practice. There is a need for students to accept some responsibility for learning, to move beyond a reliance on the teacher for the right answer. There is also a need for the teacher to use appropriate pedagogy to create opportunities for students to be challenged by the constructions they, and their colleagues, are forming. But still, underlying all of this is the dilemma, 'to tell or not to tell'. Perhaps an important extension of this dilemma is 'when to tell or not tell'.

In learning, a time arrives when knowing whether or not the right answer has been determined is important. Further, being incorrect can be equally as informative in learning as being correct. At some stage, observations need to be drawn together, ideas and inferences formed and hypotheses need to be tested. There is a time when knowing becomes a prerequisite to understanding. Little wonder that science teachers genuinely struggle to create these conditions in their classrooms. Schools are organised so that teachers meet their students through brief encounters across a range of times and days, an organisational feature of schools which makes linking the ideas and activities from one lesson to another a difficult and demanding task. From one perspective, it is clearly much easier to present information to students and to know that they can simply copy it down in their notebooks. That concept can then be marked off as delivered and completed. From both the teacher's and the students' perspective, this approach would make schooling much easier. It is an approach which is clear, is measurable and is achievable. The difficulty for science teachers like Barry is that it does not sit comfortably with their understanding of quality learning. Transmitting information does not equate to teaching, copying notes does not equate to learning.

A colleague and I recently spent a considerable period of time interviewing Grade 9 students about their understanding of electricity. Their teacher had taught with a similar pedagogical intent to that which Barry had employed and it was interesting to hear the students explain how they thought a range of circuits worked. They had constructed their understanding by being engaged in a number of activities that challenged their thinking. They had not been told what was right or wrong, they had been told to think about how to justify their thinking and how to challenge the thinking of others (their teacher included).

Somewhere in the development of an understanding of electricity, the teacher had responded to a query about the flow of electrons so he introduced an analogy. He spoke about a circuit being like a road and that on the road there were a number of trucks which travelled around. Beside the highway was a warehouse (battery) where the trucks picked up their load (energy) and carried it away along their journey. At certain points along the highway their energy load was dropped off (resistors) so that on their return to the warehouse they were able to be reloaded. The analogy was interesting because it raised many questions about 'thinking' trucks which 'knew' when to drop off their load and when to reload. The students recognised this and asked about it. The teacher's response was that the analogy offered a way of understanding current in a circuit, but that it was an analogy and so was inevitably inadequate but that it was needed because although science knew what electricity did, it was difficult to really know how it happened. The students appreciated that what they were doing was working with a concept that was complex and difficult, and that there were 'things' that were able to be explained, and others that were reasonable assertions as a result of many observations. They were learning to construct an understanding, to build their knowledge base beyond the recall of definitions and facts.

How quickly all of this could have changed if, after the effort of trying to work things out, the students were then told what they had learnt. They would have rightly questioned the purpose of the teaching approach if they were then to be told what they had learnt.

Therefore, in many science classes, Barry's dilemma persists. It persists because it is tied to another question, 'Where does the responsibility for learning reside?' If the responsibility for student learning is solely the teacher's, then the idea that one should deliver the correct information is not such a problem; particularly when science appears to have so much to be so easily delivered. If the teacher is responsible for the learning then learning is more a matter of knowing than understanding. Alternatively, if students are responsible for their own learning, then the role of the teacher is considerably different. For many it might even mean that the teacher's role is no longer quite so important, that only the students' views matter. Clearly, there is a middle ground. A pedagogical approach that recognises the need to mediate between the two extremes. An approach which is responsive to the learning demands of the situation while also respecting the differences between individuals. An approach which cannot be delivered but needs to continually be developed.

This is what we are seeing in Barry's dilemma. The development of his approach with this class, in this context, at this time. It will no doubt be an extension of his learning about teaching through experience. It will involve considerable reflection on that experience across a range of classes, grade levels and content matter. He is striving to help his students come to understand the science of electricity and to do this he needs them to see what it is, how it is understood and constructed, and how they can come to use that knowledge in a useful and meaningful way.

To tell or not to tell is a question which must arise in science teaching if the learning is to be more than the acquisition of information. Students need to be challenged by the content they are learning and need to be helped by their science teacher to develop their understanding through the challenges created as they become engaged in their learning.

To tell or not to tell involves a wealth of pedagogical understanding and reasoning. Telling can be very important when the need to know arises. Not telling can frustrate learning just as telling can stifle any need to know to begin with. It really is a dilemma; to tell or not to tell.

It seems to me that an important element of good teaching is attempting to address dilemmas. It would be much easier to ignore but would involve far less challenge and engagement for the learners and the teacher. I am not so certain that such a dilemma arose when I was 'doing' electricity in my science classes. However, I have a feeling that Barry's students are not 'doing' electricity, I think they are learning about electricity. I think that would be a good way to learn science.

★ ★ ★

Students make their own sense of what you tell

Reinders Duit, IPN at the University of Kiel

> Not even the simple electric circuit is simple.

> Never take for granted that students just store what you tell.

Yes, I fully understand Mr Krueger's disappointment. He surely did his best in Grade 9 to make students familiar with what he calls the 'correct' view of current flow in the electric circuit. And yet, Janet, one of the better students in the class, presented a theory that was not at all in accordance with the view that she had been taught. And what was even more worrying to the teacher, Janet did not give up her idea easily and was even able to persuade some of her peers that her view is right.

It is well known from many studies[1] that at the end of an instructional unit students frequently present ideas that surprise the teachers given all the effort made in class to guide students to the science view. Quite often, science instruction fails to change students' preinstructional conceptions substantially. To make matters worse, a considerable number of what Mr Krueger likes to call *misconceptions* are created or at least supported by science instruction. Research on students' conceptions of the simple electric circuit clearly illustrates that when the topic comes up in the science class for the first time students have alternative conceptions already, for example, about how current flows in the circuit. Driver and Easley (1978) called these conceptions *alternative* and not *mis-conceptions* as they are not (at least not totally) in accordance with the science view but do make good sense to students in a similar way as our science conceptions make to us. Telling the correct science view in such a situation will not help. Of course, some students will just learn that by heart and may be able to repeat it in a somewhat parrot-like manner later. But are students with such an alternative view really able to understand what the teacher tells? They can't. The constructivist view of learning may be brought into play here (Treagust *et al.*, 1996). Understanding, that is sense making, is possible only on the grounds of certain interpretive frameworks the students hold. Hence, the preinstructional conceptions that students bring into class provide the framework to make sense of the teacher's words. We know from numerous studies that discourse between students and the teacher may be an endless chain of misunderstandings. On the one hand the students do not understand what the teacher tells, at least not in the intended way, as they lack the 'background knowledge' that the teacher associates with the topic in question. On the other hand, the teacher also does not understand the students' responses as he or she tries to make sense of them from the science point of view.

Let us have a closer look at Janet's idea of current flow. Her idea is well known from studies on students' conceptions of the electric circuit. Young students especially argue, for instance, that a 'plus' and a 'minus' current flow to the bulb and clash together there – sparks are created, the bulb shines.[2] Others think that there is some sort of chemical reaction that results in the light. Again other students hold that the current goes to the bulb, is used up there and then goes back to the battery. Sometimes it appears that these students draw an analogy to gas given to a motor and exhaust flowing away from the motor. Crazy or childish ideas? Viewed from the correct science view it appears to be so. But viewed from the perspective of the students they are not stupid or childish at all. On the contrary, the ideas are ingenious and creative. These students really think about what they see and they try to make sense themselves of what may be behind what they observe, by drawing on processes already familiar to them.

If we try to look at the simple electric circuit with the students' eyes, we have the following situation. There is a battery (or another 'source'), there are two different terminals (+ and −) and there is a light bulb shining if the two terminals of the light bulb are connected in the appropriate manner with the terminals of the battery. Appropriate means that a shortcut has to be avoided and that the connections have to be so called 'conductors'. That is all the set up and the observation may tell. The students do not *see* electrons. Nor does the teacher. He or she may *think* of electrons. If we look at the above ideas of students it becomes quite clear that these ideas explain what they observe: There are two connections between the terminals of the battery and the bulb; as the two terminals of the battery are called + and − it makes good sense to think that there are also different kinds of current; finally their views explain why the bulb shines. It appears also that Janet's ideas are based on convictions supported by what may be observed. Further, she clearly expresses a need to explain why the bulb shines. After Stafford 'won the day', Janet was embarrassed and asked: 'Just where do they think the heat comes from?' In fact, Janet asked a very thoughtful question, the explanation given by Stafford did not address this issue.

If the teacher in such a situation tells the students the correct view, that electrons flow from the minus-terminal through the bulb to the plus-terminal, it is most unlikely that they will understand this explanation. He has to show the students that his, or the science view respectively, is more valuable than students' alternative views.[3] In other words, he has to persuade students that the science view makes more sense. It should also be made clear to the students that the teacher actually presents a *model* of current flow and not the ultimate truth. Mr Krueger clearly made no attempt to explain to his class that his view of electron flow is merely a model.

Is the view discussed in the class under inspection here, the electron flow view, *correct* (as Mr Krueger points out several times)? It appears that this may be only justified under certain conditions. There are a number of hidden assumptions involved. It is assumed, for instance, that the conductors are metals (or at least materials where electrons really form the current). What about a slight variant? If the circuit also contains semi-conductors or electrolytes or if the bulb is replaced by a light-emitting diode (which has become a quite familiar kind of 'bulb' these days), what about the current flow in this case? Surely, things become much more complicated – and there may be truly *positive electricity* (as Janet called it) now (e.g. positive ions). To make things even more complicated, what is the view that we implicitly evoke in students' minds when we *tell* them that electrons come out of the negative terminal and flow in a circle? Does this view include the conceptualisation of the electrons moving as a chain of interrelated particles like the parts of a bicycle chain? It appears from literature that often electrons are viewed as particles moving *individually* through the wires – but they don't. Also, where do the electrons come from when a battery is driving them? And where do they end? Surely they do *not* come out of the negative terminal of the battery and they do *not* go back into the positive terminal of the battery. Clearly, in the battery the circuit is closed by ions moving.

It is certainly appropriate to stop making things more and more complicated now and to come back down to earth and to Janet, Stafford and Mr Krueger. The simple electric circuit surely is not simple for young students and also is not for students at college level who have severe difficulties understanding the science view. But the simple circuit is not simple also from the physics point of view. Certainly, matters usually are not that simple as presented in science classes. Of course, often we have to make things simple in order to allow a chance for learning. But we have to be aware of the ways in which we trivialise the science point of view. Viewed from this perspective it is difficult to say, for instance, whether Stafford really holds the *correct* science view. Of course, the way he argues is convincing. Surely, in metal wires there are no positive charges that may move. But does his view go beyond that idea? Is he able to apply this idea in other more complicated cases?

To tell or not to tell? Mr Krueger worries whether in the end he has to *tell* the students the correct view. His idea in the lesson under inspection is that students are required to develop their own theories about current flow in the electric circuit. This certainly is a valuable strategy – if students may draw on solid previous knowledge about electric circuits. Students then are encouraged to actively think about what they know and what they remember. In other words, they have the chance to reconstruct what they learned in an active manner. Of course, there is a certain risk in this strategy. Namely, if students like Janet draw on alternative ideas deeply rooted in everyday experiences, the teacher has to provide arguments in favour of the science view. Even so, just to tell the correct view will fail as becomes clear in the case of Janet.

To conclude, Mr Krueger is most worried about the 'false' view that Janet holds and about her resistance to giving up the idea that is so convincing and obvious for her. Maybe he should be more worried about those in the class who speak as if they hold the scientifically acceptable view by simply following opinion leaders or present an item stored in memory. Janet apparently struggles hard with the conflict between her conviction and the consensus of the class. It is quite likely that at the end of her struggle she understands what current flow in the electric circuit is about much better than her peers.

★   ★   ★

Editors' synthesis

Barry Krueger's classroom provides a setting familiar to most science teachers – students working with materials carefully selected by the teacher to provide a structured experience designed to scaffold students' knowledge towards a scientific view of the world. Teachers will also recognise that critical point in the lesson when it becomes obvious that the students' understanding falls short of the teacher's intentions (and the textbook assertions). It is at this point – often towards the end of the lesson – that many science teachers are faced with the dilemma, 'to tell or not to tell?'

What Krueger's story and the accompanying commentaries provide is a deeper understanding of the complexity of this dilemma. Several issues emerge from these analyses. The first issue concerns the status of scientific knowledge. On the one hand, the authors acknowledge the tentative and complex nature of science. Loughran, for example, explains that the truck analogy provides a different way of understanding electricity. Duit reminds us that the simple circuit is not simple – electron flow explains some conditions of electrical flow but not all. It is a model and not the ultimate truth. On the other hand, all three commentators speak about the importance of moving students towards the 'correct' or 'right' answers or 'the science view'. Clearly, the question of what constitutes a correct view of science and how to qualify this view remains one of the core issues in trying to teach for understanding (Louden and Wallace, 1995).

A second and related issue concerns the importance of the process of coming to understand. Both Loughran and Duit applaud Krueger's attempts to promote theory building or sense making in his classroom. Indeed, each commentator argues that understanding is as much about this struggle to make sense as it is to come to the 'correct' view. Duit claims that – notwithstanding her imperfect knowledge – Janet is more likely than her peers to understand what current flow is about. However, as Krueger's experience with Janet illustrates, students are unlikely to respond positively to this approach without some preparation. As Loughran says, students need to get used to 'justifying their thinking and challenging the thinking of others (their teacher included)'.

The third issue concerns the powerful effect of school structures – school timetables, syllabus requirements, textbooks and assessment procedures – on the teaching and learning of science. Reforms based on constructivist or other ideas are unlikely to succeed in the face of these powerful regularities of schooling which compel teachers to adopt a 'teach and test' regime. Students, too, understand the rules of what Krueger calls 'the learning game'. Experience tells them that, in due course, the teacher will more than likely provide them with the correct answer. There is enormous pressure on even the most innovative teacher to conform to students' expectations.

Finally, there is the issue of responsibility for learning (and teaching). In order to move beyond a reliance on the teacher for the right answer, there is a need for students to accept some responsibility for learning. For Loughran, this issue of responsibility for learning lies at the heart of the dilemma, 'to tell or not to tell'. Good teachers tread the 'middle ground' on this issue, mediating between the two extremes of telling (and therefore taking on some of the responsibility) and not telling (and encouraging students to take more responsibility). According to Loughran, different situations call for different responses – deciding what to do and when involves a 'wealth of pedagogical understanding'.

Notes

1   There are some hundreds of studies on students' conceptions of the electric circuit and on their learning processes towards the physics view in the bibliography by Pfundt and Duit (1998).
2   'Clashing current' is Osborne's (1981) term for such a conception.
3   See the model of conceptual change by Posner et al. (1982) for arguments about convincing students that science conceptions are more valuable than their own conceptions (see also, for a summary of a more recent interpretation of that model, Duit and Treagust, 1998).

References

Champagne, A. B., Gunstone, R. F. and Klopfer, L. E. (1985). Effecting changes in cognitive structures among physics students. In L. West and L. Pines (eds), *Cognitive structure and conceptual change* (pp. 163–186). Orlando, FL: Academic Press.

Driver, R. and Easley, J. A. (1978). Pupils and paradigms: A review of literature related to concept development in adolescent science students. *Studies in Science Education*, 5, 61–84.

Duit, R. and Treagust, D. (1998). Learning in science – From behaviourism towards social constructivism and beyond. In B. J. Fraser and K. G. Tobin (eds), *International handbook of science education* (pp. 3–25). Dordrecht, The Netherlands: Kluwer.

Feyerabend, P. K. (1975). *Against method: Outline of an anarchistic theory of knowledge*. London: Verso.

Lakatos, I. (1970). Falsification and the methodology of scientific research programs. In I. Lakatos and A. Musgrave (eds), *Criticism and the growth of knowledge* (pp. 91–181). Cambridge, UK: Cambridge University Press.

Lawson, A. E. and Renner, J. W. (1975). Piagetian theory and biology teaching. *The American Biology Teacher*, 37, 336–343.

Lorsbach, A. and Tobin, K. (1992). Constructivism as a referent for science teaching. *NARST News*, 30, 9–11.

Louden, W. and Wallace, J. (1995). What we don't understand about teaching for understanding. Paper presented at the annual meeting of the National Association for Research in Science Teaching, San Francisco, CA.

Osborne, R. (1981). Children's ideas about electric current. *New Zealand Science Teacher*, 29, 12 ff.

Osborne, R. and Freyberg, P. (1985). *Learning in science: The implications of children's science*. Auckland, New Zealand: Heinemann.

Pfundt, H. and Duit, R. (1998). *Bibliography – Students' alternative frameworks and science education*. Kiel, Germany: Institute for Science Education (IPN).

Pines, A. L. and West, L. H. T. (1985). Conceptual understanding and science learning: An interpretation of research within a sources-of-knowledge framework. *Science Education*, 70, 583–604.

Popper, K. R. (1972). *Conjectures and refutations: The growth of scientific knowledge*. London: Routledge & Kegan Paul.

Posner, G. J., Strike, K. A., Hewson, P. W. and Gertzog, W. A. (1982). Accommodation of a scientific conception: Toward a theory of conceptual change. *Science Education*, 66, 2, 211–227.

Solomon, J. (1994). The rise and fall of constructivism. *Studies in Science Education*, 23, 1–19.

Tobin, K. (1990). Social constructivist perspectives on the reform of science education. *Australian Science Teachers Journal*, 36 (4), 29–35.

Treagust, D., Duit, R. and Fraser, B. (eds) (1996). *Improving teaching and learning in science and mathematics*. New York: Teachers College Press.

Chapter 14

Science for all

Contributions by Anna Blahey, Ann Campbell,
Peter J. Fensham and Gaalen L. Erickson

Editors' introduction

Science for all has been a catch cry for science education since the mid-1980s (Fensham, 1985, 2000). Science for all, and its associated movement, scientific literacy, takes the position that science education is a fundamental right to be accorded every member of the population, regardless of background, nationality, language, sex, cultural origins and/or socio-economic circumstances. The stance here is that scientific literacy is essential for the personal, intellectual, social and economic well-being and futures of all students. While there is broad, in-principle, agreement about the desirability of science for all, there are different orientations to the issue depending on whether the focus is on goals (ends) or processes (means).

The goals orientation to science for all places emphasis on a broad set of aims or outcomes for school science, usually organised around the acquisition and application of science knowledge and procedures. Lists of such goals can be found in many publications on scientific literacy (Bybee and Ben-Zvi, 1998; Bybee and DeBoer, 1994; DeBoer, 2000; Fensham, 1985; Roberts, 1988). While commentators also refer to the processes required to achieve those goals, alluding to the importance of attending to differences among students, the basic premise is that scientific literacy is a concept that should be broadly applied to the school population. According to Stinner and Williams (1998, p. 1,028), for example, science for everyone is 'science that is comprehensible to most students, that students find meaningful and interesting, and that relates to the everyday lives and experience of most students'.

Another perspective on this issue focuses on the processes of teaching school science, particularly the cultural consequences of terms such as science for all (Aikenhead, 1996; Lee and Fradd, 1998; Tobin, 1998). Commentators point out the difficulty of using terms such as 'comprehensible', 'most students', 'meaningful' and 'everyday lives'. These terms are particularly problematic when used to describe the characteristics and learning of students who come from marginalised communities. What is comprehensible and meaningful for one community may not be so for another. Further, the embodied practices and predispositions for thought and action – what Bourdieu (1977) call the habitus – of students from marginalised communities are often far removed from the lives and experiences of those who design and deliver the curriculum. According to the process perspective, science for all can only be achieved through a recognition, particularly on the part of teachers, of the cultural capital brought to the learning of science by all students, particularly those from marginalised communities (Tobin, 1998).

These two (equally defensible) perspectives, one about ends and the other about means, provide a set of ongoing dilemmas for the practising science teacher. It is not possible to teach science without some content, skills and application goals in mind. Equally, one must consider that different students and groups of students come to class with different experiences – so goals for some may not be appropriate for others. The danger is that, in the quest to achieve particular goals, teachers may come to regard the habitus of certain students as a deficiency to be overcome rather than a resource to be used. There is a further danger, as Gallard and colleagues (1998, p. 951) warn, of 'watered-down curricula, which ask less of minority students or provide a laissez faire environment'. Either way, if the goals are too remote from the students or too remote from the scientific norms, students may engage in passive and/or active resistance to the enacted curriculum.

This dilemma sets the context for the story that follows. In *All work and no play makes school hell*, Anna Blahey describes her experience of teaching science in a weekly research period to 10R, a group of Grade 10 students from low socio–economic circumstances. By Anna's account these students have a history in the school of poor learning, absenteeism and disruptive behaviour. Anna describes her attempts to juggle the competing demands of providing a meaningful, school science experience with her own survival. The story is followed by commentaries by a school colleague, Ann Campbell, and by Peter Fensham and Gaalen Erickson.

All work and no play makes school hell

Anna Blahey

Friday, Period 6, Grade 10 Science. This class contains some of the roughest students at Township High School. A mixture of behaviour problems, low self-esteem students, low ability, some almost illiterate, sometimes aggressive with a long history of truanting, abusive language and not a very high regard for teachers or education in general. These were the kind of students I was facing for a 'research period' once a week. I must admit, not all the kids were as difficult as this. There were at least two or three reasonably nice kids, but as a whole I was not exaggerating. Needless to say, I was not looking forward to 'fighting' this class to impart a small amount of knowledge.

I was not their regular teacher and therefore we had not built a relationship or developed any mutual respect. We were also placed in a room, Lab 6, which was a demonstration lab, poorly equipped and reasonably small (not their usual room, so they were in an unfamiliar environment and unsettled). Even though this was only one period a week it caused me quite a lot of thought and worry. I had come to the realisation that this could not be handled or even approached as any other teaching period.

My first thought was to keep them suitably occupied with practical work allowing for the limited facilities and space. Our first period of the term involved measuring the lung capacity of certain students (with their regular teacher the class were doing the topic Circulatory and Respiratory Systems so this activity fitted in perfectly). The lesson went much better than I had expected. The students were enthusiastic and quite cooperative. I set up the measuring as a sort of competition. Along the way I posed certain questions, such as, would a tall person have a greater lung capacity than a short person, a male greater than a female, or a large-framed person greater than a small-framed person? The students then chose the next person for testing with these questions in mind.

After we tested each student we recorded the lung capacity and the height of the individual on the blackboard and in the students' books (if they had them) or on paper. I introduced the class to the word 'correlation', and we looked for any obvious patterns in our results. The class really enjoyed the competition aspect of the measuring and wanted to out-do their first attempts. I was pleased to do this for the next week on the provision that every member of the class graphed the first set of results (peer pressure can be a wonderful tool). When the next lesson came they made no complaints about having to graph the results – even the ones who caught onto the graphing exercise quickly helped those who were having trouble. I checked all the students' books and kept my end of the bargain; we had lung capacity finals. I knew we couldn't do lung capacity readings all year, but I realised I had found the key to 10R/Science.

The following week I introduced 10R to a game called Fictionary. The students were given an unknown word from the dictionary and they made up a definition for the word (in groups) on a piece of paper. I collected the definitions and added the correct definition to the collection of false ones. I then read out all the definitions to the class. A team could score points either by choosing the correct definition or having another team accept its incorrect definition. I was stunned at some of the definitions written by these seemingly low-ability, almost illiterate, students. Granted the spelling was awful, the imagination they used in some of the definitions was surprising. The students thoroughly enjoyed the game and they actually remembered some of the words and the correct definitions the following week.

10R/Science and I have reached a happy medium. Every week we do either a small experiment, where they learn basic skills and science concepts, talk about science issues that appear on the news or in the papers or discuss interesting science facts. I usually quiz them at the end of the activity and, if they have paid attention and can answer the questions for the last ten minutes or so of the period, we play a round of Fictionary or watch a video. However, they always have to do some work first.

So far, this approach has worked extremely well with 10R. I have had no behaviour problems in class (granted they do get a little noisy at times but it's working noise and that's acceptable to me) and virtually no truanting from this lesson each week. Friday, sixth period is no longer as big a concern or worry as it has been in the past – it is now reasonably enjoyable and is proving to be an ongoing challenge.

★   ★   ★

Colleague commentary

Ann Campbell

I thoroughly enjoyed reading the scenario about 10R Science. This case study demonstrates that a teacher must review a situation and determine appropriate strategies to best deal with the particular problem in order to gain confidence of students and to have settled lessons. Teachers must be prepared to take risks and to adopt untraditional methods and be prepared to innovate if they are not immediately successful with a difficult class. I believe that Mrs Blahey has been successful in the approach which she has taken with this class.

Mrs Blahey certainly was posed with a difficult dilemma. The allocation of a mixed-ability group for a single period each week in a less than adequate room was a problem. She has solved the problem in an interesting manner. She has examined the situation and determined a strategy which is favourable to both the students and to the teacher. She has successfully established a climate within the room which is conducive to learning in a non-threatening manner. This climate was developed by encouraging the students to think for themselves and to be successful. The students emerged with an enhanced self-esteem and a greater motivation to participate.

The major problem with these students is that they have a deeply entrenched history of failure and as a means of coping they adopt recalcitrant behaviour patterns. Mrs Blahey's approach has started to make these students aware of the fact that science is not limited to the confines of the classroom. Science is an important and useful part of our daily lives and designing lessons which are less stressful and relevant can change the students' perceptions of science. Future lessons can build on this initial interest and provide a stimulus for motivation.

A suggestion for follow-up lessons could be to have small groups of students prepare short talks about interesting aspects of science, which they have read or heard about outside the school, and to present these to the class. Another possibility could be to organise debates or role plays among the students. Certainly once interest is captured and behaviour becomes less of a problem, the possibilities are endless.

Congratulations on an innovative approach which has involved a certain amount of risk taking. Teachers cannot rely on traditional approaches with many students and the adoption of this type of unconventional approach is one way to make school, and particularly science, more relevant and enjoyable to the students. Certainly students who enjoy learning allow teachers to exist in a 'stress free' environment.

★   ★   ★

Surviving science lessons is not science for all

Peter J. Fensham, Monash University

When I read this story, I was reminded of my visit to talk to a science teacher of Grade 10 in what was then a Junior Technical School (boys only) in a Melbourne suburb. Finding nobody in the classroom to which the front office directed me, I was rescued by another teacher who told me I would find John and Grade 10 in or near the last shelter shed behind the main school buildings. Sure enough there were Grade 10, beavering away, making fibre glass canoes which were to be completed in time for a race on the river in the last week of term.

Now at Township High School the science teacher solved her problem of engaging 10R in Science Research with the same motivational ploy – competition. You can build fibre glass canoes for a term, but you can't 'do lung capacity readings all year long'. Competition also loses its motivational edge if the same students are always the winners and losers – a lesson 10R knew only too well since they as a group had learnt it the hard way through their many years of schooling. Furthermore, it is not easy, if you have to parallel and complement a traditional science syllabus (Circulatory and Respiratory System suggests this was the case), to come up with a series of practical exercises that have an equally attractive competitive aspect.

So, in the Township High School case the teacher needed an additional motivational carrot. To her surprise and delight, a strategy she had obviously used before, short sessions of the party game Fictionary were swallowed by 10R. Hence their less compelling science tasks were completed with the faster students helping the others through – an admirable and spontaneous example of perhaps cooperative learning or, at least, of shared task completion. Anna is to be congratulated on handling a difficult situation so capably and she may well say 'this approach has worked well with 10R', 'no behaviour problems', 'no truanting' and 'Friday 6th period no longer as big a concern as it has been in the past'.

It is undoubtedly a case of skilful teacher survival in a designated Science Research period. Can more be claimed for it? Is it an example of gender-inclusive science teaching and learning? Is it an example of teaching for scientific literacy? Has it some of the characteristics of what the slogan, science for all, has been challenging science educators to bring to the classroom for the last fifteen years? Let me try some of these criteria on this story before setting the story in terms of a more recent curricular approach to teaching science.

Gender inclusivity

Topics in personal biology tend to rate highly on interest for both middle secondary boys and girls. Competition is a stronger motivator for boys than for girls but girls cooperate more easily in learning than boys. The measures for the teacher-directed search for correlations were restricted to general factors of which only sex (as any standard textbook or encyclopedia would report) is likely to show a clear correlation. This correlation makes the boys the consistent winners in science whatever the outcome of the Fictionary might be.

Scientific literacy

While there are a number of ways of defining scientific literacy, and hence of setting up criteria for its teaching and learning, the seven emphases Doug Roberts (1988) set out will suffice to indicate that this story hardly rates in terms of this contemporary goal for school science. These emphases are learning for (i) Everyday Coping, (ii) Solid Foundation for Future Learning, (iii) Science Skill Acquisition, (iv) Correct Explanations, (v) Self as a Confident Explainer, (vi) Science/Technology Decisions, and (vii) Understanding the Nature of Science.

Without even enlarging the definitions of these categories of purpose for learning science in school, it will I think be apparent that the story does not score well. Only on the seventh of these, Nature of Science, does it probably score at all. The students did carry out measures of one variable in relation to some others to see which pairs correlated together. However, these ideas all seemed to be teacher-defined and teacher-directed. The students were simply passively (in a minds-on sense) carrying out the measurement, recording and calculating tasks. If the students had been asked to suggest variables that might be related to lung capacity, to come up with a variety of ways of measuring it and to think how they could test their ideas about it, the beginning into the nature of science could have been rather larger and open-ended in a way that may actually have taken off.

Science for all

Two criteria that were identified early in the debates about science for all are (i) the likely usefulness of the learning in the students' everyday life out of school and (ii) the chance that it will produce a response of wonder and curiosity about nature. Not much of a score on these.

Another criterion is the students' awareness of the worth of the knowledge they were acquiring. My encounter with the fibre glass canoe builders coincided with the introduction of polymers and plastics into the senior syllabus for Chemistry. The academic stream of students were learning, for several types of monomer, about chain and condensation mechanisms of polymerisation, and about the distinctions between thermoplastic and thermosetting plastics. On a test-tube scale most of them also made a crude sample of a nylon-like polymer. The canoe makers learnt, on a practical scale, about the conditions of concentration, catalyst, temperature, and time that led to effective polymerisation and how their product could be reinforced, shaped, worked and finished in an aesthetically decorated form.

In the academic class, the successful students would have acquired a sense of having been introduced, at the atomic scale level, to a new class of macro substances of great social importance to a vast field of chemical knowledge that went far beyond school chemistry. They acquired no useful practical knowledge. The Grade 10s who made the canoes, in contrast, all had a sense of having acquired a powerful and useful new practical skill, and were able to talk confidently about what they had learnt about the process of polymerisation. Fibre glassing has a high potential, particularly for boys, in a society like Australia where surfing and cars (often with small dents needing repair) are common among school leavers. There are no obvious counterparts in the case of the lung capacity lessons of knowledge, theoretical or practical, that would make the students feel their learning in the science tasks was worthwhile.

Setting the story in a more recent curricular approach to teaching science

Many of the science concepts in traditional school science have application in a variety of real-world contexts that are part of the lives of the school students. These concepts exist in science itself because they have useful relationships (for science) with a number of other concepts. For example, force is a useful concept in physics because it relates to acceleration, to work, to current, to pressure, etc. It is part of a network of relationships. In traditional school science we often create special laboratory situations that enable these relationships to be taught independently of each other. This simplifies the learning in one sense but, in another sense, makes it unreal or abstract. A major development in curricula to make science more meaningful to more students is embodied in the slogan, 'Networks of concepts in networks of contexts'.

Large-scale real-world contexts like transport or sport are made up of a large number of smaller contexts which share some elements and not others. In this sense they are a 'network of contexts'. Many of the smaller contexts involve applications of the relations between force and those other science concepts to which it is related. Science teachers using this curriculum approach start with real-world contexts that are familiar and of significance to their students to provide motivation and to assist the learning of the science concepts and their relationships. The contexts give these concepts immediate meaning for the students before the elegance of their role in science has been appreciated by most of them. Conversely, at whatever level of meaning the science concepts and relationships are learned, the students gain an expanded sense of their understanding and confidence to live and act in the everyday situations these contexts involve.

Lung capacity does no doubt have applications in human performance and hence in a number of significant real-world contexts for students. The 'concepts in contexts' approach may have provided the extrinsic and intrinsic motivation for the students and their learning that could have made this story of 10R an exemplar of science for all.

★   ★   ★

Playing around and creating learning conditions

Gaalen L. Erickson, University of British Columbia

Anna's short case story about a class of 'reluctant learners' raises a number of interesting pedagogical issues about the demands and the diversity of classrooms today. On reading this story we, as readers, might ask ourselves: 'What is this a case of?' As with all stories or descriptions of classroom practice, this case can be framed in many different ways depending upon the types of issues that we wish to bring to the foreground and those which we will leave to recede into the background. The aspects of this case that I intend to foreground relate to some important issues about the nature of student and teacher learning. Some of these issues are fairly transparent, while others are deeply embedded in the language, practices and institutional structures alluded to in the story. I will discuss what I consider to be the more interesting of these explicit and implicit issues in my brief commentary.

The initial 'framing' of the case by Anna is that she was working with a 'difficult class' – that is, one containing students with a variety of traits which teachers typically associate with management and behavioural problems. While the curricular or institutional context for this case is not revealed to us, we can speculate that it represents an attempt by the administrators in the school to keep a group of non-academic students gainfully 'occupied' for one period a week. All we are told is that Anna has inherited this class of 10R students for a once-a-week 'research period' and that it would be a bonus if she could relate her curricular activities to those of the regular science teacher. Thus, the very ambiguity of the description of the context allows for a significant degree of speculation on the part of both the commentator and the reader.

I was initially struck by Anna's preoccupation with establishing the management structures for 10R. This preoccupation is not surprising, as I suspect that all of us have had the deeply unsettling experience of working with a group of students who had little to no interest in what we were trying to accomplish with that class. What I find to be refreshingly honest was Anna's description of her own expectations and assumptions about her 'low-ability students'. It appears that Anna did have some prior experience with difficult classes since she immediately decided that the students needed: to be engaged with some form of practical work; to be motivated through the use of relevant activities, which often included some kind of competition; and that appropriate classroom behaviour would be rewarded with the use of games.

I found Anna's description of the 'happy medium' that she achieved with this class to be interesting in terms of what it seemed to reveal about what she learned from teaching this class. She registered surprise in their genuine interest in meaningful activities, in their ability to write imaginative definitions when given the opportunity, and their ability to remember terms and definitions which were elicited in a context that had some significance for the students. It seems as though Anna had 'discovered' some of the conditions for effective learning for all learners – engagement in meaningful activities, providing some ownership over the learning process, demonstrating a respect for the thinking of her students – to name several such conditions. I suspect that Anna's teaching in her 'regular classes' was informed by these intuitions about learning, but she did not appear to realise that these conditions of learning also apply to so-called 'low-ability' students. In fact, this case illustrates clearly the important role played by various types of scaffolding activities and by other affective relationships in the learning context. These factors, then, are particularly important for the kinds of students that Anna was teaching in 10R – students who do not respond well to more traditional forms of transmissive teaching.

So what lessons might we draw from such a case? It seems to me that aspects of this case point us in some potentially fruitful directions for the design and enactment of classroom practices. First, as indicated earlier, the case does illustrate some of the important learning conditions that ought to be considered when creating productive learning environments. Hoban (1996), in his study of teacher learning, drew upon Cambourne's (1988) analysis of how young children learn to talk in a family learning environment. Cambourne identified eight such conditions which were: immersion, engagement, demonstrations, expectations, responsibility, practice, approximation and feedback. While these conditions are clearly interactive and not mutually exclusive, we can see some strong parallels in this case as Anna struggled to create an environment that worked for her and her reluctant learners. They became *immersed* in a set of *engaging* tasks that were at least somewhat relevant to them. Anna endeavoured to set up clear *expectations* for their response to these tasks and held them *responsible* for their behaviour through the use of peer pressure. Furthermore, she also recognised the need for opportunities to *practise* their developing skills and understanding through continued experimentation along with extensive *feedback* on their work through class discussion and the use of quizzes.

In closing, this brief case captures some aspects of the challenges as well as the complexity of teaching in contemporary classrooms with a large diversity of students in terms of background, interests and abilities. Anna's comment that the 10R class is 'now reasonably enjoyable and is proving to be an ongoing challenge' speaks to the attributes that I think that teachers must develop if they are to be successful in addressing these complex settings – attributes which portray the important attitudinal and inquiry aspects of teaching.

★   ★   ★

Editor's synthesis

The situation described in *All work and no play makes school hell* is one familiar to many who have experienced the highs and lows of teaching science to students with a history of resistance to schooling. The key issue for each of the commentators is whether or not there is something productive – in terms of the goals and/or processes of science education – going on in Blahey's class. While this may seem to be a straightforward question, the answers provided by the commentators reveal a more cloudy picture.

In Fensham's commentary, he uses several criteria for judging the worth of the science learning in Blahey's class. These criteria include some of the standard goals for science literacy and science for all, including whether the science learning was valued by, useful to, and created a sense of curiosity among, students. While acknowledging the teacher's skill in motivating these difficult students, Fensham concludes that the learning falls short on almost all the criteria he proposes. At the heart of Fensham's critique is his sense that the science learning is absent of context. He cites missed opportunities to connect the lung capacity activity, for example, to real-life contexts such as sport. By contrast, he relates another example of a group of Grade 10s who were learning about polymers by making canoes. According to Fensham, it is context (or networks of contexts) which provide the meaning for learning about science concepts.

Fensham's point about the importance of scientific context is well made and well illustrated by the canoe-building example. Erickson, in his commentary, takes a different view of context, choosing to highlight what he calls the 'important learning conditions that ought to be considered when creating productive learning environments'. Erickson suggests that classroom productivity results from the complex interaction of a number of learning conditions – including immersion, engagement, demonstrations, expectations, responsibility, practice, approximation, and feedback. His generally positive assessment of Blahey's teaching on these criteria indicates that context is a complex notion, with social, attitudinal and emotional, as well as scientific dimensions. Blahey's own head of department, Campbell, seems to take a similar line, praising her colleague for 'successfully establish[ing] a climate within the room which is conducive to learning in a non-threatening manner' and 'encouraging the students to think for themselves'.

Given these differing assessments of Blahey's teaching, how are we to judge the worth of the science learning? What appears as disconnected science teaching to one commentator is considered a productive learning environment by others. Granted, each commentator chose to view the case from a slightly different perspective. However, the different views again highlight the difficulty of teaching science for all, particularly when students come from peripheral communities. Here, we see the dilemma for the teacher resurfacing. Should the focus be on recreating 'real-life' versions of the subject matter, as advocated by Fensham, or creating a set of conditions for learning, as advocated by Erickson? The answer, of course, lies somewhere in the middle, nicely captured by Blahey's comment that '10R and I have reached a happy medium'. One could easily envisage a few refinements to Blahey's teaching, such as making better subject-matter connections and moving towards a more cooperative (and less competitive) environment, with teachers and students working as coparticipants (Schön, 1985; Tobin, 1998) to shape the science learning. However, we must not underestimate the challenge and complexity of teaching science in contemporary classrooms, of accommodating diverse students' worlds while moving towards an increasingly scientific discourse.

References

Aikenhead, G. S. (1996). Science education: Border crossings into the subculture of science. *Studies in Science Education*, 27, 1–52.

Bourdieu, P. (1977). *Outline of a theory of practice*. (Trans. Richard Nice). Cambridge: Cambridge University Press.

Bybee, R. W. and Ben-Zvi, N. (1998). Science curriculum: Transforming goals to practices. In B. J. Fraser and K. G. Tobin (eds), *International handbook of science education* (pp. 487–498). Dordrecht, The Netherlands: Kluwer.

Bybee, R. W. and DeBoer, G. E. (1994). Goals for the science curriculum. In D. Gabel (ed.), *Handbook on science teaching and learning* (pp. 357–387). Washington, DC: Macmillan.

Cambourne, B. (1988). *The whole story*. New York: Ashton Scholastic.

DeBoer, G. E. (2000). Scientific literacy: Another look at its historical and contemporary meanings and its relationship to science education reform. *Journal of Research in Science Teaching*, 37 (6), 582–601.

Fensham, P. J. (1985). Science for all. *Journal of Curriculum Studies*, 17, 415–435.

—— (2000). Providing suitable content in the 'science for all' curriculum. In R. Millar, J. Leach and J. Osborne (eds), *Improving science education: The contribution of research* (pp. 147–164). Buckingham, UK: Open University Press.

Gallard, A., Viggiano, E., Graham, S., Stewart, G. and Vigliano, M. (1998). The learning of voluntary and involuntary minorities in science classrooms. In B. J. Fraser and K. G. Tobin (eds), *International handbook of science education* (pp. 941–953). Dordrecht, The Netherlands: Kluwer.

Hoban, G. (1996). A professional development model based on interrelated principles of teacher learning. Unpublished doctoral dissertation, The University of British Columbia, Vancouver, BC.

Lee, O. and Fradd, S. (1998). Science for all, including students from non-English-language backgrounds. *Educational Researcher*, 27 (4), 12–21.

Roberts, D. (1988). What counts as science education? In P. Fensham (ed.), *Development and dilemmas in science education* (pp. 27–54). New York: Falmer.

Schön, D. (1985). *The design studio*. London: RIBA Publications.

Stinner, A. and Williams, H. (1998). History and philosophy of science in the science curriculum. In B. J. Fraser and K. G. Tobin (eds), *International handbook of science education* (pp. 1,027–1,045). Dordrecht, The Netherlands: Kluwer.

Tobin, K. (1998). Issues and trends in the teaching of science. In B. J. Fraser and K.G. Tobin (eds), *International handbook of science education* (pp. 129–151). Dordrecht, The Netherlands: Kluwer.

Chapter 15

Teaching out of field

*Contributions by Gerald Carey, Allan Harrison,
Diane Grayson and Uri Ganiel*

Editors' introduction

A decade and a half of research highlights the critical influence of teachers' subject-matter understandings on their pedagogical orientations and decisions (Ball and McDiarmid, 1990; Feiman-Nemser and Parker, 1990; Gess-Newsome and Lederman, 1999). Much of this work arises from Shulman's (1986, 1987) insights about the importance of teachers' content knowledge. In highlighting the importance of content knowledge in teaching, Shulman posits that teachers' understandings need to extend beyond specific topics of the curriculum. Teachers' capacity to pose questions, select tasks, evaluate student understandings and make curriculum choices all depend on how they understand the subject matter.

These understandings, according to McDiarmid and colleagues (1989), involve more than 'staying one chapter ahead of the students'. They include understanding how knowledge progresses in the field, how phenomena are related, and the fundamental ideas which underlie interpretation of events (Grossman *et al.*, 1989). It is argued that teachers have a better chance of being able to help their students to develop flexible understandings of subject matter if they themselves understand the subject matter well. Moreover, such understandings enable teachers to develop a variety of ways of representing their understanding for their students who bring with them very different experiences and knowledge.

These issues have particular poignancy for those teachers who are teaching in a field outside their subject discipline. Studies of the problems faced by science teachers when teaching out of field (Carlsen, 1991; Gess-Newsome and Lederman, 1995; Hashweh, 1987; Lee, 1995; Millar, 1988; Sanders *et al.*, 1993) show that out-of-field science teachers lack a repertoire of pedagogical content knowledge tricks. When planning for teaching, they do not know how long activities might take and lack a confident sense of how the activities are connected to the content. Activities are often planned with the idea of determining if or how things work. As one teacher in the Sanders *et al.* (1993, p. 729) study commented, '[you] just watch and see if they get it, you know, if it works'. Out-of-field science teachers often make rapid and frequent changes to their lessons. Frequently, they encounter difficulties with explanations, leaving both teachers and students confused (Sanders *et al.*, 1993). These teachers spend more time on teacher talk and plan less risky activities than their in-field counterparts (Carlsen, 1991). After the lesson, out-of-field teachers often reflect on the (in)adequacy of their content representations and are consistently uncertain about whether their students understood the content (Sanders *et al.*, 1993).

However, unlike their novice counterparts, experienced out-of-field science teachers have a solid base of general pedagogical knowledge (Sanders *et al.*, 1993). They are, for example, aware of the importance of interactive strategies in teaching, of keeping the class intact and engaged, and of the need to focus on student understanding. Through the authority of their experience, they have a meta-awareness of what needs to be done to teach well and the limitations on teaching imposed by their lack of content knowledge. This awareness provides a dilemma for the experienced out-of-field science teacher – whether to deliver a predictable, well-scripted, teacher-centred lesson following closely the textbook or curriculum guide, so as to remain 'faithful' to the content, or to allow the lesson to follow interesting side-issues or student questions, with risky consequences in terms of explaining, understanding and connecting with the science content. In this chapter, we illustrate this dilemma with the case of Gerald Carey, an experienced biology teacher, who finds himself teaching physics. The case, titled *Galileo revisited*, is followed by commentaries by Allan Harrison, Diane Grayson and Uri Ganiel.

Galileo revisited

Gerald Carey

Physics has always been of interest to me, but understanding the basic ideas is not one of my strong points. I had taught Grade 10 physics sporadically over the last couple of years, and, as a teacher of biology, had always found it tantalisingly interesting yet frustratingly boring. I am sure it came across this way to my Grade 10 students. I could never get a total grip on the subject. It seemed to me to be a collection of vaguely connected concepts swamped by inexplicable formulae. As my grasp of basic ideas such as light or the laws of motion was both tenuous and superficial, I could not teach the subject with much confidence. Never was this more apparent than when it came to physics practicals. All the trolleys, ticker timers and light boxes meant little to me – they seemed to attempt to illustrate a small aspect of the theory but never really illuminate it. How could I challenge my students' understanding of the subject if my own had such a feeble basis? This year was different. Close contact with a dedicated physics teacher and access to a great textbook (without too many equations) has brought greater understanding for me. I actually looked forward to teaching the topic. However, would my new-found interest lead to better understanding for my students? Would they be able to learn something of significance and relevance? Let me recount one of my experiences this year and you be the judge.

Initially, the unit started with Newton's First Law of Motion – objects at rest will stay at rest, and objects moving at a constant speed or velocity will stay at that speed unless acted on by a force. Understanding of this law depended on an understanding of the term 'inertia' as well as the effects of friction and air resistance. This particular day I ventured into the Grade 10 class with the aim of trying to show as many examples of this Law as I could. These included the following examples:

- if you are travelling in a go-cart when it hits a log, the cart will stop but you keep moving at a constant velocity until stopped by a force (namely the ground);
- it is important that children are properly restrained in the back seat of a moving car – if the car stops suddenly, their inertia will carry them through the front window; and
- if you are carrying a large bowl of water and have to stop suddenly, there is a good chance that the water will spill over the side, because it is continuing to move at a constant velocity even though you have stopped the bowl.

So it went on. I was not sure if I was making an impact on them until we started discussing the role of air resistance in stopping objects from travelling at a constant velocity. Now, the class was not even sure what the air was made up of, let alone how air particles might act as a force to slow objects down. I gave the example of riding a bike into the wind. 'What is it in the wind that is slowing the bike-rider down?' I asked. I then offered the idea that the molecules of gases in the air together exerted enough force to be able to do this and was greeted by nodding heads, but blank looks.

Briefly, I then talked about the experiment Galileo was purported to have done on the Tower of Pisa – that is, drop two objects of similar size but different weight. I said we could illustrate this in the classroom to help us understand the effects of air resistance. I held up a flat, wide folder and a piece of paper around the same dimensions and I asked the class to predict which would hit the surface of the desk first. Most students said that the folder would, because it had greater weight. I dropped both and sure enough the folder hit the desk first. I then put the piece of paper on top of the folder and again asked the class how quickly both objects would fall. Again, most said the folder would reach the ground much more quickly, because of its greater weight. I dropped both and, counter-intuitively, the paper did not float off the top of the folder, but fell with it at the same speed. They thought I was tricking them – that I had stuck it on the folder in some way. So, for my *coup-de-grâce*, I scrunched up the paper into a ball, held it next to the folder and asked for another prediction. They still said the folder would be first to hit the surface. I dropped both and, lo!, the paper and folder hit the desk simultaneously (well nearly!).

When I asked for explanations for their observations, many students were quite confused. Their own experience would indicate that the more you weigh, the faster you will fall. However, they had just seen that this was not the case. This confusion was good, because it was a confusion that came when currently held beliefs were being challenged and not simply because they did not understand my explanation. It was important that they go through this confused stage because it meant that they might be open to hearing a scientific explanation of the structure of air and how this might exert a force on objects, a force we call air resistance. From the discussion that occurred as some of the students left the class, it appeared that some of the ideas I had presented had hit home, and that some of their intuitive ideas were being challenged. I can still remember the buzz in the laboratory with students leaning over to watch the folder and paper fall, arguing among each other about their predictions, and asking more questions about what they were observing. What a difference this lesson had been to ones on the same topic last year!

★　　　★　　　★

Nodding heads and blank looks
Allan Harrison, University of Central Queensland

Gerald's account of his physics teaching is refreshing for two reasons – first the candour with which he describes his subject-knowledge weaknesses, and second, the way he went about remediating both his teaching and his students' misconceptions. I'm sure every school has teachers teaching outside their area of expertise, but how often does the struggling teacher admit his or her problem and do what Gerald did – get help from an expert in the field and find a textbook he could understand? By resolving his conceptual difficulties, Gerald came to appreciate the conceptual impasse faced by many of his students in this topic.

Gerald's problem was very real: 'How could I challenge my students' understanding . . . if my own had such a feeble basis?' And he did challenge the students' prior conceptions of motion. He wasn't prepared to 'endure' the physics topic, he refused to just go in there, go through the motions, give some notes, some pracs and a test; he was committed to changing the students' inappropriate conceptions. For instance, he says that when he explained air resistance, he 'was greeted by nodding heads, but blank looks'. The students' nominal agreement wasn't very convincing so he decided to show them a discrepant event using pieces of paper.

The problem he used contained the basic elements of the predict–observe–explain (POE) approach. As Gerald wrote 'It was important for them to go through this confused stage because it meant that they might be open to hearing a scientific explanation of the structure of air and how this might exert a force on objects.' At the same time, he confronted the Aristotelian notion that heavy objects fall faster than light objects. Gerald's account of his students' responses suggests that some of these students did undergo a degree of conceptual change.

I feel that he could have enlivened the lesson earlier on by physically demonstrating two of the three examples he cited. (Gerald's description left me thinking these examples were only talked about.) A dynamics trolley with a doll on it could have been run into a large block of wood to demonstrate inertia. Give a student a glass filled to the brim with water, tell him or her to walk fast and stop suddenly. Even the whole class could do it outside. Actually doing these things should lead to increased student learning.

Nevertheless, I found this story exciting because here was a teacher who was aware of his limited understanding and who was also cognisant of his students' alternative conceptions. He set out to do something about both problems. Sure, he probably wasn't the most knowledgeable physics teacher in that school but he was a more effective teacher than he had been and his approach suggests that he would continue to improve and that augurs well for his students.

★   ★   ★

Ways of making physics make sense
Diane Grayson, University of South Africa

I can really appreciate Gerald's comment about finding physics 'tantalisingly interesting yet frustratingly boring'. In retrospect, this is probably a good description of my experience as a physics student. I found the ideas fascinating – like the quantum mechanical notion that the observer influences what is observed, or the astrophysical idea that we are made up of atoms that came from exploding stars. Yet so much time seems to be spent on fiddling around with boring equations and doing cumbersome manipulations.

When I was a student I used to love the ideas, yet I could never do terribly well on the tests. I had come to think that perhaps I just wasn't a very good physics student. But then I spent seven years in the Physics Education Group at the University of Washington. After being exposed to the approaches developed by Arnold Arons (1990), Lillian McDermott (1996) and their colleagues – focused on developing physical understanding of concepts – I realised that I could understand physics. I discovered that given a conceptual rather than a mathematical approach to physics, I was able to develop very good intuition about, in the words of a colleague, 'what the little particles in there are doing'.

A few years ago I went back into a university physics department that taught in the traditional way. When I looked at their first-year tests I realised that I would not be able to pass them. The reason? They required students to memorise vast numbers of equations, something I had never been able to do. Now I could see how it was possible to understand the physics but do poorly in the tests.

Today more and more physicists are changing the way they present physics, from a collection of equations to a set of concepts and principles that help us explain the world around us. There are a number of excellent curricula developed in recent years that help students construct just such an understanding of physics (e.g. Laws, 1996; Sokoloff and Thornton, 1990). The people who develop such curricula subscribe to a constructivist theory of learning. In other words, they believe that all knowledge, including physics, has to be constructed by individual learners. Knowledge, by its very nature, cannot be transferred from one person's head to another person's head. So these curricula involve students in doing physics, rather than hearing about it.

I should not give the impression that we can dispense with the mathematics altogether. I am sure that many brilliant physicists look at the mathematics and see the physics. However, for mere mortals like me more words, pictures and experiments are needed to be able to see and understand the physics. Nonetheless, there are times when one needs a precise mathematical description or an actual numerical value. Then the mathematics must be brought in. Even then, far fewer equations are really necessary than students are often led to believe. Many times there is one central equation, and another half dozen or so equations are merely special cases of it. One of the reasons I went into physics in the first place was because I loved ideas and hated memorising. Memorising equations takes all the fun out of physics.

Another problem with learning physics is that physicists tend to believe that our subject is simple because we can explain a lot of the workings of the world in terms of a few basic concepts. The problem for non-physicists is that these basic concepts have very precise meanings and often differ from each other in subtle ways, ways that are not always readily apparent to the uninitiated. To make matters worse, many of these concepts are labelled by words taken from everyday language. Somehow we expect students to set aside their everyday understandings of these words, and think of them only in terms of the physics definition. For example, in everyday speech 'accelerate' means go faster, but in physics it means change velocity. Since velocity means speed in a certain direction, either a change of speed or a change of direction results in acceleration. So we get the highly non–intuitive situation where an object going round and round in a circle at a constant speed is said to accelerate because it is constantly changing direction.

On the other hand, there are some words that have a clear meaning in everyday language but are not precisely defined in physics. 'Inertia' is one such word, and so I would tend to avoid using it in class. Gerald, in one of his examples, says that children's inertia will carry them through the front window if they are not properly restrained in a moving car. Since there are so many technical terms that students need to learn I tend to avoid introducing unnecessary terms. Inertia is not used much in good, modern textbooks because it is not needed. Another problem with the term is that it is all too easy for students to think that there is some intrinsic property that makes an object move, instead of understanding that an object will keep moving at the same speed unless something exerts a force on it to change its speed.

Perhaps it is not surprising that so much of the research literature labelled 'constructivist' has come out of a physics context. Physics teachers know very well that students come into classrooms with many ideas about the concepts we are trying to teach already in place. One reason is because of the use of everyday terms by physics, illustrated above. Another reason is that a large body of elementary physics is part of students' daily life experience – force, power, energy, electricity, heat, and so on – and so students do not approach the subject *de novo*. Thus the instructional model that views science teaching as a process of facilitating conceptual change is particularly appropriate when it comes to teaching physics.

Physics teachers' first challenge is to make sure that they understand the basic concepts themselves. Often these concepts look deceptively simple, yet the subtleties may be of crucial significance. For example, in physics it is often critical to distinguish between a quantity and the change in the quantity. When heat is transferred from a hotter object to a cooler object, the amount of heat absorbed depends not on the temperature of the cooler object but on its change in temperature in the process. Another challenge physics teachers face is to try to help students develop a solid understanding of a number of concepts and, particularly difficult, learn to separate out individual concepts from a tangled bundle of related concepts. Then students need to be helped to interpret their experiences of the world in terms of physics concepts.

So let's think about Gerald's students. Gerald tells us 'their own experience would indicate that the more you weigh, the faster you will fall'. In fact, this is not the experience students would probably have had. More likely, they would have seen objects of different mass going down a hill, and seen the difference. For example, they probably know that if a truck and a car both roll down a hill starting from the top, by the time they get down to the bottom of the hill the truck would do a lot more damage to anything it hit than the car would. They might say that is because the truck was going faster, when it wasn't. The reason the truck would do a lot more damage is that it has a lot more mass and therefore a lot more momentum than the car. Thus the truck can transfer much more momentum to anything it hits, causing much more damage. Here is an example where students need to be helped to disentangle related concepts, in this case speed and momentum, in order to explain their everyday experiences using physics.

So Gerald is right to present them with demonstrations in which their non-physics beliefs were challenged. I worry about leaving the students in this state, though. I don't think that presenting them with the scientific explanation alone will be enough to remove their discomfort and confusion. That is why I advocate trying to help them explicitly link their naive conceptions to physics concepts, as well as trying to disentangle related concepts (Grayson, 1996). It seems to me that there are three different ideas that students need to clarify in Gerald's sample lesson – the force of the earth on an object causes all objects to accelerate the same amount, the force of air on an object depends on the surface area of the object, and the effect of mass is that heavier objects acquire greater momentum for the same velocity and therefore can do more damage when they hit something. So I would like to see a discussion in Gerald's class in which students compare and contrast Galileo's experiment with the experiment with the folder and flat sheet of paper and then the folder and crumpled paper. To further reinforce the idea that the difference in time of fall is caused by differences in air resistance rather than mass, it would be nice to do a demonstration in which a heavier object with a large surface area falls more slowly than a lighter object with a small surface area (e.g. a piece of flat blotting paper versus a small bit of crumpled paper).

★   ★   ★

Free fall, air resistance, Galileo and Newton: why are students confused?

Uri Ganiel, The Weizmann Institute of Science, Israel

> You can no more teach what you don't know than you can come back from where you haven't been.
> (A quote from an old teacher in the North Carolina mountains in the USA)

In many places all over the world, the teaching of physics in high schools suffers from an unfortunate state of affairs. All too often, teachers without an adequate preparation and understanding of the subject matter are assigned to teach physics, one of the more difficult topics in the school curriculum. Lacking the necessary confidence, such teachers project uncertainty and apprehension towards the subject. Their students are quick to identify these sentiments, and so many of them too are lost to physics. They become scared of it before they have had a chance to taste it and they do their best to avoid it.

In this short vignette, Gerald Carey, a biology teacher, describes his personal experience in teaching physics. His introductory remarks, describing his situation prior to the present experience, are very revealing. He admits to having been in a situation of the type described above. He has taught physics, he even found it 'of interest', yet by his own admission, he did not really understand the subject. His 'grasp of the basic ideas' was 'both tenuous and superficial'. His case, however, is somewhat more subtle. First, I was somewhat puzzled by his description of physics as being 'tantalisingly interesting yet frustratingly boring' − is there not a contradiction here? How can a 'frustratingly boring' subject be 'tantalisingly interesting'? There seems to be an ambivalence in Carey's attitude towards physics. Yes, he would have liked to understand it in depth, but alas, he did not, or could not. Things did not hang together for him, and so physics seemed to him like a 'collection of vaguely connected concepts swamped by inexplicable formulae'.

To his credit I note that he did recognise his own deficiencies. When it came to practical work, he may have understood an isolated experiment, but his understanding stopped there. It would be for him an 'attempt to illustrate a small aspect of the theory but never really illuminate it'. By his own admission, then, his understanding was fragmented at best, and he was not able to synthesise the fragments into a coherent picture. Again, he did recognise that this was a bad situation for a teacher to be in. He would not be able to 'challenge his students' understanding of the subject' given the 'feeble basis' of his own.

The way Carey tells it, he claims to have undergone something of a transformation. This was due to a combination of his interaction with a dedicated physics teacher and access to what he describes as a 'great textbook (without too many equations)'. Carey's description of the textbook as 'great', with the classification of 'not too many equations', is an important indicator. Is the book 'great' *because* it has fewer equations? If so, this connects to his previous view of physics ('swamped by inexplicable formulae'). In reality, however, physics is a science that deals with quantitative information. Mathematics, being the language used to manipulate and process such information, is indispensable in the practice of physics. Apparently, Carey is not very comfortable with mathematics, and this may be a partial explanation for his uneasiness with physics. Now he feels that matters have improved. He thinks he understands the topic he is going to teach, and wonders whether his newly found understanding, interest and confidence will be passed on to his students. However, in reading Carey's narrative one is left with serious doubts whether such a dramatic transformation has indeed occurred.

Carey's formulation of Newton's First Law is flawed, in that he does not differentiate between *speed* and *velocity* and uses them interchangeably. Speed is a *scalar*, equal to the magnitude of the *vector* entity which is the velocity. (In circular motion at constant speed, to name just one example, a force — commonly known as the centripetal force — is acting on the moving body. Without it, the body would not move in a circle. The velocity in such motion changes continuously, while the speed is constant.) Even so, he gives a number of examples from everyday life in order to illustrate the First Law. While the examples are helpful, his usage of the term *inertia* is rather vague. He wants his students to understand this term, because he believes (wrongly, I submit) that it is essential to the understanding of the First Law. Yet he himself uses inertia in an incorrect way in his second example: When a moving car suddenly stops, children who sit in the back seat but are not restrained properly will continue moving and may get hurt. This is a direct manifestation of Newton's First Law. However, it is not 'their inertia' which 'carries them through the front window'. From this formulation it would seem that inertia is some sort of force associated with the motion — a familiar misconception rooted in an Aristotelian world view.

It is, perhaps, appropriate to remark here that terms used in physics will usually carry an exact meaning or definition, which is often more limited than their use in everyday language. Energy, work, power, force are only a few such examples. So is the term inertia.

Following the examples illustrating the First Law, Carey gets into discussions of the role of air resistance. Here is a dilemma which occurs again and again in the teaching of science — most phenomena we attempt to understand are complex, involve many parameters, and cannot be fully explained in simple terms, by a single parameter or definition. Physics is that part of science which deals with the inanimate world, and which furthermore is concerned with trying to identify the most fundamental and unifying principles. The First Law is one such principle. However, it is almost always masked by additional factors. In real life bodies do not continue to move at constant speed indefinitely. If students are to accept the First Law, we owe them an explanation why that is so. Indeed, that is why the First Law was so late to be discovered — it is not intuitive at all. The Aristotelian world view, which contradicted it, is much more intuitive.

That is why Carey goes into air resistance. But he faces here a situation which is well documented in many studies — the structure of matter in general, and gases in particular, is not something which schoolchildren understand or have a clear picture of. The topic is not easy, since what is being discussed are microscopic structures and processes. These cannot be observed directly, so their explanations are far from intuitive. We are confronted here with a rather paradoxical situation — in attempting to explain a very basic, yet not at all obvious, First Law, which deals with macroscopic objects, we are drawn into much more complex issues, belonging to the realm of microscopic phenomena. No wonder Carey 'was greeted by nodding heads, but blank looks'.

Attempting to clarify the mysteries of air resistance, and the molecular structure of air as an explanation for it, Carey gets drawn into additional complications. Now he deals with objects undergoing free fall. Aristotle (384–322 BC) made the famous assertion that 'a weight which is twice as great will fall from the same height in half the time' (Carey's students made a similar guess in response to his questions). This assertion could have been disproved by a single experiment, but Aristotle did not study phenomena first hand. It was not until the seventeenth century that Galileo (1564–1642) established, by a combination of experiment and theory, the correct picture of free fall. Carey tries to go a similar route – he actually performs some experiments. However, the experiments he chooses to perform are 'contaminated', in the following sense: They are not demonstrations of free fall but rather of the dependence of the force of air resistance on an object on its form.

Carey finds that his students are now confused. Indeed, the sequence he describes is such that confusion is unavoidable. Carey expresses satisfaction with the way things evolved in his lesson, including the confusion, which in his opinion is good. It is true that some confusion may be good. Educators like to speak of 'cognitive dissonance' as a way to establish new knowledge in students' minds, knowledge which challenges existing beliefs. However, when phenomena are demonstrated in a teaching sequence, in order to challenge students' beliefs, they must be carefully chosen. In what Carey describes, at least three difficult issues are mixed up: *Newton's First Law*, the *molecular structure of air* meant to lead to an explanation of *air resistance*, and the rules governing *free fall*. Carey seems to be jumping from one to the other, and in the process things get hopelessly entangled.

Instead, it would have been much preferable to separate the issues. Here is a possible sequence: free fall could be demonstrated independently, in a 'clean' experiment with no air resistance. If that is too difficult, a readily available film loop can be used. It shows an astronaut on the moon, who drops a feather and a hammer simultaneously from the same height. They reach the ground together. Once the rules of free fall are clarified, air resistance can be dealt with separately. The molecular structure of air deserves a separate, extended treatment. Once air resistance is better understood, the First Law begins to make sense. Note that in this sequence, complicated phenomena are broken down into simpler ones, in tune with the spirit of physics alluded to above – trying to identify the simplest and most fundamental principles.

Students should perform experiments and be asked to interpret what they see. However, what they are asked to observe and explain should be carefully chosen.

From Carey's description of his lesson, one gets a feeling of such a heavy cognitive load, that one must doubt whether the students will be able to get out of the confusion he created, apparently on purpose. Clearly the lesson described was well intended. However, Carey's admitted weakness in understanding the subject matter leads to a deficient pedagogical subject-matter knowledge, and hence to a rather confused presentation of the physics he wants to teach.

★   ★   ★

Editors' synthesis

Galileo revisited reflects many of the characteristics of out-of-field science teaching described in the literature. And yet, in the rush to judgement, it is all too easy to see the problems of teaching science out of field in black and white terms. One response to Gerald's teaching might be that this is simply a case of a teacher out of his depth, struggling with the content and methods of teaching physics, with the result that he and his students are left in a state of conceptual confusion. Another response is that Gerald has made a genuine attempt to engage his students in a spirit of inquiry, resulting in a healthy state of wonderment and respect for the subject matter. In truth, as Gerald's story and the accompanying commentaries reveal, the problems of teaching out of field are rich and complex, encompassing aspects of both positions.

While all three commentators praise Carey's critique of his own teaching, they offer different responses regarding the success of his lesson. Harrison, for example, applauds Carey for his 'refreshing' approach to remediating his teaching and his students' understandings, inferring that the subject matter is secondary to the process of inquiry. In his commentary, he highlights several strategies used by Carey, including discrepant events and predict–observe–explain (POE), to challenge students' alternative conceptions. Harrison concludes that the lesson represents a small, but significant, step on the road to improving Carey's teaching. Grayson is also sympathetic with Carey's predicament. Like Carey, she seeks to move the subject beyond 'boring equations and cumbersome manipulations' towards what she calls a 'conceptual' approach, emphasising understanding over algorithms. She praises Carey for his attempts to challenge students' non-physics beliefs. However, she seems more concerned than Carey about leaving the students in a confused state about the relationships between the various physics concepts. The challenge, according to Grayson, is for physics teachers to understand the basic concepts before presenting them to students. Ganiel goes further, offering a detailed explanation of the relationship between Newton's First Law, air resistance and the rules of free fall, and a strong critique of Carey's 'well intended' but 'confused' attempts to teach these concepts. For Ganiel, the principles of the subject matter should guide the teaching strategies, and he warns that deficiencies in pedagogical subject-matter knowledge may lead to deep and lasting confusion on the part of students.

The teaching dilemma illustrated in this story is a complex one. Carey faces a delicate balancing act between too much cognitive dissonance and too little (leading to much confusion or too little), between safe and risky approaches to teaching unfamiliar content, and between minimising and maximising student engagement. We know that Carey is an experienced science teacher, albeit in a different field. The decisions he makes at each point in the lesson are informed by his extensive general pedagogical knowledge and his limited physics pedagogical content knowledge. Armed with this web of knowledge, he exercises professional judgement in making moment-to-moment decisions about appropriate courses of action. While we may criticise Carey's knowledge base, and offer constructive suggestions for improving the lesson, we must acknowledge that these decisions are Carey's responsibility and not ours.

References

Arons, A. B. (1990). *A guide to introductory physics teaching.* New York: Wiley.

Ball, D. L. and McDiarmid, G. W. (1990). The subject-matter preparation of teachers. In W. R. Houston, M. Haberman and J. Sikula (eds), *Handbook of research on teacher education* (pp. 437–449). New York: Macmillan.

Carlsen, W. S. (1991). Subject-matter knowledge and science teaching: A pragmatic perspective. In J. E. Brophy (ed.), *Advances in research on teaching: Vol. 2. Teachers' subject matter knowledge and classroom instruction* (pp. 115–186). Greenwich, CT: JAI Press.

Feiman-Nemser, S. and Parker, M. B. (1990). Making subject matter part of the conversation in learning to teach. *Journal of Teacher Education*, 41 (3), 32–43.

Gess-Newsome, J. and Lederman, N. (1995). Biology teachers' perceptions of subject matter structure and its relationship to classroom practice. *Journal of Research in Science Teaching*, 32 (3), 301–325.

—— (1999). *Examining pedagogical content knowledge.* Dordrecht, The Netherlands: Kluwer.

Grayson, D. J. (1996). Concept substitution: A strategy for promoting conceptual change. In D. F. Treagust, R. Duit and B. J. Fraser (eds), *Improving teaching and learning in science and mathematics* (pp. 152–161). New York: Teachers College Press.

Grossman, P. L., Wilson, S. M. and Shulman, L. S. (1989). Teachers of substance: Subject matter knowledge for teaching. In M. C. Reynolds (ed.), *Knowledge base for the beginning teacher* (pp. 23–36). Oxford: Pergamon Press.

Hashweh, M. Z. (1987). Effects of subject-matter knowledge in the teaching of biology and physics. *Teaching and Teacher Education*, 3, 109–120.

Laws, P. (1996). *Workshop physics activity guide.* New York: Wiley.

Lee, O. (1995). Subject matter knowledge, classroom management, and instructional practices in middle school science classrooms. *Journal of Research in Science Teaching*, 32, 423–440.

McDermott, L. C. (1996). *Physics by inquiry.* New York: Wiley.

McDiarmid, G. W., Ball, D. L. and Anderson, C. W. (1989). Why staying one chapter ahead doesn't really work: Subject specific pedagogy. In M.C. Reynolds (ed.), *Knowledge base for the beginning teacher* (pp. 193–205). Oxford: Pergamon Press.

Millar, R. (1988). Teaching physics as a non-specialist: The in-service training of science teachers. *Journal of Education for Teaching*, 14, 39–53.

Sanders, L. R., Borko, H. and Lockard, J. D. (1993). Secondary science teachers' knowledge base when teaching science courses in and out of their area of certification. *Journal of Research in Science Teaching*, 30 (7), 723–736.

Shulman, L. S. (1986). Those who understand: Knowledge growth in teaching. *Educational Researcher*, 15 (2), 4–14.

—— (1987). Knowledge and teaching: Foundations of the new reform. *Harvard Educational Review*, 57, 1–22.

Sokoloff, D. and Thornton, R. (1990). *Tools for scientific thinking*. Portland, OR: Vernier.

Chapter 16

Curriculum change

*Contributions by Garry White, Tom Russell
and Richard F. Gunstone*

Editors' introduction

It has long been argued that curriculum change is primarily a matter of changing the conditions of teacher learning (Darling-Hammond and Sykes, 1999). Teacher professional development, reflection, collaboration and classroom experimentation have been identified as contributing to teacher learning and improvements in classroom practice. However, teachers form only one side of the teaching and learning equation. A few years ago, for example, we observed the Grade 11 classroom of an experienced teacher who was trying to implement a new physics syllabus based on constructivist underpinnings. What we found was, that in spite of excellent professional support and the teacher's best efforts, the students resisted his attempts to use more student-centred practices (Wildy and Wallace, 1994). The students were more comfortable with teacher-centred practices – lots of teacher talk, clear delineation of course content and practice in examination techniques – than they were with more inquiry, context-based approaches. The new strategies were seen by the students in this class as 'wasteful digressions' causing the teacher to quickly revert to his old ways of teaching.

This episode demonstrates the difficulty faced by teachers wishing to change their practices in the face of the norms of classroom life – whole-class instruction, teacher centredness and emotional flatness (Goodlad, 1984). Teaching strategies aimed at promoting understanding, for example, will have little impact when students hold competing beliefs about teaching and learning. Models of learning that focus only on student cognition ignore students' motivational beliefs about themselves as learners (Pintrich *et al.*, 1993). When teachers attempt to apply strategies designed for personal and social meaning making, students frequently adopt passive roles for themselves in line with their transmissive views of teaching and learning (Gunstone, 1990, 1992). Students may simply deny the legitimacy of the strategies or, at best, undertake tasks in ways that minimise the demands made of them. Students opt for ready-made solutions rather than making their own meaning because they have been conditioned by the school system and the type of science knowledge it promotes (Larochelle and Désautels, 1992).

Thus teachers are caught between a desire to change and improve their practice and pressures to conform to long-established patterns of classroom organisation and student learning. It is this dilemma – about balancing the risks and the rewards of change – which is the focus of the following story by Garry White who writes about his experience of returning to the classroom after a four-year absence. The story, called *Re-establishing level ground*, is followed by comments from Tom Russell and Richard Gunstone.

Re-establishing level ground

Garry White

I was nervous. I'd been out of the classroom for four years, but I was determined to spend more time listening and asking more questions. I had left my job in education administration as a consultant in a teachers' training program to take up a position as head of the science department in a metropolitan school. It was in a low socio-economic area and had an enrolment of about 500.

I suppose you could say I was cautious, even uneasy, I guess. But I had taught in schools in low socio-economic areas before and I thought I still had the skills I needed. Dealing with difficult students and coping with management problems was something I had done before. Certainly, I was aware that there would be some students with family background problems but, as I said, I'd dealt with that before, so it didn't concern me much. I also had experience as a head of science, and my recent work in the teacher-education program gave me a certain level of confidence, so I couldn't see that the administrative part of the job would worry me overly.

At my previous schools I had pretty much been an outspoken and active teacher. But conscious that I had four years' absence from teaching, I resolved to be less so. As a consequence of this decision I was less than forthcoming with any new ideas and took a back seat in order to familiarise myself with my new school's procedures, policies and organisational approaches. It would be safe to say, I think, that my first priority was to get back into teaching and re-establish the kinds of approaches that I had used in my classroom before. These were student-centred, and represented a considerable change from the methodologies that the students were currently experiencing.

The first task that I undertook was to achieve a sound working relationship with the resource centre staff and laboratory assistants. This was essential because I needed to rely upon their goodwill in supporting the kind of access that students would need when operating within the framework I envisioned establishing. In addition to this, I also set about determining the prevailing level of school-wide expectation of such issues as student movement, assessment, reporting and curriculum development. This involved quite a considerable amount of investigation and groundwork.

The student-centred approaches I had previously employed relied on a number of important things like student access to resources. I appointed student monitors responsible for classroom tasks. Naturally, there was considerable student movement to various resource areas in the school – the library, technical studies, physical education facilities, etc. Of course, the cooperation of the laboratory staff was vital, because often there were unusual requests from the students as they planned and conducted their own practical activities from the available resources or textbooks. After students did this sort of thing for a while, they developed skills in independent learning, problem-solving, information literacy and planning their own work programmes.

I had enjoyed support in these strategies from other teachers who were experimenting with different methodologies in their own classrooms. I had changed classroom methodologies before and so had developed some useful skills, such as negotiating the curriculum, and I had used a range of descriptive assessment and reporting procedures. My own methodologies that I had used for seven years in my previous school focused on shifting the responsibility for learning away from me as the teacher towards the students. They gave the students scope to negotiate aspects of the course content, as well as processes and outcomes. I had seen them work before and I was confident they could work for the staff as well as the students in my new school.

So when I went back to the classroom, despite my nerves, I felt that I could achieve the student-centred goals I was hoping for. But it was like stepping into a time machine. I hadn't been in a school with a system like it for over ten years. I inherited a junior science curriculum that was constructed of short topics, each intended to be taught for three to five weeks. They were taken from set texts and the assessment was based on fairly standard topic tests. These were the key factor in the students' grades, which were A, B, C$^+$, C, C$^-$, D and U. Each grade level was divided up into Advanced, Standard and Basic. The students were assigned to the 'appropriate class' by teacher recommendation, and it wasn't uncommon for the Basic and Standard classes to have several students repeating the subject. I thought it was confining in the way that it was defined. So I thought the best, or at least the most appropriate, way to start initiating change would be by modelling some classroom methodologies.

Beginnings are such important times and my first day was an eye opener. I had forgotten the joys of Grade 9 classes. There I was, standing in front of a class who just did not want to know. They had no interest in me or science, and taking responsibility for their own science learning was the last thing on their minds.

The only thing they seemed remotely interested in was trying the patience and persistence of their new teacher.

My first real mission was to establish some sort of two-way communication with the well-known 'problem students' of the school without unreasonable interruptions. This was a lengthy process, not made any easier due to my unfamiliarity with the school's multi-step discipline process. But while I was doing that I started to experiment with some of the classroom activities that I hoped would demonstrate the students' independence and problem-solving abilities. The first three activities were, at first sight at least, total disasters.

I started with an exercise I had used before. It was a problem-solving exercise that I hoped would give me an idea about where the students were as far as those skills went. The activity required the students to make an electromagnet using a nail, insulated wire and a battery. At first sight, you wouldn't think that would be too difficult, but you wouldn't believe how hard they seemed to find it. There was a remarkable lack of initiative and a seemingly total dependence on me as the teacher to tell them what to do. They asked questions like, 'What do I write on this sheet?', 'How can we change the electromagnet?' and 'What should we do now?'

Of course my first thought was that perhaps the instructions were too complicated, given the students' lack of previous practical experience, but that was not the case at all. The instructions were brief and we had done practical activities, directed ones admittedly, for the three weeks before this. Several of the students displayed real difficulties completing the basic construction. The level of reliance on me as the source of all ideas, solutions and answers was amazing! So after that, I decided that perhaps it was wrong to assume or expect the students to display such high-level skills as group work, planning, practical manipulation, organisation and documentation when they probably had not been given the opportunity to develop and practise them. So, I looked upon this electromagnet session as more of a training session, for both the students and me.

I gave it another week before I tried anything else, and then I introduced the idea of concept mapping. I had used it many times in the preceding six years, both in the classroom and in the teacher-training programs, so I was comfortable with it. I should have known better. What a flop! Those Grade 9s showed no sign of ever wanting to think for themselves! I couldn't work it out: were they deaf, lazy or just totally uninterested? However, as I was having some modicum of success using concept maps with my Grade 11 chemistry class, I kept at it for three periods – a total of two and a half hours – only to discover at the end that the Grade 9s were still very dependent and very lazy.

Not to be deterred, I had another go at trying to shift the emphasis away from me to the students taking more responsibility for their learning. The last thing I tried was a 'directed student contract'. This acted as the introduction to the next unit. The objective of the contract was to expose the students to my broad expectations and then allow them opportunities to make decisions about the sequence of their work. I gave them an introductory lesson with a demonstration and some discussion and then I gave the students the chance to complete the contract in a sequence determined by their own planning.

What a mess that turned into! After two lessons I had to stop all the practical work simply because of poor behaviour. It was easy to identify just exactly the type of behaviour too. There was student apathy, very poor student communication skills, very short student attention span, and apparent lack of student interest and minimal experience with the practical approach to science. And that's not all, believe it or not. There was also apparent student reliance on teacher notes, demonstration and lecture, and not to forget a total student disregard for basic safety procedures.

With all that staring me in the face and the lack of success of the contracts, I was forced to focus on developing student communication, group work and safety skills before the students could experiment with more freedom for decision making. After five lessons of teacher-directed demonstrations and note taking, they actually asked me for another try at the practical activity again. And, believe it or not, after the first few lessons, it went quite well. Eight weeks it took us, but I was quite pleased with the results I was beginning to see.

$$\star \qquad \star \qquad \star$$

Taking responsibility for learning

Tom Russell, Queen's University, Kingston, Ontario

I cannot imagine a more interesting story to comment on. In 1991 I returned to the classroom (one-third time for half the school year, an arrangement I repeated in 1992). I had been away from the secondary school classroom for twenty-four years! The intervening time included Ph.D. studies, in-service work with teachers (three years) and pre-service and M.Ed. teaching at my present university (fourteen years). I, too, was nervous, wondering how the students would respond but perhaps even more concerned about how my new colleagues would view someone stepping from the 'crystal palace' (where they don't know what teaching is really like) back into the classroom. Like Garry, I resolved to listen; I was the outsider moving in. Like Garry, I felt that I had once been a student-centred teacher and I resolved to be such a teacher again.

Perhaps the similarities end there. I was not in a low socio-economic area, and Canadian secondary schools generally do not have laboratory assistants. Practical work is important in a ritualistic kind of way, as I learned when I shifted the requirements for students' reports on their second prac of the year. I asked them to write a report that told me what they had learned from the experience, and virtually no one had a clue how to respond. I had agreed to teach at exactly the same (fast-moving) pace as the other person teaching the course, and I also relied extensively on that teacher for equipment for demonstrations as well as materials for practical work. I was eager to follow Garry's dream of 'shifting the responsibility for learning away from me as the teacher towards the students', yet the pace at which content had to be covered imposed severe restrictions. I never managed to return to helping students tell me what they learned from personal experience with equipment.

I was facing Grade 12 students, a far cry from the Grade 9s who quickly showed Garry that they had no interest in learning. Even so, I can identify with his observations: 'a remarkable lack of initiative' may not have been the case, but I did sense 'a seemingly total dependence on me as the teacher to tell them what to do'. My first leap was to remove myself from the role of 'giver of notes' and we joked from the first day to the last about my inability to organise work clearly on the blackboard. I had read Damien Hynes' (1986, pp. 30–31) account of nonsense notes that students copied without question, and I resolved to deny the 'pencil theory of learning', despite my students' conviction that they *did* learn by copying from the board.

I never reached the stage of concept mapping or contracts. I was pedalling too fast just to keep a day ahead of the students. One student, whose parents assured me he had always been outspoken, told me to my face (how refreshing, yes, he had my attention!) at the end of one class that he expected my lessons to prepare him completely to do the problems set for the next day, yet he found that my lessons did not prepare him. Later in the term there was a lesson that I (and many students) felt was significantly different from most others, as I took a large motor-generator into the centre of the room and told them to ask me anything and everything they could think of. The next day, when I solicited short written comments about how that lesson had been different, the outspoken student assured me he had seen nothing different at all!

Why is it that Garry and I can work with apparently different students in very different parts of the globe and find such powerful resonance in our classroom goals as well as in our difficulties in achieving those goals? I have taught in schools in Canada, Nigeria and the USA, and I have observed science lessons in the UK, Sierra Leone, Trinidad and Tobago, and Australia. One of my simplest conclusions is that anyone from the English-speaking countries of the world who is dropped into any other such country could never fail to recognise a school classroom. And everywhere one goes, teachers seem to either face or give up on the same challenge: *'How can I get students to take more responsibility for their own learning?'*

For two decades, I faced a similar challenge in my classroom in a pre-service teacher education programme. All that has finally begun to change because the programme at Queen's University has changed dramatically this year. Gone is the traditional assumption, expressed in three three-week blocks of teaching practice, that learning to teach involves being told how to teach and then going into schools to 'put theory into practice' (Loughran and Russell, 1997a). In its place is a nine-month programme that *begins* with *four* months in one school, interrupted for two weeks to return to the university to refocus and set goals for the remaining time. When my science method course began in earnest at the half-way point of the programme, after four months of teaching experience, I rejoiced that 'experience first' had trans-formed the people I was to teach. They knew what they wanted to learn, and they were prepared to direct their own learning. A few had even gone so far as to attempt an 'experience first' approach to science teaching in the second half of their four-month placement.

The central theme I see in Garry's account of the challenges he faced is a group of students who have given up on the standard teaching practice in which teachers ask students to provide and listen to 'the answers to questions they have not learned to ask' (O'Reilley, 1993, p. 34). I faced the same challenges when I began teaching, when I returned to the secondary school classroom, and in years of pre-service teaching where experience came too little and too late. How did schooling become so removed from personal experience, when so much of the knowledge in the school curriculum has its roots in the experi-ences of those who have preceded us? How did schooling shift from being problem-centred to being answer-centred (Holt, 1964, pp. 88–9)?

When Sarason (1971) first published his analysis of the school culture in relation to efforts to change (improve) schooling, I was drawn instantly to his sense that everything hangs on the fundamental pattern of teachers asking questions and students answering them. Now I find it even more compelling that he has concluded, twenty-five years later, that he did not state his initial conclusions strongly enough:

> What I am saying here I said in the book but, I have since concluded, I did not sufficiently emphasise how bedrock the asker–answerer relation-ship is for school change. *Any effort at systemic reform that does not give top priority to altering that relationship will not improve educational outcomes. ... Teachers cannot create and sustain contexts for productive learning unless those conditions exist for them.*
>
> (Sarason, 1996, p. 367, italics in original)

Personally, I pin my greatest hopes on a uniquely Australian invention – the Project for Enhancing Effective Learning (PEEL) that began in a suburb of

Melbourne where students had attitudes much like those that Garry describes. By good fortune that I cannot explain clearly in hindsight, my university has been fortunate to have had significant visits by no fewer than five different individuals closely associated with PEEL. The project is a rich and intriguing one that has achieved a unique blend of practical theory and theory-laden new practices (Baird and Northfield, 1992). Perhaps the central point of entry for those new to PEEL is expressed in a chapter constructed by Judie and Ian Mitchell (1992) that categorises and illustrates the 'classroom procedures' developed over many years by teachers working in cross-curricular school groups.

Garry writes as a teacher new to a particular school context who is eager to resume his pursuit of goals for students that are shared by many beginning teachers. It would be valuable to learn how his professional goals have played out as he comes to know the other teachers and they come to know him. I believe PEEL has survived, succeeded, spread, and moved on to new dimensions of teacher research by achieving what Sarason argues is essential for change in schools – the conditions for student learning must shift hand in hand with the conditions for teacher learning. For both teachers and students, the central activity of schooling must shift from answering other people's questions to taking a significant responsibility for one's own learning.

Linking my understanding of conditions for the development of school innovations to a major innovation in the structure of the teacher education programme where I work has added the essential ingredient of personal experience. That new structure places experience before extended course work, helping me to understand the potential of 'experience first' teaching procedures as well as the authority that comes with personal experience (Munby and Russell, 1994). Garry and I sought to capture the power of experience in our teaching of science, and we both found that working alone with individual classes is a steep uphill battle against the 'culture of the school'. PEEL has shown the creativity that is generated when teachers work in school groups. Just as there are thousands of teachers who share the goal of having students take more responsibility for their own learning, so there are hundreds of teacher educators who share a similar dream for those learning to teach (Loughran and Russell, 1997b). I hope that both Garry and I will come to know the support that is possible in groups within the schools where we teach. I wish the same for those I teach who are just beginning their teaching careers. Thank you, Garry, for sharing your experiences so clearly.

★   ★   ★

Innovation is relative

Richard F. Gunstone, Monash University

Garry White's narrative is rich in issues of significance for science classrooms.

For me, the central (and the most personally relevant) one relates to understanding what we could call 'the shock of starting afresh'.

In his narrative Garry is unduly modest about his teaching abilities. At the time he began in this school, the time the narrative commences, I had just finished working closely with him for a number of years. Here was a teacher who was bursting with energy, articulate, highly informed, deeply thinking, widely experienced. ... Yet his first few months in this new school with this Grade 9 seemed like none of this. This is a common experience for teachers changing schools. Teachers often talk about it. My personal identification with the issue is because the biggest and most difficult management problem I had in my twelve years of high school science teaching came early in my ninth year. This problem came in my first year in a new school, rather like the scenario Garry describes (and also with a Grade 9 class).

There are obvious, and basically trite, 'explanations' for this difficulty of starting afresh – statements of the form 'kids need to get to know who you are and how you want to do things'. But such statements are not of much use to gaining an understanding of these situations. Nor do such statements give any notion of why the problem is so much more acute in circumstances such as Garry's where he was attempting to implement approaches that, it seems clear, these students had not experienced before. We can do better than 'they need to get to know you' by way of analysis and understanding of these situations.

Students bring to classrooms ideas and beliefs about teaching, about learning, about roles seen as appropriate for teachers and learners, and about the purposes for being in the classroom. And there are frequent instances of these ideas and beliefs being different from the ideas and beliefs of the teacher about teaching, learning, roles and purposes. A common example of such dissonance between teacher and student ideas is found in undergraduate science study. When we were studying science at university all of us knew (and some, like me, were) students whose views of learning, teaching, and roles were that the teacher (lecturer) had a responsibility to provide a set of excellent notes (which we believed we should obtain by copying clearly written and well-organised things from a blackboard) and access to many old exam papers, and the learner then had to 'learn' (basically that meant memorise) these notes and reproduce relevant pieces for the examination. The purpose of this process was singular and clear – to pass the examination. None of this matches with the views of learning, teaching, roles, purposes held by most of those who teach undergraduate science. Yet, in this context, it is the views of the students that determine what these students do; this is largely because of the nature of the assessment in this context – the assessment rewards the student ideas and beliefs that I have just briefly described.

It seems reasonable to label the students in Garry's class, at the beginning of the year of Garry's narrative, as being passive learners. That is these students had much in common with the undergraduates I characterised in the previous paragraph: the job of the teacher is to give clear notes, the job of these students is to 'learn' (memorise) these notes, the role of assessment is to see if students can reproduce these notes. Once the test is finished then one can forget all about the topic. The passiveness of Garry's students was, it appears, being strongly reinforced by the assessment practices of the school because these practices rewarded the reproduction approach just described.

But it is still not enough to label the students as passive learners. This does not help us understand why problems of dissonance between teacher views and student views of learning, teaching, roles and purposes should be so much more difficult when the teacher attempts to introduce different approaches with different purposes, as Garry did. To understand this we need to consider what is known about the introduction of innovations in terms of the student perspective. I do this via a number of points. Each of these points applies to both teachers and students when one is considering innovation in the classroom, and all are interrelated. There is a substantial literature about each of these points in terms of the teacher perspective, but little has been written about the student perspective. Here I will briefly discuss only the student perspective because the narrative Garry White has written involves a situation where the innovation is a change for the students, not for the teacher.

The logic of existing practice   Students in classrooms have practices that they use and have some understanding of in terms of their ideas and beliefs about learning, teaching, roles and purposes. These existing practices have, for the large majority of students, evolved to meet the constraints, demands and expectations that the students experienced before the change was introduced. Most students behave in classrooms in ways that they see as appropriate in terms of their ideas and beliefs, and these constraints, demands and expectations. Thus, according to this position, the students in Garry's class were reacting with some personal logic in their very negative and difficult responses to his innovations.

Change involves taking risks and initially becoming less expert   A logical consequence of the preceding point is that change requires of the students that they no longer use at least some of the well-developed skills and approaches that were previously acceptable. This requires them to take risks in their classroom approaches and become less skilful, less expert than previously as a learner in the classroom. A common reaction of course is that the students do not abandon the skills and approaches that have been appropriate in the past. This then distorts the innovation from the intentions of the teacher, or even prevents the innovation from being implemented in any form.

Experience precedes understanding   The two points just outlined say much about the problems described by Garry White resulting from his introduction of alternative approaches and purposes. That experience precedes understanding says much about the time Garry found was needed before any signs emerged of student change. This point is a necessary consequence of the importance of experiential knowledge in the understanding of any innovation. Students need to form personal meaning for the innovation before there is any chance of them seriously reconsidering their ideas and beliefs about learning, teaching, roles and purposes. And sometimes here is a very difficult form of vicious circle. It is not until the students experience the innovation as intended by the teacher that there is any possibility of them genuinely understanding the value of the innovation; if the students do not see the value of the innovation it is difficult to have them experience the innovation as intended. One of the many consequences of this is that, in any context, adoption of an innovation is an early point in any change. Sadly adoption is often erroneously seen as the end point of any change.

Assessment In all contexts of innovation this is a very significant example of the first two of the above points (the logic of existing practice, change involves risk taking and loss of expertise). For students, assessment is an absolutely central constraint/demand/expectation that involves the use of well-developed skills and approaches. If an innovation does not consider appropriate changes to assessment it is very likely doomed to failure; if assessment changes are introduced then there is a further set of changes required of students.

Levels of concern and the processes of change Much has been written about levels of concern and teacher change in the introduction of innovations. These levels of concern are usually described as 'self' (crudely 'how does the change affect me?'), 'task' ('what is the nature of the change?'), 'impact' ('what are the consequences of the change?'). I know of no attempt to consider levels of concern among students involved in an innovation, yet I am convinced that this is a potentially valuable way of considering students and change. Certainly what we know of students and innovations is quite consistent with a 'self' concern being dominant.

In conclusion Much of what I have written in this commentary[1] could be simply summarised as 'Innovation is relative' – you as a teacher might well have come to a clear and cohesive position with respect to broad philosophy and related strategies, materials, and so on; each new class you teach is potentially quite unfamiliar with your approaches and purposes. Thus each new class needs to come to understand and see the purposes of what you are doing (and, we intend, come to value these purposes). Garry's title for his narrative – *Re-establishing level ground* – is most appropriate for his perspective on the situation; for his students it was much more 'Breaking new ground'.

★   ★   ★

Editors' synthesis

White's sobering account of the difficulties he encountered upon his return to teaching seems to strike a chord with Russell and Gunstone. Both commentators draw parallels with their own similar experiences in different settings and with students of different age groups. What all three authors have in common is the experience of trying to introduce new teaching strategies to groups of students who seem totally dependent on the teacher for their learning. Russell observes that everywhere he goes, teachers seem to 'either face or give up on the same challenge' of how to get students to take more responsibility for their own learning.

Facing or giving up is bound up in what Gunstone calls a 'vicious circle' for the teacher. Students will only understand the value of accepting responsibility by experiencing more responsibility. However, if students do not see the value of the innovation, it is difficult for them to have the experience of responsibility. The dilemma for the teacher is how far to push the idea with a resistant group of students without it becoming self-defeating (that is, for the classroom to become even more teacher-centred in the process). In White's case, for example, at one point he was forced to stop all practical work and revert to note taking, demonstration and lecture because of poor student behaviour. In our own research in a physics classroom, described at the beginning of this chapter, the teacher reverted to lots of teacher talk and practice at examination technique in the face of student resistance to student-centred approaches (Wildy and Wallace, 1994).

Gunstone argues that it is not enough to blame students for this problem by using simple labels such as 'passive learners'. He observes that students' ideas, beliefs and expectations about teaching and learning have been conditioned by particular kinds of teaching and assessment practices that promote dependency. Both commentators suggest that change in schools requires a fundamental change in the relationship between teacher and students – what Sarason (1996) calls the asker–answerer relationship. For both teachers and students, argues Russell, 'the central activity of schooling must shift from answering other people's questions to taking significant responsibility for one's own learning'.

As Gunstone points out, for both parties, this approach requires a good deal of risk-taking and initially becoming less expert. Whether or not teachers and their students judge that taking the risk is worth the effort depends on many factors. There is plenty of evidence that this challenge is too much for some teachers who choose a settled existence based on comfortable patterns of practice (Wallace and Louden, 1992). However, both Russell and Gunstone point to examples of where, with appropriate supports, teachers and students have made the transition from dependency to responsibility. The challenge set by these three authors is how to find ways of making this practice more widespread in the science education community.

Note

1 There are many other issues of significance in the narrative that I (Gunstone) have not directly considered. Obvious examples are student motivation, how one can increase this, and likely general characteristics of 14–15-year-olds (particularly the influences of hormones and group pressures). There is much about the problems with passive learning, approaches to making learners more active in the work, appropriate forms of assessment and so on in the products of the Project for Enhancing Effective Learning (Baird and Northfield, 1992).

References

Baird, J. R. and Mitchell, I. J. (eds) (1986). *Improving the quality of teaching and learning: An Australian case study – the PEEL project* (1st edn). Melbourne: Monash University Printing Services.

Baird, J. R. and Northfield, J. R. (eds.) (1992). *Learning from the PEEL experience.* Melbourne: Monash University Printing Services.

Darling-Hammond, L. and Sykes, G. (eds) (1999). *Teaching as the learning profession: Handbook of policy and practice.* San Francisco: Jossey Bass.

Goodlad, J. I. (1984). *A place called school: Prospects for the future.* New York: McGraw-Hill.

Gunstone, R. (1990). 'Children's science': A decade of developments in constructivist views of science teaching and learning. *The Australian Science Teachers Journal*, 36 (4), 9–19.

—— (1992). Constructivism and metacognition: Theoretical issues and classroom studies. In R. Duit, F. Goldberg and H. Niedderer (eds), *Research in physics learning: Theoretical issues and empirical studies* (pp. 129–140). University of Kiel: Institute for Science Education.

Holt, J. (1964). *How children fail.* New York: Dell.

Hynes, D. (1986). Theory into practice. In J. R. Baird and I. J. Mitchell (eds) (1997), *Improving the quality of teaching and learning: An Australian case study – the PEEL project* (1st edn, pp. 28–44). Melbourne: Monash University Printing Services.

Larochelle, M. and Désautels, J. (1992). The epistemological turn in science education: The return of the actor. In R. Duit, F. Goldberg and H. Niedderer (eds), *Research in physics learning: Theoretical issues and empirical studies* (pp. 155–175). University of Kiel: Institute for Science Education.

Loughran, J. and Russell, T. (1997a). Meeting student teachers on their own terms: Experience precedes understanding. In V. Richardson (ed.), *Constructivist teacher education: Building a world of new understandings* (pp. 164–181). London: Falmer Press.

—— (1997b). *Teaching about teaching: Purpose, passion and pedagogy in teacher education.* London: Falmer Press.

Mitchell, J. and Mitchell, I. (1992). Some classroom procedures. In J. R. Baird and J. R. Northfield (eds), *Learning from the PEEL experience* (pp. 210–268). Melbourne: Monash University Printing Services.

Munby, H. and Russell, T. (1994). The authority of experience in learning to teach: Messages from a physics methods class. *Journal of Teacher Education*, 45, 86–95.

O'Reilley, M. R. (1993). *The peaceable classroom.* Portsmouth, NH: Boynton/Cook Heinemann.

Pintrich, P. R., Marx, R. W. and Boyle, R. A. (1993). Beyond cold conceptual change: The role of motivational beliefs and classroom contextual factors in the process of conceptual change. *Review of Educational Research*, 63 (2), 167–199.

Sarason, S. B. (1971). *The culture of the school and the problem of change*. Boston: Allyn & Bacon.

—— (1996). *Revisiting the culture of the school and the problem of change*. New York: Teachers College Press.

Wallace, J. and Louden, W. (1992). Science teaching and teachers' knowledge: Prospects for reform of elementary classrooms. *Science Education*, 76 (5), 507–521.

Wildy, H. and Wallace, J. (1994). Understanding teaching or teaching for understanding: Alternative frameworks for science classrooms. *Journal of Research in Science Teaching*, 32 (2), 143–156.

Contributors

Editors

John Wallace, Science and Mathematics Education Centre, Curtin University of Technology, GPO Box U1987, Perth, WA 6845, Australia, j.wallace@smec.curtin.edu.au

William Louden, Community Services Education and Social Sciences, Edith Cowan University, Bradford St, Mt Lawley, WA 6050, Australia, w.louden@cowan.edu.au

Storytellers and commentators

Sandra K. Abell, Southwestern Bell Science Education Centre, University of Missouri-Columbia, MO 65211, USA, AbellS@missouri.edu

Glen S. Aikenhead, College of Education, University of Saskatchewan, 28 Campus Drive, Saskatoon, SK S7N 0X1, Canada, glen.aikenhead@usask.ca

Mary Monroe Atwater, The University of Georgia, Science Education Department, 212 Aderhold, Hall, Athens, GA 30602–7126, USA, matwater@coe.uga.edu

Angela Barton, Science Education, Department of Scientific Foundations, 412A Main Hall, Box 210, Teachers College, Columbia University, 525 West 120th Street, New York, NY 10027, USA, acb33@columbia.edu

Paul Black, School of Education, King's College, London, Franklin-Wilkins Building, 150 Stamford Street, London SE1 9NN, UK, paul.black@kcl.ac.uk

Anna Blahey, 14 Rutherglen Place, Macquarie Hills, NSW 2285, Australia, blahey@ses.curtin.edu.au

Nancy W. Brickhouse, School of Education, University of Delaware, Newark, DE 19716, USA, nbrick@UDel.Edu

Gerald Carey, 18 Thornton Rd, Green Acres, SA 5086, Australia

Jan Crosthwaite, Philosophy Department, University of Auckland, Private Bag 92019, Auckland, New Zealand, jan.c@auckland.ac.nz

Vaille Dawson, Social Science, Humanities and Education, Murdoch University, South St, Murdoch, WA 6150, Australia, v.dawson@murdoch.edu.au

Reinders Duit, Institute for Science Education at the University of Kiel, Olshausenstr. 62, D 24098 Kiel, Germany, duit@ipn.uni-kiel.de

Gaalen L. Erickson, Department of Curriculum Studies, Centre for the Study of Teacher Education, Faculty of Education, University of British Columbia,Vancouver, BC V6T 1Z4, Canada, gaalen.erickson@ubc.ca

Peter J. Fensham, Faculty of Education, Monash University, Clayton, Victoria 3168, Australia, peter.fensham@education.monash.ed.au

Uri Ganiel, Department of Science Teaching, The Weizmann Institute of Science, Rehovot 76100, Israel, uri.ganiel@weizmann.ac.il

David Geelan, Department of Secondary Education, 341 Education South, University of Alberta, Edmonton, Alberta, T6G 2GS, Canada, david.geelan@ualberta.ca

John K. Gilbert, Department of Science and Technology Education, University of Reading, Bulmershe Court, Reading RG6 1HY, UK, J.K. Gilbert@reading.ac.uk

Wendy Giles, St Hilda's Anglican School for Girls, Bayview Terrace, Mosman Park, WA 6012, Australia, wendy.giles@shildas.wa.edu.au

Penny J. Gilmer, Department of Chemistry, Florida State University, Tallahassee, FL 32306–4390, USA, gilmer@chem.fsu.edu

Noel Gough, Deakin Centre for Education and Change, Deakin University, 221 Burwood Highway, Burwood, Victoria 3125, Australia, noelg@deakin.edu.au

Diane Grayson, Faculty of Science, University of South Africa, PO Box 392, UNISA 0003, South Africa, graysdj@unisa.ac.za

Joan Gribble, Science and Mathematics Education Centre, Curtin University of Technology, GPO Box U1987, Perth, WA 6845, Australia, j.gribble@smec. curtin.edu.au

Richard F. Gunstone, Faculty of Education, Monash University, Clayton, Victoria 3800, Australia, dick.gunstone@education.monash.edu.au

Allan Harrison, School of Education and Innovation, Central Queensland University, Rockhampton, Queensland 4702, Australia, a.harrison@cqu.edu.au

Brent Kilbourn, OISE/University of Toronto, Department of Curriculum, Teaching and Learning, 252 Bloor St W., Toronto, Ontario M5S IV6, Canada, bkilbourn@oise.utoronto.ca

Barry Krueger, Living Waters Lutheran College, PO Box 997, Rockingham, WA 6168, Australia, b.krueger@m140.aone.net.au

Marie Larochelle, Département d'études sur l'enseignement et l'apprentissage, Faculté des sciences de l'éducation, Université Laval, Québec (Qc) G1K 7P4, Canada, marie.larochelle@fse.ulaval.ca

Norman G. Lederman, Department of Mathematics and Science Education, Illinois Institute of Technology, 226 Engineering I, 10 W 32nd St, Chicago, IL 60616, USA, lederman@iit.edu

Jay L. Lemke, City University of New York, New York, USA, jlemke@gc.cuny.edu

Roger Lock, School of Education, The University of Birmingham, Birmingham B15 2TT, UK, r.j.lock@bham.ac.uk

J. John Loughran, Faculty of Education, Monash University, Wellington Rd, Clayton, Victoria 3800, Australia, john.loughran@education.monash.edu.au

Cathleen C. Loving, Texas A&M University, Department of Teaching, Learning and Culture, College Station, TX 77843–4232, USA, cloving@tamu.edu

J. R. Martin, Department of Linguistics, University of Sydney, Sydney, NSW 2006, Australia, jmartin@mail.usyd.edu.au

J. Randy McGinnis, Science Teaching Center, Department of Curriculum & Instruction, Room 2226 Benjamin, University of Maryland, College Park, Maryland 20742, USA, jm250@umail.umd.edu

Bevan McGuiness, Wesley College, South Perth, WA 6151, Australia, bmcguiness@wesley.wa.edu.au

Karen McNamee, 15 Rowland Crt, M.S. 1436, Toowoomba, Queensland 4350, Australia

Catherine Milne, Department of Chemistry, University of Pennsylvania, 231S 34th Street, Philadelphia, PA 19104–6323, USA, cemilne@gse.upenn.edu

Sharon E. Nichols, Science Education, 357 Flanagan Hall, East Carolina University, Greenville, NC 27858, USA, nichols@soe.ecu.edu

Nel Noddings, 3 Webb Ave, Ocean Grove, NJ 07756, USA, noddings@stanford.edu

Léonie J. Rennie, Science and Mathematics Education Centre, Curtin University of Technology, GPO Box U1987, Perth, WA 6845, Australia, l.rennie@smec.curtin.edu.au

Wolff-Michael Roth, Applied Cognitive Science, MacLaurin A548, University of Victoria, PO Box 3010, Victoria, BC V8W 3N4, Canada, mroth@uvic.ca

Tom Russell, Faculty of Education, Queen's University, Kingston, Ontario K7L 3N6, Canada, russellt@educ.queensu.ca

Clive R. Sutton, Leicester University, School of Education, 21 University Road, Leicester, LE1 7RF, UK, crs@leicester.ac.uk or clive.sutton@btinternet.com

Peter C. Taylor, Science and Mathematics Education Centre, Curtin University of Technology, GPO Box U1987, Perth, WA 6845, Australia, p.taylor@smec.curtin.edu.au

Deborah J. Tippins, University of Georgia, Science Education/Elementary Education Department, 212 Aderhold Hall, Athens, GA 30602, USA, dtippins@coe.uga.edu

Kenneth Tobin, Graduate School of Education, University of Pennsylvania, 3700 Walnut St, Philadelphia, PA 19104–6216, USA, ktobin@gse.upenn.edu

Grady Venville, Science and Mathematics Education Centre, Curtin University of Technology, GPO Box U1987, Perth, WA 6845, Australia, g.venville@smec.curtin.edu.au

Other contributors

Ken Atwood (pseudonym, by request), **Sue Briggs**, **Lyn Bryer**, **Ann Campbell**, **Peter Leach** (pseudonym, by request), **Garry White** (deceased).

Index